Learning to Program

Addison-Wesley Learning Series

Addison-Wesley

Visit informit.com/learningseries for a complete list of available publications.

The Addison-Wesley Learning Series is a collection of hands-on programming guides that help you quickly learn a new technology or language so you can apply what you've learned right away.

Each title comes with sample code for the application or applications built in the text. This code is fully annotated and can be reused in your own projects with no strings attached. Many chapters end with a series of exercises to encourage you to reexamine what you have just learned, and to tweak or adjust the code as a way of learning.

Titles in this series take a simple approach: they get you going right away and leave you with the ability to walk off and build your own application and apply the language or technology to whatever you are working on.

Addison-Wesley · **informIT** · **Safari** Books Online

ALWAYS LEARNING · **PEARSON**

Learning to Program

Steven Foote

Addison-Wesley

Upper Saddle River, NJ • Boston • Indianapolis • San Francisco
New York • Toronto • Montreal • London • Munich • Paris • Madrid
Cape Town • Sydney • Tokyo • Singapore • Mexico City

Library of Congress Control Number: 2014951063

Copyright © 2015 Pearson Education, Inc.

ISBN-13: 978-0-7897-5339-7

33614081581521

ISBN-10: 0-7897-5339-1

Text printed in the United States on recycled paper at Courier in Westford, Massachusetts.

6   17

Editor-in-Chief
Mark Taub

Acquisitions Editor
Mark Taber

Managing Editor
Sandra Schroeder

Project Editor
Mandie Frank

Copy Editor
Krista Hansing

Indexer
Ken Johnson

Proofreader
Jess DeGabriele

Technical Reviewers
Seth McLaughlin
Jeremy Foote

Editorial Assistant
Vanessa Evans

Designer
Chuti Prasertsith

Compositor
Jake McFarland

❖

For Paige

❖

Contents at a Glance

Table of Contents

Acknowledgments

I wish to thank the following people for their help in the preparation of various versions of this text: Jimmy Chan, Prash Jain, and Jim Gourgoutis.

At Pearson, I'd like to thank Mark Taber and my project editor, Mandie Frank. Thanks also to my copy editor, Krista Hansing, and my technical editors, Seth McLaughlin and Jeremy Foote. Finally, I'd like to thank all the other people from Pearson who were involved on this project, even if I did not work with them directly.

About the Author

Steven Foote is a web developer at LinkedIn. A self-taught programmer who loves technology, especially the Web, he has a Bachelor's degree and Master's degree in Accountancy from Brigham Young University. While working on his Master's degree, he built all aspects of two AJAX-y web applications, from visual design to server and database maintenance, and everything in between.

We Want to Hear from You!

As the reader of this book, *you* are our most important critic and commentator. We value your opinion and want to know what we're doing right, what we could do better, what areas you'd like to see us publish in, and any other words of wisdom you're willing to pass our way.

We welcome your comments. You can email or write directly to let us know what you did or didn't like about this book—as well as what we can do to make our books better.

Please note that we cannot help you with technical problems related to the topic of this book, and that due to the high volume of mail we receive, we might not be able to reply to every message.

When you write, please be sure to include this book's title and author, as well as your name and phone number or email address.

Email: feedback@developers-library.info

Mail: Reader Feedback
          Addison-Wesley Developer's Library
          800 East 96th Street
          Indianapolis, IN 46240 USA

Reader Services

Visit our website and register this book at www.informit.com/register for convenient access to any updates, downloads, or errata that might be available for this book.

Introduction

Why I Wrote This Book

Like most great (accountant) stories, mine starts with an Excel spreadsheet. The year was 2008, and I was studying accounting at Brigham Young University in Provo, Utah. I was also working as a clerk at the Law School library. One day my boss asked me if I knew how to randomize a list of names in Excel. "Of course," I lied and then proceeded to do what every well-intentioned overpromiser knows to do. Google showed me at least three different ways to randomize a list in Excel, and within 2 minutes, I returned the randomized list to my boss. At that point, she decided that I was good with computers and should work for the library systems department. I'm not certain that an aptitude to Google stuff equates to being good with computers, but I'm grateful that she thought so.

It was there in the law library systems department that my programming journey began. On my first day, my boss gave me a 25-year-old book called *Programming Perl* and showed me to my desk in a windowless room cluttered with old computers, keyboards, and monitors. He was busy with some other things, he told me as he left, but the Perl book would keep me busy until he came back. I opened the book and started reading, and I've never been the same since.

The book was written before Windows even existed, so it expected the reader to be using the UNIX Operating System (which I had never heard of). I ignored that and kept using my Windows XP computer, which had recently been retired from the library's computer lab (before that day, I had no idea there was such a thing as a computer too old for a library computer lab). The book told me to get a copy of Perl by sending a self-addressed, stamped envelope to some address and then getting a floppy disk mailed to me. I decided to use my Google skills instead and found instructions on downloading and installing Perl. I had downloaded software before, but I had no idea you have to download and install programming languages. I was getting a bit nervous that I might be destroying my computer, but I figured it wouldn't really be missed, so I kept going.

The first chapter of the book showed some sample code that was supposed to print `Hello, world!` It looked something like this:

```
print("Hello, world!");
```

I was supposed to save the sample code to a file named `hello_world.pl`. The only software I had ever used to input text into my computer was Microsoft Word, so I opened Word and started typing. It took me about 45 seconds to realize that Microsoft Word was the wrong place to be writing code and 45 minutes to figure out the right place. For all of my Google know-how, I couldn't figure out what to search for to find the right place to type code. I was in a new and unfamiliar world now, and the search terms I was accustomed to were useless. Eventually, I found an answer in Notepad (as you will learn in Chapter 1, "'Hello, World!' Writing Your First Program," Notepad was not the right answer, but it did work), and I continued trudging along, only a little discouraged.

Finally, I typed the code from the book into Notepad and saved the file. Nothing happened. But I was "good with computers," and I knew that if something isn't working, you should try restarting it. So I closed the file and tried to open it again by double-clicking it. A little black box with white text flashed on the screen for a fraction of a second; then it was gone, and Notepad never opened. By this point, I was sure I had broken the computer, and I wasn't quite as confident that my boss wouldn't be upset with a broken computer, however old. Then the idea crossed my mind that my program had actually worked. I ran to the printer across the room to see if I had successfully printed Hello world!. The printer sat idly, with no freshly printed paper in the tray. I tried restarting the printer, just in case. No luck. (I didn't find out until much later that print means print to the screen, not print on a piece of paper.) The rest of the afternoon proceeded in a similar, frustrating fashion.

By the end of the day, I was feeling like I was *not* good with computers; indeed, the computers were having their way with me, and they seemed to be enjoying it. I was ready to quit, but I needed the job—and I don't like quitting. I wasn't about to let the computers win. Over the following weeks and months, I made slow and sporadic progress. I backtracked a lot, and I had to keep learning the same things over and over again. The only people who might have been able to guide me and answer my questions were either too busy or too experienced to be helpful. Like the Perl book I was reading (which assumed I already knew how to program in C, whatever that was), these potential mentors assumed I knew a lot more than I did. I didn't want to let on how little I knew, for fear of losing my job (probably not a smart move). However, even in those frustrating early days, I could see how powerful programming would be, and I was even having fun. Eventually, the pieces started to come together, and understanding began to emerge.

My introduction to programming was wrong in so many ways, and I realized that anyone trying to teach themselves how to program would have a similar experience. Several times, I wanted to quit, thinking that programming was just for nerdy computer science students anyway. Starting to learn to program is daunting, and the experienced programmers know so much that they seem too intimidating to ask questions. But despite how hard it can be and how many times you might want to bang your head against your desk or throw your computer across the room, programming can be amazingly fun and rewarding. When I realized how great programming can be, I left a Master's degree in accounting and a job at a top accounting firm to pursue it. And I've never looked back. I wrote this book to be the book I wish I'd had when I started programming.

Why You Should Read This Book

Computers are all around us, in almost every aspect of our lives, yet most of us don't really understand how they work or how to make them work for us. We are limited to what the computer already knows how to do. But computers have always been intended to be programmable machines. You can program the computer that is already on your desk to do whatever you want it to do. As the world moves to relying more on computers, programming skills will become essential for everyone, not just professional software engineers and developers. This book will help you learn to program—and have fun doing it.

In the pages that follow, you will build a foundation in programming that will prepare you to achieve all your programming goals. Whether you want to become a professional software programmer, you want to learn how to more effectively communicate with programmers, or you are just curious about how programming works, this book is a great first step in helping to get you there. Learning to program will still be hard, but it will be possible—and hopefully it can be fun instead of frustrating.

Your Project

The best way to learn how to program is to actually program. Throughout this book, you will be programming a complete Chrome extension. A Chrome extension is a program that enhances (or extends) the functionality of the Chrome web browser. The extension we will be building together will ask a user for a name and phone number, then change all the images in the user's Facebook newsfeed to kittens or puppies, based on the user's location (as determined by the phone number). This extension (which we call kittenbook) might not be particularly useful, but it will be fun to build, and it will help you learn a lot of important programming concepts along the way.

1

"Hello, World!" Writing Your First Program

Note

Project: Create a Google Chrome Extension.

Welcome to the world of programming! I believe that the best way to learn how to program is to actually program (but you already know that because you totally didn't skip the introduction), so we're going to build a program in this chapter. The program will be the first part of a larger project that we will build throughout this book. Go get in front of your computer if you're not already there—you have some code to write!

One word of warning before we get started: We are going to cover a few things in this chapter that you won't immediately understand. Not understanding what you are doing is (for me at least) a big part of programming computers. By the end of the book, all the mysteries will be revealed. For now, trust me.

Choose a Text Editor

One of the most important parts of programming is writing code (but, as discussed in the sidebar, coding and programming are not exactly the same thing). When I say *code*, I mean instructions for a computer written in a programming language that the computer can understand. Code is written in plain-text files using a text editor. Your text editor is perhaps your most important tool (like Robin Hood's bow, King Arthur's Excalibur, and Susan Boyle's voice). You have many text editors to choose from, so choose wisely.

Programming vs. Coding

The difference between programming and coding might be subtle, but it is significant. Coding is just a part of programming. In fact, coding is probably the *easiest* part of programming. Programming includes such tasks as creating an environment in which your code can successfully be executed, organizing your code in a logical way, testing your code to identify errors, debugging your code to find what is causing those errors, working with code and frameworks that others write, and packaging your code in a way that others can use it. When you know how to program, coding can be a lot more fun.

Tip

My first mistake in learning to program was my choice of text editors. I had previously used only Microsoft Word for putting my words and thoughts into a computer, so I tried programming in Word. It didn't take long for me to realize that didn't work. Next, I opened up Notepad and used that for months before I discovered the amazing alternatives I could have been using. Notepad doesn't include any of the core features every good text editor should have. Learn from my mistakes. For crying out loud, don't use Notepad for programming.

Core Features

Several text editors are designed specifically for coding. The next section outlines some of the more popular text editors and their most important features. All these editors share a few core features: monospace type font, syntax highlighting, text completion, and extensibility.

Monospace Type Font

Monospace type font is a font style in which every character takes up the same amount of space. In other words, an *i* is as wide as a *w* and also as wide as a space. At first you'll think the characters look ugly and awkward, but with time, you will come to tolerate, appreciate, then find beauty in the formatting that monospace type font brings to your code.

Syntax Highlighting

Just as the English language has nouns, verbs, adjectives, and so on, programming languages are made up of different parts (such as *variables*, *reserved words*, and *strings*). A good text editor differentiates the various parts of programming languages, usually with different text colors. Take a look at Figures 1.1 and 1.2. Even without knowing what the code means, you can see that Figure 1.2 is much easier to look at. Syntax highlighting can also help you find typos in your code.

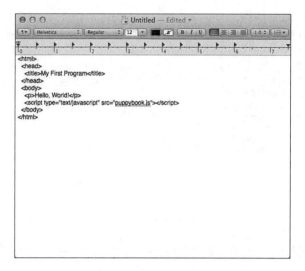

Figure 1.1   An HTML document in a nonmonospace type font.

Figure 1.2   The same HTML document with monospace type font. Is this not much easier to read (and much prettier, too)?

Text Completion

When writing code, you need to type the same words over and over again. For the code to work properly, the words must be typed exactly the same way every time (for example, `myCode` is not the same as `MyCode` or `mycode`). Tiny misspellings and typos are hard to find and can cause major headaches. Every good text editor includes text completion of some sort—similar to the way Google can guess what you're going to search for, your text editor can guess what you're going to type (see Figure 1.3). Using text completion helps you write code faster and can also help you avoid typos and other errors.

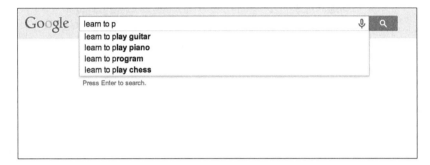

Figure 1.3   Good text editors guess what you want to type, just as Google guesses what you want to search for.

Extensibility

Text editors that are meant for programmers should allow those programmers to build extensions and plug-ins to enhance and modify the behavior of the editor. For example, extensions can modify the appearance of the editor, check code for errors, or quickly add a "snippet" of code to a file. As you will see throughout this book, extensibility is important not only for text editors, but for nearly all software. Almost certainly, there are some features the original creator didn't think of, didn't have time to build, or didn't want. Extensibility makes it possible for those features to be built by anyone who wants to build them.

Making Your Choice

Choosing the best text editor for you depends on your preferences (and your willingness to pay), as well as the project you are working on. I use Vim for most of my coding, but I use IntelliJ when I write Java code, and I use Xcode when I work on iOS apps. The following overview of text editors should help you make your decision.

What Is an IDE?

In the next chapter, you learn about how your computer actually executes the code you write in your text editor. Part of that process involves having an environment that can understand and execute your code. In this book, we use a programming language called JavaScript; the environment that can understand and execute JavaScript is a web browser. For some other programming languages, the text editor is also an environment that understands and executes the code. These special types of text editors are called integrated development environments, but their friends call them IDEs. An IDE is a powerful tool for languages that need an IDE. Your web browser can be just as powerful for writing JavaScript code.

Sublime Text

- Sublime Text has a wide array of plug-ins that can help make you more productive. It is easy to use and has an attractive (dare I say sublime?) user interface.

- It is available on Windows, Mac, and Linux.

- Sublime Text is a good choice for beginners. It is simple and intuitive, and it follows many of the conventions you are familiar with from using a word processor.

- A Sublime Text license costs $70, but you can try it for free.

- Sublime Text is a simple text editor, not a full-fledged IDE.

- You can download Sublime from http://www.sublimetext.com/.

TextMate

- TextMate and Sublime Text have many of the same plug-ins—a plug-in for one usually works with the other. TextMate is easy to learn and easy to use.

- It is available only on Mac.

- As with Sublime Text, TextMate is a good choice for beginners. You can get started and be productive without needing to learn anything new.

- A TextMate license costs $55, but you can try it for free.

- TextMate is a simple text editor, not a full-fledged IDE.

- You can download TextMate from http://macromates.com/.

Notepad++

- Notepad++ is a great option if you are using Windows. The "++" (pronounced "plus plus") comes from the programming language C++; the idea is that C++ is like C, but better—so Notepad++ is like Notepad, but better.

- It is available only on Windows.

- Notepad++ is easy to use and great for beginners.

- Notepad++ is free.

- NotePad++ is a simple text editor, not a full-fledged IDE.

- You can download Notepad++ from http://notepad-plus-plus.org/download/.

Gedit

- Gedit is a good basic editor, but it's not as visually appealing as some of the other editors. If you're using Linux, it is probably already installed.

- It is available on Windows, Mac, and Linux.

- Gedit is easy to use and easy to learn.

- Gedit is free.

- Gedit is a simple text editor, not a full-fledged IDE.

- You can download Gedit from https://wiki.gnome.org/Apps/Gedit/.

Vim

- Vim takes a while to learn, but once you know what you're doing, you can work quickly, with a wide range of shortcuts and plug-ins. Additionally, Vim is compatible with nearly every operating system and is often already installed, so working on an unfamiliar OS is less unfamiliar when you use Vim. I used to be afraid of Vim, but now it's my favorite editor.

- It is available on nearly every operating system ever created (it comes preinstalled on Mac OS X and Linux, but you have to install it yourself on Windows). Vim is like a cockroach: It can survive nearly anywhere, and it will still be around long after the rest of us are gone.

- Vim is not easy to learn and is probably not a great editor for beginners. If you want to learn Vim, though, you can find plenty of resources, including a built-in tutorial (type **vimtutor** on the command line).

- Vim is free.

- Vim is a simple text editor, not a full-fledged IDE.

- You can download Vim from www.vim.org/download.php if it's not already installed.

Eclipse

- Eclipse is a full-featured IDE generally used for Java programming. If you are working on a Java project, this is a great choice.

- It is available on Windows, Mac, and Linux.

- Eclipse is not particularly easy for beginners to start using because it is far more than a simple text editor. However, learning to program Java using Eclipse or IntelliJ is much easier than using one of the simple text editors listed previously.

- Eclipse is free.

- Eclipse is an IDE focused on Java development.

- You can download Eclipse from www.eclipse.org/downloads/.

IntelliJ

- IntelliJ is a full-featured IDE for Java that is a bit more lightweight (and, arguably, better looking) than Eclipse. IntelliJ also offers support for other languages, such as Scala and JavaScript.

- It is available on Windows, Mac, and Linux.

- IntelliJ is about as easy to learn as Eclipse.

- IntelliJ is available in a free Community Edition. A license for the Ultimate Edition costs $199.

- IntelliJ is a full-featured IDE.

- You can download IntelliJ from www.jetbrains.com/idea/.

Xcode

- If you are writing an iOS or Mac OS X app, Xcode is the IDE for you. Xcode is an IDE built by Apple for the purpose of building software for Apple platforms.

- It is available only on Mac.

- Xcode is not easy to learn, but Apple has extensive documentation and you can find a lot of community support. If you want to learn to build iPhone apps, you need to learn to use Xcode.

- Xcode is free.

- You can download Xcode from https://developer.apple.com/xcode/ or the Mac App Store.

Visual Studio

- Visual Studio is a full-featured IDE mostly used for .NET development (C#, Visual Basic, and so on), but it can also be used for other languages.

- It is available only on Windows.

- Visual Studio is as easy to learn as any other full-featured IDE—not too easy.

- Visual Studio is available for free as an Express Edition, which is both good and usable. The paid editions of Visual Studio range in price from $1,200 to $13,300.

- You can download or purchase Visual Studio from www.visualstudio.com/downloads/download-visual-studio-vs.

I haven't mentioned all the editors here, but this list should be enough to get you started. For the purposes of this book, I recommend Sublime Text (unless you have experience with one of the other editors). Sublime Text is more than good enough for our purposes and is easy to start using.

Create a Project Directory

Before we start writing our code, we need a place for it to live. Computer programs are usually a collection of multiple files working together, so it is a good idea to group all the files you will need for a project in a single folder (folders are often called directories—I use *folder* and *directory* interchangeably in this book). I have a directory called `projects` where I group all such project directories. Create a directory called `kittenbook` somewhere on your hard drive. You can create a new directory by using your file browser (Finder on Mac, Windows Explorer on Windows, and Nautilus on Linux) and clicking File → New Folder.

Start Small: Create a Test File

Now that you have your project directory, let's start programming. The first thing you're going to do is create an HTML file in your `kittenbook` directory called `kittenbook.html`. You can create a new file in a few different ways, but the easiest is to open your chosen text editor, create a new file (click File → New File), and then save it as `kittenbook.html` (File → Save As, then find your `kittenbook` directory, type in **kittenbook.html** as the filename, and click Save). Now fill in `kittenbook.html` with the code in Listing 1.1.

Listing 1.1   **kittenbook.html**

```
<html>
    <head>
        <title>My First Program</title>
    </head>
    <body>
        <p>Hello, World!</p>
    </body>
</html>
```

Save the file and then open it in a web browser by double-clicking it in your file browser. You should see something similar to Figure 1.4.

Take a break to enjoy this moment. Now look back at your code and compare it to what you see in the web browser. You should see `Hello, World!` in the window body, and you should see `My First Program` in the tab. HTML (Hypertext Markup Language) is made up of elements. An element consists of an opening tag, an optional body, and a closing tag. For instance `<p>` is an opening tag for the paragraph element, `Hello, World` is the content, and `</p>` is the closing tag. The body of an element can also contain other elements. For instance, see Listing 1.2.

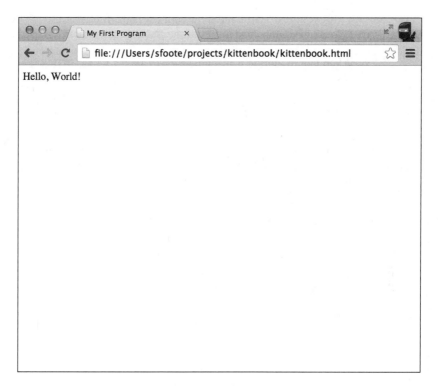

Figure 1.4   You told the computer to do something, and it worked!

Listing 1.2   **The `<head>` Tag of `kittenbook.html`**

```
<head>
    <title>My First Program</title>
</head>
```

The head element contains a title element. This tells the web browser the title of the HTML page, and most web browsers display that title in the tab. You have plenty more to learn about HTML, but we'll leave it at that for now.

How HTML and JavaScript Work Together in a Browser

You've just created your first web page. Now let's make the page a little more interactive. Create another file in your `kittenbook` directory called `kittenbook.js`. This will be a JavaScript file, and it will make your web page more interesting.

Open `kittenbook.js` with your text editor and fill it with the code in Listing 1.3.

Listing 1.3   **Hello, Friend!**

```
alert('Hello, [your name]!');
```

Replace `[your name]` with your real name. For me, this would be `alert('Hello, Steven!')`.

Now open your web page again (or reload it) and see what happens. It's a trick! The page should look exactly the same as it did before. The HTML doesn't know that the JavaScript exists, and that's because we didn't tell the HTML about the JavaScript. Update `kittenbook. html` by adding the line from Listing 1.4 inside the `<body>` element.

Listing 1.4   **Add Your JavaScript to `kittenbook.html`**

```
<script type="text/javascript" src="kittenbook.js"></script>
```

Now `kittenbook.html` should look like Listing 1.5.

Listing 1.5   **`kittenbook.html` with JavaScript**

```html
<html>
    <head>
        <title>My First Program</title>
    </head>
    <body>
        <p>Hello, World!</p>
        <script type="text/javascript" src="kittenbook.js"></script>
    </body>
</html>
```

This time, you should see something similar to Figure 1.5.

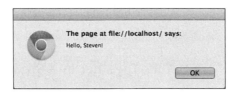

Figure 1.5   Hello, you wrote a real program!

That was awesome! You made a window appear with your name in it. You could type whatever you wanted, and it would show up in that window. Let's talk about what you just did; then we'll take it to the next level.

The JavaScript you wrote is a single instruction for your computer. alert is something called a function that tells the web browser to open a window with an OK button. You can add some text to the window by adding an argument to alert. A function is a piece of code that can be called to perform a task. An argument can modify how the function performs the task. The semicolon at the end of the line indicates to JavaScript the end of an instruction. Programs usually have many instructions, so the semicolons separate the instructions.

The Value of Small Changes

Now we're going to enhance our program so that we can say hello to anyone, instead of just "Hello, World!" As you make the enhancements, make small changes. Then test those small changes before you make more changes. At first, this process might seem tedious and unnecessary. However, if you make many changes before testing and find that your program isn't working, you will have a hard time determining which of your changes broke the program. If you make one small change before testing and see that your program is broken, you will know exactly what you did to break it.

Our first small change is to ask for a name. A personalized greeting isn't much good without a name. For this example, we use a function called prompt because it is simple and it works well here. However, I beg you not to use prompt (or alert) with a real website. Although prompt and alert are convenient for testing and learning, they make for a poor and outdated user experience. We cover alternatives for them in Chapter 8, "Functions and Methods." For now, update your kittenbook.js to use prompt instead of alert, and change the message to say "Hello, what's your name?" (see Listing 1.6).

Listing 1.6 **Prompt for a Name**

```
prompt('Hello, what\'s your name?');
```

You might be wondering why this code says what\'s instead of what's. A group of characters such as 'Hello, World!' is called a string. A string starts with a quote and ends with a quote. If I type prompt('Hello, what's your name?');, then I have three quotes (even though one of them is intended to be an apostrophe), which confuses the computer. The computer sees the string 'Hello, what', then sees some other characters that it doesn't understand, and then sees another string: ');'. I use a backslash before the single quote in what\'s to tell the computer that I don't mean the apostrophe to signify the end of the string. The backslash is called an escape character.

Now if you refresh your page, you should see a window with a place for you to type your name (see Figure 1.6).

Notice that when you type in your name and click OK, the page still says Hello, World! What gives? Why ask for a name if you're not going to show it? Well, we haven't told the computer what to do with the name. We made a small change: We switched the alert window for a prompt window. It worked, so now we can tell the computer what to do with the name.

Figure 1.6   What's your name?

One of the most important tools in programming is the variable. A variable is a place to store some data that affects how the program works—Chapter 5, "Data (Types), Data (Structures), Data(bases)," discusses variables in great detail. In this case, we want to store the name from the prompt window. (See Listing 1.7.)

Listing 1.7   **Your First Variable**

```
var userName = prompt('Hello, what\'s your name?');
```

All variables have names, and we have called our variable `userName`. To tell the computer that we are creating a variable, we use a reserved word: `var`. A reserved word is a word that has special meaning to a programming language. It is reserved, so you cannot use that word as the name of a variable; you don't want to confuse your computer.

Now that we have stored our variable, refresh the page to see that everything still works. The web page should look the same as the last time you refreshed. We have stored the username, but we haven't told the computer to do anything with it yet. The next step is to insert the username in the web page (see Listing 1.8).

Listing 1.8   **Put Your Variable to Work**

```
var userName = prompt('Hello, what\'s your name?');
document.body.innerHTML = 'Hello, ' + userName + '!';
```

We add a new instruction to change the HTML document's body. Remember the `<body>` element from `kittenbook.html`? `document.body.innerHTML` refers to everything between the opening tag and the closing tag of the `<body>` element. `document.body.innerHTML = 'Hello, ' + userName + '!';` effectively changes the HTML to look like Listing 1.9 (assuming that I type `Steven` when the prompt asks for my name).

Listing 1.9   **kittenbook.html When Your JavaScript Is Done with It**

```
<html>
    <head>
        <title>My First Program</title>
    </head>
    <body>
```

```
      Hello, Steven!
    </body>
</html>
```

Congratulations! You just created a real program. Admittedly, this is not the most useful program that has ever been written, but it is certainly not the *least* useful—and you learned a lot along the way.

Build on Your Success

Now we take the program that you just built and turn it into a Chrome extension. A Chrome extension is a small program that can be installed in Google Chrome to enhance the user's Chrome experience. A Chrome extension can be powerful; some companies' main product is a Chrome extension. The extension that we start in this chapter serves as the basis of the project for the rest of the book.

The first step is to create a new file called manifest.json. This file gives Chrome information about the extension and how it works. JSON is a type of document that stores data in an efficient way and that both computers and humans can easily read. Fill in your manifest.json file to look like Listing 1.10 (remember that every character is important, including the funny-looking characters called curly braces on the first and last lines).

Listing 1.10 **Example manifest.json for a Chrome Extension**

```
{
    "manifest_version": 2,
    "name": "kittenbook",
    "description": "Replace photos on Facebook with kittens",
    "version": "0.0.1"
}
```

Now that you have a manifest.json file, you have everything you need to create a Chrome extension. At this point, your extension won't do anything, but you can still add it to Chrome to make sure your manifest.json file doesn't have any problems. To add your extension to Chrome, you need to open the Chrome web browser (download it if you haven't already) and then enter **chrome://extensions** in the address bar. You should see something similar to Figure 1.7.

Click the checkbox next to Developer Mode (because you're a developer now!) to be able to add your extension. Now you should see a button that reads Load Unpacked Extension (see Figure 1.8).

Figure 1.7   The Chrome Extensions page

Figure 1.8   The Chrome Extensions page in Developer mode

When you click that button, you want to select your entire project directory (instead of a single file within the project directory). If you have selected the correct directory and the `manifest.json` file has no problems, you should see your extension added to the list of extensions (see Figure 1.9).

If your `manifest.json` file has a problem, you get a message like the one in Figure 1.10. If you do see such a message, you should copy the contents of `manifest.json` and paste them into a JSON validator such as http://jsonlint.com/, which shows you just where your error is and how to fix it.

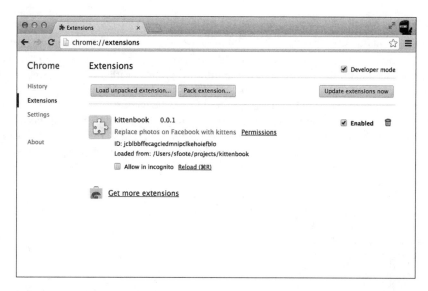

Figure 1.9   Kittenbook making its debut in Chrome

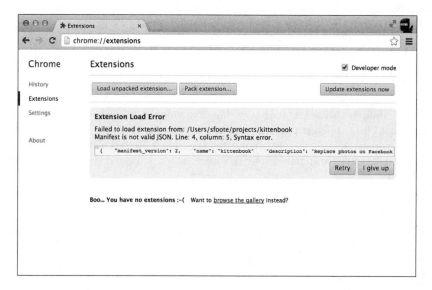

Figure 1.10   When `manifest.json` is busted

Reference Your JavaScript in `manifest.json`

After the kittenbook extension is successfully installed, you are ready to make it actually do something. You already have a JavaScript file written, so all you need to do is make that JavaScript available on Facebook.com. We ran into this problem earlier when we tried to add the JavaScript file to `kittenbook.html`. To solve that problem, we had to tell `kittenbook.html` about the JavaScript file. In this case, we need to tell `manifest.json` about the JavaScript file. We also need to tell `manifest.json` the website to which our JavaScript file should be added. We can do this by using a property called `content_scripts` (see Listing 1.11). Content scripts are JavaScript files that should be added to the content of a given web page or set of web pages.

Listing 1.11   **`manifest.json` with Content Scripts**

```
{
    "manifest_version": 2,
    "name": "kittenbook",
    "description": "Replace photos on Facebook with kittens",
    "version": "0.0.1",
    "content_scripts": [
        {
            "matches": ["*://www.facebook.com/*"],
            "js": ["kittenbook.js"]
        }
    ]
}
```

With the addition in Listing 1.11, our extension now adds `kittenbook.js` (`"js"`: `["kittenbook.js"]`) to every page that contains www.facebook.com in the URL (`"matches"`: `["*://www.facebook.com/*"]`). For your extension to pick up the changes you made to `manifest.json`, you need to reload your extension, which you can do by clicking the Reload link in Figure 1.9.

Let It Run!

If your extension has successfully reloaded, you can make one last change to `kittenbook.js` to make the greeting look a little nicer (see Listing 1.12).

Listing 1.12   **Updated `kittenbook.js` for Use in the Chrome Extension**

```
var userName = prompt('Hello, what\'s your name?');
document.body.innerHTML = '<h1>Hello, ' + userName + '!</h1>';
```

Adding the `<h1>` tag styles the greeting as a heading (big and bold text). Now reload the extension and open Facebook to see what happens. You should see your prompt window open and then see something similar to Figure 1.11.

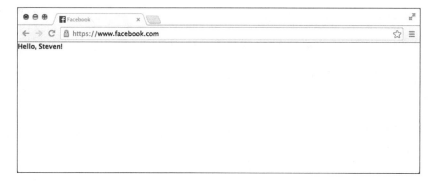

Figure 1.11   Hello, Facebook!

That was amazing—you just changed Facebook. *The* Facebook is showing *your* greeting. That is really cool but not useful at all. In fact, the extension we just built will prevent you from seeing any real Facebook page. That's really annoying. While I was building the extension, my wife tried to check Facebook on my computer; she was not particularly impressed with the greeting that took over her Facebook page. When you're not working on your extension, you can disable it by unchecking the Enabled check box (refer to Figure 1.9).

Great Power, Great Responsibility

By reading this chapter, you have started to acquire remarkable power. You are beginning to learn that you can give your computer instructions and that your computer will do what you say. Software is no longer something you just buy; you can *make* it.

The Chrome Extension that we started in this chapter will be a great tool to help you learn about many different concepts in programming. However, in its current state, the extension is a nuisance. It would be unkind to share it with friends (especially if you don't tell them how to disable it). You have power to create useful, helpful, and fun programs, but you also have the power to create annoying, harmful, and malicious programs. Always use your power for good.

Summing Up

In this chapter you learned about:

- Text editors, the place where computer programs are created
- Project directories to keep your program organized
- HTML and JavaScript, and how they work together
- Small iterations for finding problems early
- Variables and escape characters

Oh, and you built a real, functioning program. Then you turned that program into a Chrome Extension that actually changes Facebook.com. Just think, 40 minutes ago, you didn't even know what a variable was. You should be proud—and probably a bit tired. Now might be a good time for a break.

In the next chapter (after your break), you will learn about:

- How software works
- Compiled software
- Interpreted software
- Input and output
- Memory and variables

2

How Software Works

Note

Project: Create a good directory structure and split JavaScript code into different files.

In the last chapter, you built a real software application, but we hid the details of how that software (or any software) actually works. A big part of programming is figuring out why your program is not currently working. You will have a difficult time figuring out why your software isn't working if you don't understand how software works. Understanding how software works will also help you make better decisions about how to build your programs.

I want to be up front with you: This chapter is going to be difficult, even painful. Learning to program is painful, and the topics in this chapter can be especially difficult. You might not understand them fully by the time you're done reading, and that's fine. You can keep moving, if you want, or you can read this chapter again. The important thing is that you become aware of these concepts.

You might think "I want to quit" as you go through this chapter (or any chapter in this book). I completely sympathize with you. Programming is hard, and your head probably hurts. When I first started learning, I wanted to quit several times. I also wanted to throw my computer across the room several times (that still happens). But every time I finally got something to work, all the pain was worth it. I have asked several professional software engineers if they ever wanted to quit, and the answer is almost always "Yes!!!" Then comes a story about a missing semicolon or comma that nearly drove them crazy. If you feel like you want to quit, you are in good company. If you don't quit, you are in better company. Hang in there.

What Is "Software"?

From a consumer's point of view, software is a product that you can buy to run on your computer or smartphone. You are not just a consumer anymore, though; you have already written a program, so you are a programmer. In this book, we take the point of view of a programmer. From our point of view, software is a set of instructions to be executed by a computer. A program might have very few instructions in a single file, or it might have millions of instructions spread across thousands of related files.

In another sense, software is any part of a computer's functionality that is not hardware (that is, the physical components of a computer). Hardware and software are closely related: One isn't much good without the other. Hardware doesn't know what to do with itself without the software, and software can't execute itself.

The First Software

Hardware and software aren't much good without each other, but one of them had to come first. In this particular chicken-and-egg problem, we know which came first, and it's a bit of a surprise. In 1842, Ada Lovelace wrote the software to calculate Bernoulli numbers. Her software was meant to run on Charles Babbage's mechanical computer, the Analytical Engine. But in 1842, the Analytical Engine didn't even exist; in fact, the Analytical Engine was never completed, so Ada's code (the world's first computer program) was never tested.

Software Life Cycle

The way in which software runs on a computer can be broken down into 3 basic steps (see Figure 2.1).

1. The computer receives a set of instructions.

2. If those instructions are not in a form that the computer can understand (binary), the computer must try to transform them into binary (using other instructions that are already in binary).

3. The computer hardware executes instructions in binary.

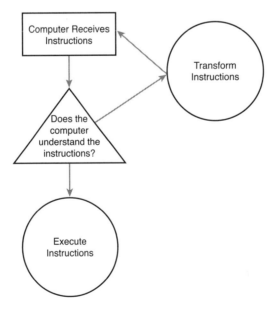

Figure 2.1   How software makes the computer do stuff

Source Code—Where It All Starts

In your kittenbook project, you wrote source code. Specifically, the instructions you wrote in `kittenbook.js` are the source code of your project. The other files (`manifest.json` and `kittenbook.html`) can also be considered source code, but they don't really contain instructions. `manifest.json` is used to make Chrome understand how your program works (a type of input), and `kittenbook.html` describes what should be on your web page and in what format (a type of output).

A Set of Instructions

Every program is a set of instructions. Sometimes the instructions exist in a single file, and sometimes they are spread across multiple files and even multiple computers. Each instruction on its own is simple. Using `kittenbook.js` as an example, you can see three instructions (see Listing 2.1).

Listing 2.1 **`kittenbook.js` Instructions**

```
var userName = prompt('Hello, what\'s your name?');
document.body.innerHTML = '<h1>Hello, ' + userName + '!</h1>';
```

From these two lines of code, we can break out three distinct instructions:

1. Ask the user for a name.

2. Tell the computer to save that name to a variable called `userName`.

3. Replace the contents of `document.body` with the string `'<h1>Hello ' + userName + '!</h1>'`.

That seems to make sense, but which of these instructions told the computer to show a window with a Chrome icon, your message, a text input field, and two buttons? Which of these instructions told the computer *where* to save the name? Which of these instructions told the computer to update the way the web page looks when `document.body.innerHTML` is assigned a new value? If you're not telling the computer to do these things, who is? How is this magic happening?

The answer to all these questions is the same: It doesn't matter. I had a hard time accepting this answer. When I started to program, I wanted to control everything, and I wanted to understand how everything worked. The truth is, all three of the instructions are expanded into many more instructions. You don't need to know what those instructions are or understand how they work, as long as they work.

You are building on a framework. In this case, the framework is the web browser. `prompt` is a call to the framework, and the framework runs its own instructions to make the window appear. It's not magic, because someone had to actually write those instructions, but it's magic to you.

The concept of using the work of others without fully understanding it has a lot of names, including *levels of abstraction* and *black box*. The `prompt` function is a great example of a black box. You know that you can call `prompt` with a string and that a window will appear with that string, a text field, and some buttons. But when you call `prompt`, you don't need to know what instructions are executed to make that window appear. It just works, and that's all you need to know. If the people who work on Chrome find and fix a bug that affects how `prompt` works, you don't have to do anything to get the fix. If those people decide to improve the look of the window, you don't have to do anything to get the new look.

Software Magic Tricks Revealed

I have said a lot about using the work of others and how it's great. You don't have to understand anything, as long as it works. Hopefully some red flags are going up: If you don't need to understand *anything*, then what on earth are you doing reading this book? The truth is, you do need to understand your framework so you don't misuse it.

To drive a car, you don't need to understand alternators, differentials, internal combustion, or even what they put in windshield wiper fluid to make it so darn effective. You don't even need to know how to switch gears—automatic cars will do that for you. You do need to understand what the gas pedal does and what the brake pedal does and when to use each. You do need to understand P, R, N, D, and L and when to use them. If you don't take the time to understand that much of the car framework, you are likely to misuse your car. For example, you might know that you want your car to go, and you find out that R makes the car go, so you just drive around backward. You get the job done, but there is a much better way. If you don't have some understanding of the software framework you are building on, you are likely to make similar mistakes.

Programming Languages

Programming languages are an excellent example of "levels of abstraction." Computers don't understand programming languages; programming languages are meant for humans to read and write. That's right, that code that makes no sense to you, but at least the computer understands it—yeah, the computer doesn't understand it, either. A programming language is an easy way for humans to give instructions to a computer (well, easier than writing binary). The instructions still have to be transformed into something the computer can understand (a bunch of 0's and 1's). The programming language has its own set of instructions that handle that process.

You have many programming languages to choose from, each with its advantages and disadvantages. Some languages have a very specific purpose (for example, R is used almost exclusively for statistics applications), whereas other languages are general purpose (for example, Java and C++ can be used for almost anything). Deciding what programming language to use depends on the type of software application you are trying to build. In some cases, you can choose from many alternatives (if you want to build a server for a website, you can choose from Java, Python, Ruby, PHP, Perl, JavaScript, C#, and many more). In other cases, you don't have a choice at all (if you want to build an Android app, you have to use Java, and if you want to build a web app, you have to use JavaScript). The following sections compare a few of the most popular languages. The list might be a good reference for you as you are trying to decide what language you want to take the time to learn.

Bash

Bash is most used for automating command-line tasks, such as file system manipulation. Bash is one of the key tools of a system administrator.

- Every command on the Linux command line (see Chapter 3, "Getting to Know Your Computer") can be considered a small Bash program; so learning the basics of Bash can be fairly easy. Getting beyond the basics is fairly difficult

- Knowing Bash might not get you a job, but you do need to know it if you want to be a systems administrator, and it is really useful for all other professional programmers. Bash allows you to be more efficient by automating common tasks (see Chapter 3).

C

C is a general-purpose language, but it is mostly used for applications in which speed is very important. If you want to write desktop applications, this is a good language to learn.

- Many of the popular languages today inherit at least some part of their syntax from C. The syntax is mostly not difficult to understand, but I still think C is a relatively difficult language to learn, especially as a first language.

- You can still find a lot of C jobs out there, but for the most part, you will be better served by learning both C and C++.

- The Windows Operating System and many applications on Linux are written in C.

C++

C++ is much like C, with a few extra language features, including the fact that C++ is object oriented.

- C++ is a common language for entry-level computer science courses in high school and college. Learning C++ teaches a lot of fundamentals, but it can still be a relatively difficult language for beginners.

- Plenty of C++ jobs exist.

- Google Chrome, Firefox, Microsoft Word, Excel, and PowerPoint are all written in C++.

C#

C#, a part of Microsoft's .NET framework, is a general-purpose programming language with similarities to both C++ and Java. It can be used for building many types of applications and is most commonly used in in the Windows Operating System. If you love working on Windows, C# is a good choice for many types of tasks.

- As with C++ and Java, C# is not particularly easy to learn for beginners. By the time you are done reading this book, however, you will be ready to take it on.

- C# is probably the most popular language in the .NET Framework, and there is plenty of demand for C# developers.

- Windows Phone apps (among other things) are written in C#.

Java

Java is a popular general-purpose language. Many schools teach introductory computer science courses using Java. It is one of the more common languages in the industry and can be used for almost anything.

- Java is not particularly easy to learn, but it is often taught to beginners because of its popularity and usefulness—and it's easier to learn than C/C++.

- If you are a good Java developer, you shouldn't have trouble finding a job.

- Android apps and servers for many popular websites (including much of LinkedIn) are written in Java.

JavaScript

JavaScript is the language of the Web. Originally created by Netscape for use in the Netscape Navigator browser, JavaScript is now the one and only language used in every web browser for every website that needs an interactive experience. It is the language we use in this book for our Chrome extension. If you want to program websites, you need to learn JavaScript. (Be warned that, contrary to popular belief, JavaScript bears very little relation to Java. They are most certainly not the same language.)

- The JavaScript syntax is a lot like C and Java. JavaScript is arguably easier to get started with because it is a scripting language with less structure and fewer restrictions. However, the lack of structure and restrictions make it easy to learn how to write really bad JavaScript.

- Web developers are in high demand, and you must know JavaScript to be a web developer.

- Gmail, Twitter, Facebook, Amazon, and LinkedIn all use JavaScript.

Objective-C

Objective-C is mostly used for writing Mac OS X and iOS applications (see the upcoming section on Swift). It is a superset of the C language, meaning that it does everything C does and more.

- Objective-C is somewhat difficult to learn. Although it is just C with extra features, its syntax and conventions are quite different. When you accept these differences, it is no harder than learning Java, C, or C++.

- Have you seen how many iPhones are out there? Every company that wants an iPhone app needs an Objective-C developer (at least for now—see the upcoming section on Swift).

- iOS (iPhone/iPad) and Mac OS X apps (up to May 2014) are all written in Objective-C.

Perl

Perl is a general-purpose language that is commonly used for manipulating large amounts of text. Perl is the first language I learned for this very reason. In Chapter 6, "Regular Expressions," you will learn about regular expressions; Perl is the granddaddy of these regular expressions. If you have large text reports that you need to turn into something useful, Perl is your language.

- Perl is relatively easy to learn. Its syntax is very similar to C, but it is an interpreted language, which makes executing the code relatively easy. Also, Perl is a dynamic language, which means you don't have to fully understand data types to start writing— see Chapter 5, "Data (Types), Data (Structures), Data(bases)."

- You can still find Perl jobs out there, but you might want to consider learning Python or Ruby instead.

PHP

PHP is a common language for simple to complex web servers. It gained popularity because it is fairly easy to learn and can easily connect to a database (see Chapter 5). If you are just starting out and you want to build a web server, PHP could be a good choice.

- PHP is pretty easy to learn, but strange features and bugs can make developing in PHP quite frustrating.

- A lot of PHP jobs exist, but PHP is losing popularity. Python and Ruby might be better choices.

- The Facebook web server is written in PHP.

Python

Python was created to be easy to read and write. It is a powerful, general-purpose language that reads almost like plain English. Python lets you do a lot without having to write a lot of code. The online community is quite strong as well, so you can find plenty of support if you don't know how to do something.

- Python is one of the easiest languages to learn. It is a great language for beginners (many introductory computer science courses are now taught in Python).

- Learn Python well, and you will have many job opportunities available to you.
- Newer Ubuntu applications and Instagram's web server are written in Python.

R

R is a specialized language that is mostly used for statistical analysis. If you need to analyze datasets much larger than will fit on a spreadsheet, R was built for you. Because R is tuned for statistical analysis, it handles that job quickly and efficiently. Using R for other purposes is probably a bad idea.

- R is fairly easy to get started with, especially if you have a math background. If you don't have a math background (like me), you will probably have trouble understanding some of R's core features.
- R plus a solid knowledge of statistics could get you a job, but R alone probably won't get you much.

Ruby

Ruby is a relatively new language that was designed to be easy and intuitive. Ruby is a general-purpose, dynamic language. It is used for all kinds of applications, with web servers being one of the most common applications. Ruby developers love Ruby; they are a loyal group, and there is strong community support.

- Ruby is designed to be easy to learn and makes a good first language.
- Demand for Ruby programmers is high. If you learn Ruby well, you will find many job opportunities.

Swift

Swift, introduced to the world in 2014, is the language Apple has created to replace Objective-C as the officially supported language for iOS and Mac OS X development. Swift is a general-purpose, dynamic language. The world is still getting to know Swift and its features, but developers seem to really like it so far.

- As a dynamic language, Swift is probably a bit easier to learn than Objective-C.
- Going forward, iOS developers will be expected to know Swift. If you don't already know Objective-C, you should probably just learn Swift.

VBA

VBA is a language used for automating tasks in Microsoft Office products. Even with such limited scope, it can be a powerful language. I used VBA in Excel frequently when I was an auditor.

- VBA is not terribly difficult to learn, but the syntax is a bit strange compared to many of the other languages that are currently popular.

- You probably won't find many VBA jobs, but if you have a job in accounting or finance, knowing VBA will save you a lot of time. It might even get you a promotion.

From Source Code to 0's and 1's

You don't need to know the details of *how* your code becomes binary, but you do need to know that it happens, and you should understand why. A programming language is itself a piece of software: a set of instructions that transforms code written in that programming language to something that the computer can execute. If your code isn't written just right, parts of your instructions can be lost in translation and your program will not do what you want it to do. I used to think it was silly to the point of being absurd that hundreds of lines of code would not work because I had forgotten one closing parenthesis or semicolon. Knowing that my code must be translated before being executed helped me understand; if my instructions have typos or errors, the programming language will not be able to properly translate to binary.

Compiled vs. Interpreted Languages: When Does the Source Code Become Binary?

Some languages require all your code to be compiled before any of the code can be executed; other languages interpret each instruction at the time the code is executed. In fact, compiled languages are generally compiled by a programmer on the programmer's computer; when the programmer shares (or sells) the software, he or she shares the compiled 0's and 1's, not the source code.

When you are writing a program in a compiled language, you must compile the program after each change to the source code before running the program again. Working with a compiled language can be nice because many bugs are found when source code is compiled. These bugs, called compilation errors, prevent the code from compiling. Compilation errors can also be frustrating because a single compilation error prevents all your code from compiling, not just the line where the error is found.

In contrast, interpreted languages are never compiled, so you don't get the benefits or drawbacks of compilation errors. Interpreted languages require a piece of software called an interpreter, which takes the source code and executes one instruction at a time. Interpreted languages can be faster and easier to write because you don't have to recompile your source code after each change. Compilation can take a long time, so skipping this step can be a huge time saver.

Pros and Cons of Compiled and Interpreted Programming Languages

Compiled Languages

Pros

- Delivers better performance
- Offers better IDE tools
- Does not require the user's computer to know what language the software was written in because the program is already binary

Cons

- Involves lengthy compilation time
- Must be compiled in a different way for different types of processors (the processor on a PC doesn't work the same as the processor on a Mac, so the code needs to be compiled differently for each of them)
- Can be harder for beginners to get started with (more tools to learn and more cryptic errors to understand)

Interpreted Languages

Pros

- Does not require recompiling to pick up code changes
- Can be easier for beginners to get started with

Cons

- Delivers relatively slower performance
- Requires user to have an interpreter installed on their computer
- Makes some bugs harder to catch because the code doesn't need to compile

Runtime Environment

You already learned that your source code needs to be transformed into binary for the computer to understand it, and you might have guessed that each programming language has its own way of performing that transformation. Did you know that you have to install a programming language? Without installing the programming language (or, more correctly, an implementation of the programming language), the transformation from source code to binary will never happen and your code will never execute. As you are writing your code, you need a place for it to execute—a runtime environment. For JavaScript, the web browser is the most common runtime environment. For many languages, the IDE is also the runtime environment. For some languages, the command line is the runtime environment.

Figure 2.2 presents a useful metaphor for understanding compiled languages, interpreted languages, and the runtime environment. For a player piano, the source code is the sheet music. The sheet music is a set of instructions that a musician has written and that other musicians can understand. However, the player piano does not understand the sheet music. The sheet music can be "compiled" into a player piano roll that the player piano can execute. If the musician ever changes the original sheet music, the roll must be compiled again. Once compiled, the roll can be inserted into a player piano and the instructions can be "executed." If the sheet music is not compiled, a musician can act as an "interpreter" and execute the instructions on the fly, but the musician has to interpret the instructions every time she plays the song, whereas the roll needs to be created only once. Finally, a normal piano cannot execute the roll because it does not have a runtime environment installed. However, a normal piano can execute the sheet music as long as it has an interpreter (musician).

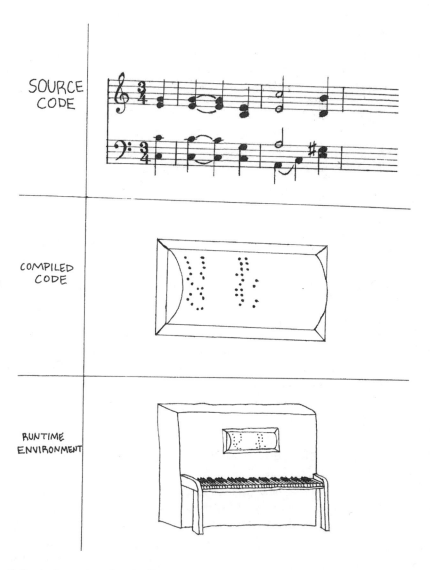

Figure 2.2   A player piano is a lot like a computer.

Execution by the Processor

The final step in the software life cycle is execution. This is the point when your instructions, translated to 0's and 1's, are fed into the computer's processor (more on the processor in Chapter 3). The processor, which knows just what to do with all those, and exectues your instructions. Your program runs!

Input and Output

Thus far, you have seen how a set of human-readable instructions in the form of source code is converted into 0's and 1's to be executed by a computer. That's great, but what if we want the program to do something different, depending on the situation? If the instructions always do the same thing every time, they might not be that useful. For instance, imagine that the source code for opening a file in Microsoft Word looked something like Listing 2.2.

Listing 2.2   **Fake Code to Open a Word Document**

```
var wordWindow = openWordWindow();
var fileContents = loadFile('C:\Documents\Intro.docx');
displayFile(wordWindow, fileContents);
```

That (fake) code is fairly straightforward:

1. Open the Word window and save a reference to it in a variable called wordWindow.

2. Load the file at the path C:\Documents\Intro.docx, and save the contents to a variable called fileContents.

3. Display fileContents in the window wordWindow.

Can you see the problem if this is the code that runs every time a Word user wants to open a file? No matter what file users want to open, they will always open Intro.docx. This code is incredibly useful if you want to open Intro.docx and utterly useless if you want to open any other Word document. I'm assuming that you want your software to be useful, so I will tell you the answer to this problem: input.

Making Software Useful (and Reusable) with Input

You might recall that we ran into this problem in Chapter 1, "'Hello, World!' Writing Your First Program." At first, your web page only greeted you (alert('Hello, Steven!');, remember?). You included input to your program by adding the prompt code. Admittedly, kittenbook is still not that useful, but at least now it can greet anyone.

Let's look back at the Microsoft Word example. How can the code be changed to open any file instead of just Intro.docx? We need input! In the prompt example, we knew just where the input was coming from: the prompt. But you can open a Word file in several different ways, and you don't want to have to rewrite your code for each of these situations. We will create a function that will solve this problem for us. We discuss functions in great detail in Chapter 8, "Functions and Methods," but for now, we can think of a function as a named mini program. Functions can accept input, and they don't care where the input comes from. That is exactly what we need for our Word example (see Listing 2.3).

Listing 2.3   **Allow Input by Using a Function**

```
function openWordFile(filePath) {
 var wordWindow = openWordWindow();
 var fileContents = loadFile(filePath);
 displayFile(wordWindow, fileContents);
}
```

Our function is called openWordFile, and we have to give it a file path (a file path is a like a file's home address on the computer). Written in this way, we can open Word files by double-clicking a file icon or using File → Open. Writing reusable code can save you a lot of time because you have to write it only once and you have to fix problems in only one place. Using input is an important part of writing reusable code.

Where Does the Input Come From?

Input to a computer program doesn't just come from computer users, although that is an important source. Input can come from many places, including other computer programs, the computer's clock, files on the hard drive, the Internet, and external devices. Some of these sources of input might seem a bit confusing, but they should make more sense with some examples.

Input from Other Programs

Perhaps the most commonly used type of input is input from other computer programs. When you save a text file to your computer (such as kittenbook.js), the software that controls the hard drive (called the file system) receives input from the text editor. The different computer programs on your computer are interacting with each other all the time.

Input from the Clock

Some software takes time as an input. One example of this type of software is called a cron job (cron comes from *chronos*, which is Greek for "time"). A cron job runs at a given time of day, week, month, year, and so on. It receives the time as its input to know when to run.

Input from the Hard Drive

Every time you open a file on your computer, the program you open is using input from the hard drive. The next section covers state, and you will understand more about how important input from the hard drive can be.

Input from the Internet

A web browser is a program that receives input from the Internet. The web browser receives HTML (similar to what you wrote in `kittenbook.html`) as input and displays it as a web page. Programs such as Dropbox and Evernote use input from the Internet to keep your files and notes in sync. Mobile applications that require a connection also use input from the Internet. The Internet is a powerful (and fun) source of input.

Input from External Devices

When you move your mouse or type on your keyboard, you are giving input to the computer. You can set up your program to pay attention to that input. For instance, you can run some code when the mouse enters a certain area of the screen or clicks on a certain button. You can also receive input from external devices such as cameras and microphones. Skype uses both the camera and the microphone as input to make video chatting possible.

How the Software Gets the Input

The process of feeding input into your code can be challenging. The process is both common enough and difficult enough that it has its own name. Performing this process is called "wiring up" your software. The difficulty lies in the fact that getting input from the mouse is completely different from getting input from the hard drive, and both of these are completely different from getting input from the Internet. As we build our kittenbook Chrome extension, we will work through wiring up a few different sources of input, and you will see how tricky (and rewarding) it can be.

Types of Output

Input is great, but at the end of the day, we want our programs to make something for us. Although there are exceptions, most software should have output. Output can take on a lot of forms. Sometimes input is a question ("Where is the nearest fast food restaurant?") and output is an answer. Sometimes input is messy data and output is organized data. Sometimes input is the name of a song and output is the song being played through the computer's speakers. Output can be extremely simple, such as displaying some text on the screen, but it can also be complex, such as displaying a video with synced audio. Often the output of one computer program is used as the input of another program and is not intended for humans at all.

Sometimes it seems that a program doesn't need any output. Some programs are meant to perform a task that does not result in any output. For instance, when you send an email, the program you are using to send the email performs a task: It takes the body of the email and sends it through the Internet to the intended recipient(s). This task does not really require any output, but it does have a result: Either the email gets sent or it does not. In both cases, you want to know what happened. An email program that performs only the send task and does not output the result of that task is not all that useful. So even when your program is just performing a task, it should still output something about the result of that task.

GIGO: Garbage In, Garbage Out

Input and output are closely related; a program's output depends on the input received. Thus, if a program receives garbage data as input, it will produce garbage as an output. In kittenbook, we ask users for their name and then (foolishly?) assume that they are actually going to enter their real name. If it's not *their* real name, we assume that they will at least provide a real name, or something that looks remotely like a name. But the text box we provide is free form, and our users can enter whatever characters they want. They could enter their address, their favorite movie quote, a math equation, or even some malicious code. If anything but a name is entered, the output won't make any sense: `Hello, Do, or do not. There is no "try"`.

You reap what you sow, and there is no way around that. If you give a program bad input, you will get bad output. However, garbage input is not always the result of a user trying to be funny or mean. Sometimes the user just doesn't know what good input looks like. Sometimes erroneous output from one program becomes garbage input in another program. Although you can't magically turn low-quality input into high-quality output, you can use some techniques to make your programs handle garbage input gracefully.

Defensive Coding

You know what happens when you assume? Bad stuff, usually. When your program receives input, you shouldn't assume that the input is good. Hopefully it is good, but you should check first. Usually your program will expect input to be in a certain format. As you will learn in Chapter 5 , "Data (Types), Data (Structures), Data(bases)" and Chapter 7, "If, For, While, and When," you can write code that checks that the input is in that format and then recovers or displays an error if it is not. Writing code that does not make too many assumptions is called defensive coding, and this is a good way to prevent garbage out, even when you get garbage in. Defensively written code is a mark of high-quality software.

Validation and Sanitization

An essential piece of accepting user input in any computer program is input validation. Validation is a specific part of defensive coding. For example, if you build a program that asks users to register with their email address, home address, and phone number, you want to make sure they enter a real email address, home address, and phone number. The initial step of validation is a sanity check: Does the user's email address look like a real address? Does it include the @ symbol? Is there text on both sides of the @ symbol? Does the phone number contain only numbers, or are there some letters in there? These checks are an important first step, and you will learn how they are done in Chapter 6. Depending on how crucial this information is to the functionality of your program, this initial step might be enough.

Checking that an email address looks like a real email address does not really tell you whether the email address actually *is* a real email address, and even if you find out that the email address is a real email address, you don't know that the email address belongs to the user who gave it to you. The next step in validation is confirmation. Whenever you get a confirmation email for a new service you have signed up for, that is the software validating your email address and confirming that it belongs to you. The same applies to getting confirmation codes in a text message to confirm your phone number.

Sanitization is the part of defensive coding that involves cleaning up input to prevent bad things from happening. When a malicious user tries to submit input that will harm your program or compromise the data of other users of your program, you can (and should) try to sanitize that input before letting your program process it. When you write programs that only you will ever use, validation and sanitization are not as crucial, but as soon as you have another user, you need to start thinking about defensive coding.

State

State is a crucial component to how software works. The concept of state in software is much like state in any other context. If you were to ask me what state I am in, I might answer with the JSON in Listing 2.4.

Listing 2.4   **My Current State in JSON Form**

```
{
 "isSitting": true,
 "consciousness": "drowsy",
 "mood": "restless",
 "heartRate": 73
}
```

After reviewing my state, you might decide that I should take a walk. Similarly, software can use state to determine how it should behave. For example, Gmail has a set of keyboard shortcuts to help users manage their emails more efficiently. One of the most commonly used shortcuts (for me, at least) is typing g and then i to go to the inbox. If I am in the middle of typing an email and I type "give me a few minutes" Gmail is smart enough not to send me to the inbox, even though I typed g and then i while I was typing give. Gmail is using state to be smart: If the user is writing an email (state), ignore keyboard shortcuts.

State is not automatically added to your program, and not every aspect of a program is significant. It is up to you, the programmer, to decide which aspects of the state you want to track, and it is up to you to keep a copy of those aspects of the state. Some aspects of the state are short term (Is the mouse over the button?) and can be forgotten almost immediately. Other aspects of the state are longer term (Is the user logged in?) and need to be remembered the entire time the user is using the software (this length of time is called a session). Some aspects of the state should never be forgotten (What is the user's name? What is the user's email address?). Regardless of how long a given aspect needs to be remembered, the software needs to keep its copy of the state in sync with the actual state. If the software's state does not accurately reflect reality, bad things happen.

Add State to Kittenbook

So far, our kittenbook software doesn't really have any state or care about it. Let's take a first step toward putting state into our extension by adding some extra information to our "Hello" page. You will add these values to a new JavaScript file called values.js, which should be put in a new directory called js. While you're at it, you can move kittenbook.js into the new directory and rename it prompt.js. The purpose of moving files and renaming them is to keep our project organized. Writing all your source code in a single file makes sense at first but quickly becomes unmanageable (I know, I've tried). A well-organized directory structure and well-organized, well-named source code files make development much easier and more logical. At this point, your kittenbook directory should look something like Listing 2.5.

Listing 2.5　**A Visual Representation of the kittenbook Directory**

```
kittenbook/
├── js
│   ├── prompt.js
│   └── values.js
├── manifest.json
└── kittenbook.html
```

The values we will be adding to values.js are the project name, the version number, and the current time (see Listing 2.6). The first two are pretty easy, but the last one is a bit trickier.

Listing 2.6　**Adding State to kittenbook with values.js**

```javascript
var projectName = 'kittenbook';
var versionNumber = '0.0.1';
var currentDate = new Date();    // Create Date object. More about objects and
                                 // Date objects in chapter 5. This object will
                                 // be used to build our date.

    // currentTime will look like '2014-01-25 at 14:45:12'
var currentTime = currentDate.getFullYear() + '-' +  // Set year
                (currentDate.getMonth() + 1)+ '-' +  // Set month
                currentDate.getDate() + ' at ' +     // Set day of the month
                currentDate.getHours() + ':' +       // Set hours (military time)
                currentDate.getMinutes() + ':' +     // Set minutes
                currentDate.getSeconds();            // Set seconds
```

Now you can update prompt.js to include the new values. We'll wrap these new values in a <p> tag to put them on a new line and make them smaller (see Listing 2.7).

Listing 2.7   **Updating `prompt.js` to Use the Values from `values.js`**

```
var userName = prompt('Hello, what\'s your name?');
document.body.innerHTML = '<h1>Hello, ' + userName + '!</h1>' +
                          '<p>' + projectName + ' ' + versionNumber +
                          ' accessed on: ' + currentTime + '</p>';
```

Now you need to change `manifest.json` to point to the new JavaScript files. You can do this by changing the `"js"` line in the `"content_scripts"` section. Note that you have to add `js/` before the filenames because the new files are in the `js` directory.

Listing 2.8   **Update `manifest.json` to Reference the New JavaScript Files**

```
"js": ["js/values.js","js/prompt.js"]
```

Now you can reload your extension from the extensions page. Go to https://www.facebook. com and, after filling in your name, you should see something similar to Figure 2.3. Great work! You have taken the first step in making your project more organized. These changes might seem insignificant now, but they will allow you to work more quickly down the road (and by "down the road," I mean "starting in Chapter 5").

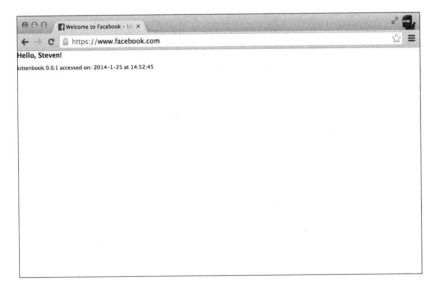

Figure 2.3   Now kittenbook shows its name, its version, and the current time.

Memory and Variables

As you will learn in the next chapter, software uses RAM to store information about itself. Everything about an executing program goes through memory: State, variables, and the actual instructions are all stored in memory.

Variables

You already know that a variable is used to store some data that is to be used at some point in the program. Variables are one of the most important tools in a programming language. A variable really can vary, which is why it is so useful. When you play a video game (such as *Mario Bros. 3*), your score is saved to a variable. When you start a new game, the variable is set to 0, and each time you score points, the value of the variable increases (see Listing 2.9).

Listing 2.9   **Keeping Score with Variables**

```
var score = 0;
// Increase the score by the amount given in points
function increaseScore(points) {
 score = score + points;
}
```

The player's score is stored in a variable called `score`. In JavaScript, you use the = symbol to set the value of a variable. The = symbol is not a statement of equality, as it is in math. Instead, the variable on the left of the = symbol receives the value on the right of the = symbol. Otherwise, a statement such as `score = score + points;` could not possibly make sense.

Comments

Programming languages are written in English, but they're not plain English (because English is too ambiguous and computers can't handle ambiguity). Every (useful) programming language has a feature called comments. Comments are not instructions, and the computer ignores them when the instructions are executed. You can use comments to explain what you are doing and why. We go into more detail on comments in Chapter 10, "Documentation," but we use them extensively before then, so you should be aware of what they are.

In JavaScript, there are two types of comments: inline and block. Inline start with two forward slashes, and everything on the line after the slashes becomes a comment (see Listing 2.10).

Listing 2.10   **Inline Comments in JavaScript**

```
// inline comment
var score = 0;   // inline comment after real code.
// score = score + 10; inline comment before real code
//                  turns the code into a comment.
//                  The value of score is still 0.
```

Block comments open with a forward slash and an asterisk (/*) and close with an asterisk and a forward slash (*/). Everything between the open and the close is a comment (see Listing 2.11).

Listing 2.11   **Block Comments in JavaScript**

```
/* The comment starts here
var score = 10; score = score + 10;
Note: this code will not actually be executed,
because it's in a comment.
The comment ends here.*/
```

Variable Storage

When a variable is created, the value assigned to that variable needs to be stored somewhere. Different programming languages handle variable storage differently, but they all store the values somewhere in RAM. We discuss RAM in more detail in the next chapter, but for now, you can think of RAM like a really big blank book with numbered pages. When the value of a variable is stored in RAM, one or more pages are set aside for storing the value of that variable. The number of pages is based on how big the program thinks that value will be (more on this when we discuss data types in Chapter 5). Similar to the index at the back of a book, the program keeps a reference to where the value of each variable is stored. Updating the value of a variable is basically updating the pages related to that variable. See Figure 2.4.

Figure 2.4   Variables are stored in a given place in RAM like pages in a book.

g on the language and situation, variables can be stored in two different ways: by
reference. Listing 2.12 will help make this clearer.

.2   **Setting Two Variables Equal to Each Other**

160

```
var myWeight = 160;
// My brother weighs exactly the same as me
var myBrothersWeight = myWeight;
```

By Value: A Variable Copy Machine

If variables are stored by value, then myWeight would point to a page in the book with the
value 160 and myBrothersWeight would point to a completely different page in the book,
which would also have the value 160. The second variable (myBrothersWeight) is a copy of
the first variable (see Figure 2.5).

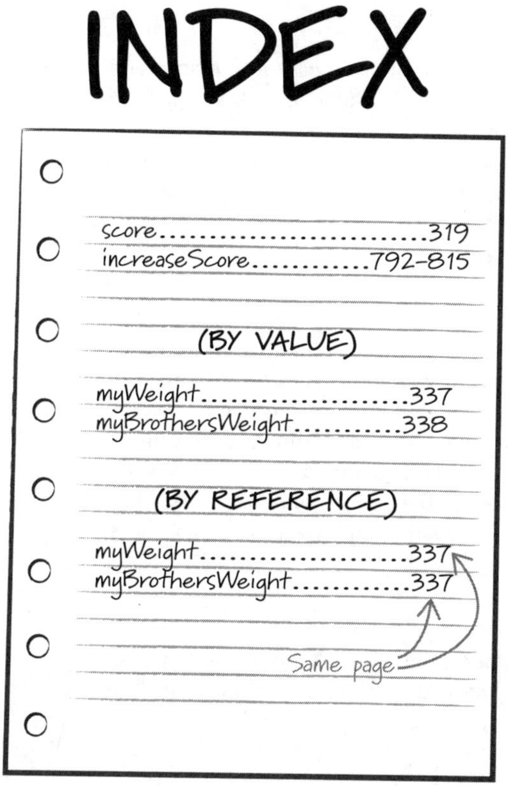

Figure 2.5   You can find the values of variables by looking at the index.

By Reference: A Rose by Any Other Name

By contrast, if the variables are stored by reference, then `myBrothersWeight` would point to the same page in the book as `myWeight`. In this case, no copies are made. Instead, both variables reference the same location in the book. This technique saves space, but it also has an interesting side effect (see Listing 2.13).

Listing 2.13   **Setting Two Variables Equal to Each Other and Then Changing One of Them**

```
// I weigh 160
var myWeight = {
 inPounds: 160
};
// My brother weighs exactly the same as me
var myBrothersWeight = myWeight;
// My brother overeats and gains 10
myBrothersWeight.inPounds = myBrothersWeight.inPounds + 10;
// Now how much do I weigh?
alert(myWeight.inPounds);
```

If two variables are pointing to the same page in the book and your code updates the value of one of the variables, that means the value of both variables changes. In the previous example, `myWeight.inPounds` would have increased to `170`, even though my brother was the one who ate too much. Totally not fair. Variables stored by reference might seem confusing and annoying (especially in this example), but this can actually be very useful, as you will see in Chapter 5. However, this behavior occurs only when variables are stored by reference.

A Finite Resource

Remember that software is dependent on hardware; every variable your program stores must take up some physical space on the computer's hardware. You program is sharing that space with every other program that is currently running on a computer, and there is only so much space. If a program takes up too much memory, it can cause that program—and possibly all other programs—to run slowly. In some cases, it can even cause the computer to shut down. For smaller programs such as the one we will build in this book, the amount of memory is rarely a concern. However, even small programs can have a big impact on memory.

Memory Leaks

One of the first programs I wrote was a Perl program that was supposed to rename a few hundred PDF files. All I needed to do was add a few characters to the end of the filenames. I used a technique called looping (see Chapter 7) to modify each filename. I made a copy of two or three of the PDFs to test my program before I let it run on all 300 files. (As a general rule, it is a good idea to make backup copies and test your code on a small scale before unleashing your code on the real stuff. This is especially true when you are working with the file system.) Everything worked as expected with the copies, so I ran the program on the full set of hundreds of PDFs. I noticed that the program seemed to be taking much longer than I expected, and then the computer just shut down. My program was so small and seemed so insignificant that I didn't believe it was my fault. I mean, I was barely learning to program—how could I do something so wrong that the whole computer would shut down? I restarted the computer and ran my program again. And it shut down again. So it was my fault. I had no idea what I had done wrong, so I deleted the file and started over.

When a program is done using a variable, the space in memory allocated to storing that variable can be made available again. A programmer creates a memory leak when the space in memory is never released, even though the program doesn't need the variable anymore. I had created a memory leak. Each time my program went through the loop, it used more memory. It seems that I also created an infinite loop (which is surprisingly easy to do). So my simple little program quickly took up all the available memory on my computer, and the computer had to shut down.

Summing Up

In this chapter, you learned about:

- The definition of software
- Source code and how it becomes binary
- Programming languages
- Input and output
- Software reusability
- Memory, variables, and memory leaks

My head hurt while I was writing this chapter, and I deal with this stuff every day in my job. Your head is probably pounding, but you made it through. You might want to come back to read through this chapter again eventually, though. The things you learned in this chapter are a big part of the foundation for everything else you will learn about programming.

When your head feels better, in the next chapter, you will learn about:

- How computer hardware works
- How hardware and software interact
- What the file system is
- How to interact with the file system using the command line

3

Getting to Know Your Computer

> **Note**
>
> *Project:* Use the command line to (1) create a new `release` directory for kittenbook, and (2) concatenate all JavaScript into a single file in the release directory.

You already know a lot about how to use your computer. You can boot it up, you can connect to a wireless network, and you can work on an online document. You are probably a poweruser in Outlook or Photoshop. When learning how to program, however, you need to go beyond understanding how to use software on your computer; you need to understand how your computer works. Let's get started.

Your Computer Is Stupid

Computers can play chess—and even beat chess grand masters every time. Computers can find the cheapest flight to wherever you want to fly and identify the shortest route with the least traffic to wherever you want to drive. Computers are pretty impressive. So now is probably the best time to bring up a rather awkward subject: Computers are pretty stupid. They really don't understand anything about the commands they are executing. They are also very obedient. They will do whatever we tell them to do, with two conditions:

1. They must be capable of executing the instructions. For instance, just because you tell a computer to make you a sandwich doesn't mean you're going to get a sandwich. Most computers just can't make sandwiches.

2. They must understand your instructions. This is where programming languages are useful.

A computer's willingness to execute any and all instructions it receives is the reason we have bad software (both low quality and malicious). A computer will never receive an instruction and think, "I'm not doing that!" Computers don't think; they just do. This is also the reason we have really high-quality and useful software. Because there are no limits to what a computer will do, there are no limits to what can be created.

Your Computer Is Magic

You might sense a contradiction. Here I am telling you that computers are magic, even though I just told you that computers are stupid. Well, they are stupid; I'm not backing down. They are magic, too, perhaps because they are stupid. Computers will do anything we ask, and fast. So we can ask them to do anything we can imagine. We have imagined some cool things: the Internet, cellphones, videoconferencing, missions to the moon, ways to find old friends and new friends, translations—the list goes on and continues to expand.

Standing on the Shoulders of Giants

Each new innovation and breakthrough builds on the last one. Program code used to be a bunch of holes in a stack of punch cards. You had to be able to write instructions in binary (and you had to keep your punch cards in order). One misplaced punch, and your entire program could fail. Eventually, programmers were able to write code in assembly, which is still really hard to understand, but is much easier than using 1's and 0's. The assembly code was translated to 1's and 0's. Then other languages were developed that are (relatively) easy to write and understand. You can write instructions in English, and other code magically converts your code into binary so the computer will understand it.

One of the most difficult parts of learning to program is realizing that you do not and will not understand everything. Someone else has figured out how to convert C code to binary; you don't have to understand binary, and you don't have to understand the process of converting C to binary. Again, this concept is called abstraction. This might not seem that great now, but the abstraction of complexity made possible by using other people's work is what makes rapid technological advancement possible.

Computer Guts

This section teaches you a few basics about computer hardware as it relates to the process of writing and executing code. By no means should this be considered a complete description of how computer hardware works. Instead, this section explains only what you ought to know to successfully start programming.

Processor

The CPU (central processing unit) is the part of the computer that actually executes the instructions. It is a small, seemingly insignificant chip that has created a multibillion-dollar industry.

It has been featured on Formula 1 cars and pro cycling jerseys. It has been the subject of several Super Bowl commercials. It's a big deal.

The CPU is the workhorse of the computer. The other pieces of hardware we discuss are used to support the CPU in some way.

Short-Term Memory

The CPU executes the instructions, and random access memory (RAM) is the place where instructions wait to be executed. Think of it as short-term memory. If I told you how to build a paper airplane, my instructions couldn't be stored in your hands, even though your hands are actually executing my instructions. Instead, the instructions are kept in your short-term memory and executed by your hands one at a time. RAM also stores any data, such as variables, that is relevant to the program's execution. We discuss this application of RAM in further detail in Chapter 5, "Data (Types), Data (Structures), Data(bases)."

If you're like me, you can hold about four instructions in your head at once, and you probably ask for these instructions to be repeated several times. Fortunately, your computer's short-term memory is much better than yours. Computers have unparalleled concentration; they don't forget until you tell them to forget, and they can hold millions of instructions at once. However, RAM does have a limited capacity, which is why more RAM means your computer tends to perform better; it doesn't have to keep going back and asking for more instructions.

The CPU and RAM work very well together. They are positioned close to each other inside the computer, so communication is fast. They have no moving parts, so performance is fast. They are a great team, but where do all the instructions come from?

Long-Term Memory

The computer isn't too picky about where instructions come from. Instructions can come from a number of places, including the command line, a file that is downloaded directly into RAM (such as a JavaScript file on a web page), or a file in the computer's hard drive. We discuss the first two methods later; now we focus on the hard drive.

A computer's hard drive is long-term memory. Hard drives are the place to put things that you don't want the computer to forget *ever*—even if the computer gets turned off. Think of a hard drive as a collection of files. All kinds of files reside on a hard drive. Yours probably has images, presentations, and rich-text documents. Your hard drive also stores files containing instructions. When the computer executes these instructions, it finds the instructions on the hard drive, reads them, and sends them to RAM, where they are fed into the CPU for execution.

As you are programming, you need to decide whether you want to store your data in short-term or long-term memory. Data stored in short-term memory is wiped out when the computer shuts down or the program ends, whereas data in long-term memory is permanent. Short-term memory is much faster, but long-term memory usually has much more storage space. Deciding where to store your data is usually quite straightforward, but you should know that you do have a choice.

Using Your Computer

Computers will do whatever you want—you just have to know how to ask. The computer you own right now can do things that no one has even dreamed of yet. But most computers aren't used to their full potential. They do only the things that the software vendors tell them they can do. When I say "using your computer," I don't intend to teach you how to use a mouse, open a file, and print a document; you will begin to use a computer as a programmer uses a computer.

The File System

A file system is the way your computer stores and organizes its files. Your hard drive, external hard drive, and USB drive are all part of your file system. When you create a file, your file system allocates space on the hard drive for that file and then creates a pointer from the filename to the allocated space (see Figure 3.1). Based on the file type, the file system tries to guess how much space will be needed for that file. If the file's data outgrows the space originally allocated, the file system allocates more space. When a file is deleted, the file system does not remove the data; it simply removes the pointer and deallocates the file's space on the hard drive, freeing it up for other files to use (see Figure 3.2). This is why even deleted files can usually be recovered: You just need to know how and where to look.

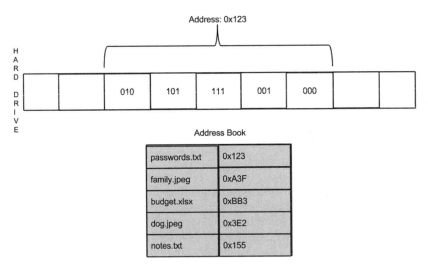

Figure 3.1   The file system keeps a sort of address book that links files to locations in the hard drive.

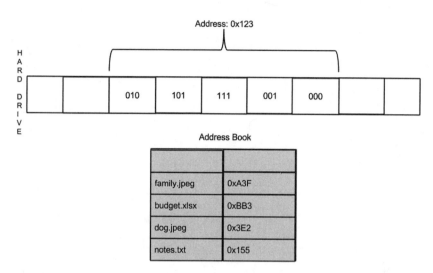

Figure 3.2   When the `passwords.txt` file is deleted, all the data is still on the hard drive, but the entry for `passwords.txt` has been deleted from the address book.

A file system is organized in directories (or folders). A good directory structure makes it easier for you to find the files you are looking for (for example, photos go in the `Pictures` directory, and documents go in the `Documents` directory) and also makes it easier for software to find the files it is looking for. A single computer can have multiple user accounts, and they all share the same hard drive. However, some users shouldn't be allowed to modify (or even read) certain files. For this reason, file systems set up a way to manage permissions. Permissions can be set on a specific file or an entire directory. The permissions that can be set are `read`, `write`, and `execute`.

Sometimes it can be convenient for two different files to point to the same data. You can achieve this by creating a symbolic link (similar to Desktop shortcuts on Windows). After it's created, the symbolic link works just like the original file. If you open the link, you see the original file (see Figure 3.3). If you modify the link, the original file is modified. However, if you delete the link, you delete only the pointer—the original file still exists. If you delete the original file but not the link, the link points to nothing (see Figure 3.4).

Another hidden feature of file systems are hidden files. On Linux and Mac, these are called dot files (because the filenames start with `.`). Dot files are hidden from view unless you explicitly ask to see them. They generally define configurations and settings and are often written directly by the software. When you select user preferences in a program, those preferences are often written to a hidden file. Humans usually can edit these configuration files as well.

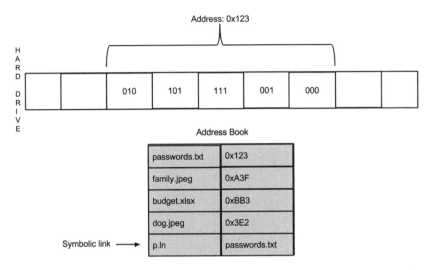

Figure 3.3   The symbolic link `p.ln` simply points to `passwords.txt`, which, in turn, points to the correct location on the hard drive.

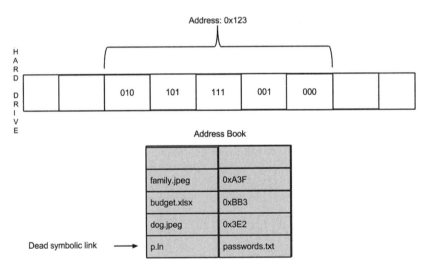

Figure 3.4   When the original file is deleted, the symbolic link points to nothing. This is called a dead link.

The Command Line: Take Control

The command line is the original and most powerful way of navigating and manipulating the file system. Many new programmers avoid the command line because it seems intimidating, confusing, and (ahem) nerdy. You can actually get pretty far without knowing anything about the command line, but eventually you will need it. You might as well learn it early on. You won't be sorry you did.

Anything UI Can Do, CLI Can Do Better

Windows Explorer (not to be confused with Internet Explorer), Mac's Finder, and Linux's Nautilus and Konqueror are all graphical representations of the file system. They show directories as little folder icons, and files as little file icons. You can click directories to show their contents, and you can click files to open them with the default application. This interface makes the file system accessible to the average user, and it provides easy-to-use features for the most common file operations. If you want to rename a file, that's slightly more difficult (and the answer is not to open the file and click Save As with the new name and then delete the old file, although that works, too). Moving a file to a different directory might not be straightforward. Deleting a file can be tricky (usually I just drag it to the trash can icon, but I can't find the trash can icon—what do I do?). For most of the basics, the GUI (graphical user interface) works great, but some things it doesn't do well, and some things it just can't do at all.

When I worked as a financial auditor, one of my first assignments was to copy each of the hundreds of files from the previous year's audit into a new folder and change the filenames to end with 2011 instead of 2010.

I started the task using the GUI. Copying the files into a new directory would have been fairly easy. I could have just highlighted all the files, pressed Ctrl+C, opened the new directory, and pressed Ctrl+V. But there was a catch: I wanted to copy only the spreadsheet files whose names ended with 2010. So I sorted the files by type, hoping the needed files would be grouped together, but of course, they weren't. I ended up copying by 3s, 4s, and occasionally 20s instead of 100s. And that was still the easy part. When I had all the files in the new directory, I had to rename them. On Windows Explorer, clicking a file once highlights that file, and clicking a highlighted file allows you to rename that file. However, double-clicking a file opens that file. So I clicked on a file, waited for a moment, clicked again, then pressed the right arrow (to bring the cursor to the end of the filename), backspaced one time, then pressed 1, and repeated a few hundred times. For about one in five files, I didn't wait long enough before the second click, Windows recognized my clicks as double-clicks, and then I had to wait as my woefully slow laptop (with not enough RAM) loaded the file in Excel; then I closed the file, went back to Windows Explorer, and started again. After about 10 minutes, I was ready to cry, quit, or both. I spent the next 30 minutes relearning how to write a Perl script to rename the files for me. I ran the script, and all the files were renamed in a fraction of a second.

Since then, I learned that I could have just used the command line for the whole thing, with just three simple commands (see Lisiting 3.1), two of which you will learn to use in the next section.

Listing 3.1   **Using the Command Line to Rename Hundreds of Files in Seconds**

```
C:\Users\sfoote> cd audit\2010
C:\Users\sfoote\audit\2010> copy * ..\2011\*
C:\Users\sfoote\audit\2010> cd ..\2011
C:\Users\sfoote\audit\2011> rename *_2010* *_2011*
```

The first command copies all files into the new directory named 2011. The second command renames the files, replacing 2010 with 2011 for every file whose current filename ends with _2010. Instead of spending an entire afternoon of mind-rotting manual work, I could have used the computer as it was meant to be used and finished the task in less than 30 seconds.

Basic Commands

I think my biggest fear of the command line was the thought of having to memorize so many commands. Although I still think this is a valid fear, I have found that a small set of basic commands makes up about 80% of all the commands I use. Before we get into the commands, take a moment to understand the command line itself.

Opening the Terminal

The first step is to open a terminal. If you already know how to do this, you can skip to the next section. On Linux, the terminal can be found in Application→System Tools. On Mac, Cmd+spacebar opens Spotlight (see Figure 3.5). From there, you can search for "Terminal." On Windows, press Start→Run, type **cmd**, and press Enter (see Figure 3.6).

Figure 3.5   Open the Mac Terminal by typing `Terminal` in Spotlight.

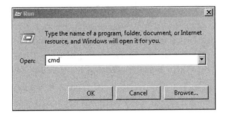

Figure 3.6   Open the Windows Command Prompt by typing `cmd` at the Run prompt.

The Prompt

When you open the terminal (or command prompt), you will see very little—no shiny buttons to click on. You just see a somewhat cryptic-looking line. Fear is usually just a lack of understanding, so let's demystify that line in Listing 3.2.

Listing 3.2 **The Prompt**

```
sfoote@sfoote-mac:~ $
```

This line has four different components: username, computer name, file system location, and mode.

1. **Username:** sfoote is my username. That's the name I use when I log in.

2. **Computer name:** sfoote-macbook is my computer's name. This is one of the ways other computers on your network can find your computer.

3. **File system location:** ~ is your home directory. That's where you start when you open the terminal. This is probably the most useful item in the line.

4. **Mode:** $ indicates that you are in the normal mode, with normal permissions. Don't worry too much about this one.

Windows gives you only the file system location (see Listing 3.3), which, again, is the most useful. Windows also gives you the full path, whereas UNIX gives you only the current directory (although you can modify this).

Listing 3.3 **The Windows Prompt**

```
C:\Users\sfoote>
```

Now on to the commands. The best way to learn these is to actually use them. So if you're not already in front of a computer, now is the time. As we go through these examples, try running each of them on your own. You don't need to type the # or anything that comes after it; those are just comments to help you understand what is going on with each command.

pwd

In your prompt, you have the name of your current directory, but you don't have the full path to the current directory. For instance, if my prompt says sfoote@sfoote-mac:js $, I know that I'm in a directory called js, but I might have multiple directories called js. pwd (for present working directory) gives me the full path to the current directory. Windows already gives you the full path, so you don't need a pwd command. See Listing 3.4.

Listing 3.4 **Using pwd**

```
sfoote@sfoote-mac:js $ pwd
/Users/sfoote/projects/website/static/js
```

When you first start your command prompt, you will likely be in your home directory. For the following exercises, you will want to be in the kittenbook directory. But how can you get there?

cd

You don't always want to stay in the home directory. `cd` lets you change directories.

Absolute and Relative Paths

When navigating the file system using the command line, you can specify the location of a file or directory in two ways. These are known as an absolute (full) path and a relative (partial) path. The full path always starts at the same place (the root directory), whereas the relative path is relative to the present working directory. Listings 3.5–3.10 should make this more clear.

Listing 3.5   **cd Using Relative Paths**

```
sfoote@sfoote-mac:~ $ cd projects   # Move into the projects directory,
sfoote@sfoote-mac:projects $ pwd    # Now run pwd to see where we are
/Users/sfoote/projects
sfoote@sfoote-mac:projects $ cd kittenbook/js  # Move into kittenbook/js directory
/Users/sfoote/projects/kittenbook/js
```

Listing 3.6   **cd Using .. to Move up a Directory**

```
sfoote@sfoote-mac:js $ cd ..          # Move up one directory.
sfoote@sfoote-mac:kittenbook $ pwd
/Users/sfoote/projects/kittenbook
```

Listing 3.7   **cd Using ~ to Go to the Home Directory**

```
sfoote@sfoote-mac:kittenbook $ cd ~   # Move to the home directory.
                                      # The ~ will always take you home.
                                      # It's like clicking your heels.
                                      # Works in Linux and Mac only.
sfoote@sfoote-mac:~ $
```

Listing 3.8   **cd Using - to Go to the Previous Directory**

```
sfoote@sfoote-mac:~ $ cd -  # Move back to the directory that we just
                            # came from. We were in the kittenbook direct-
                            # ory, so we'll go back there.
                            # Works in Linux and Mac only.
sfoote@sfoote-mac:kittenbook $
```

Listing 3.9 **cd with Complex Relative Paths**

```
sfoote@sfoote-mac:kittenbook $ cd js       # move into the js directory
sfoote@sfoote-mac:js $ cd ../../puppybook # Move up 2 directories
                                           # (../..), then from there
                                           # to the puppybook directory.
                                           # You will need to create (mkdir) the
                                           # puppybook directory for this to work
sfoote@sfoote-mac:puppybook $ pwd
/Users/sfoote/projects/puppybook
```

Listing 3.10 **cd with Full Paths**

```
sfoote@sfoote-mac:puppybook $ cd /Users/sfoote/projects/kittenbook/js
sfoote@sfoote-mac:js $ pwd
/Users/sfoote/projects/kittenbook/js
sfoote@sfoote-mac:js $ cd ~/projects/kittenbook # Use the home directory
                                                # as our starting point
sfoote@sfoote-mac:kittenbook $ pwd
/Users/sfoote/projects/kittenbook
```

> **Note**
>
> When you are writing out paths on the command line, try pressing Tab (you might need to press it twice on Linux and Mac) to autocomplete what you're typing or see a list of options.

ls (dir)

When I'm using a GUI file browser, I can see all the files and directories inside the current directory. You can use ls (or dir on Windows) to show that same list on the command prompt. This command is often used along with cd to help with navigation. See Listing 3.11.

Listing 3.11 **Using ls**

```
sfoote@sfoote-mac:kittenbook $ ls
js           manifest.json    kittenbook.html
sfoote@sfoote-mac:kittenbook $ ls -a    # List all files and directories
                                        # (including hidden files)
                                        # You probably won't see .git. I will
                                        # explain what Git is in chapter 15.
.    ..    .git    js    manfiest.json    kittenbook.html
sfoote@sfoote-mac:kittenbook $ ls js    # List all the files and directories
                                        # in the js directory (you can use
                                        # any path, relative or full, and
                                        # this will work)
prompt.js        values.js
```

Did you notice the -a in the second command? This is the first time you have seen a flag on a command. Flags modify the way the command works. Sometimes you add some text after the flag to further customize how the command works. You will see many more flags later.

cp (copy)

Copying files and directories is really easy on the command line (see Listing 3.12).

Listing 3.12   **Using cp**

```
sfoote@sfoote-mac:kittenbook $ cd js
sfoote@sfoote-mac:js $ cp prompt.js new_prompt.js
```

The cp command takes two arguments. The first is the path (full or relative) to the file you want to copy, and the second is the path to where you want the new file to be. The path in the second argument can include a filename if you want to rename the file as you copy it. Be careful; if the new file already exists, running cp overwrites the contents of that file without asking. Listing 3.12 shows the prompt.js file being copied to a new file called new_prompt.js.

In Listing 3.13, I have copied the entire js directory into js_copy. This shows that I can copy entire directories and that I can change the name of the new directory while I copy. The -r flag (for *recursive*) is necessary to copy a directory.

Listing 3.13   **Using cp to Copy a Directory**

```
sfoote@sfoote-mac:js $ cd ..
sfoote@sfoote-mac:kittenbook $ cp -r js/ js_copy
sfoote@sfoote-mac:kittenbook $ ls
js      js_copy     manifest.json    kittenbook.html
```

mv (move)

The mv command works a lot like cp, except that it also deletes the original file (see Listing 3.14).

Listing 3.14   **Moving Files with mv**

```
sfoote@sfoote-mac:kittenbook $ mv kittenbook.html js/   # Move kittenbook.html
                                                        # into the js directory
sfoote@sfoote-mac:kittenbook $ ls
js   js_copy    manifest.json
sfoote@sfoote-mac:kittenbook $ mv js/kittenbook.html .  # Move kittenbook.html back
```

You can use mv for moving files, and you can also use it for renaming files (see Listing 3.15).

Listing 3.15   **Renaming Files with** `mv`

```
sfoote@sfoote-mac:kittenbook $ cd js
sfoote@sfoote-mac:js $ mv new_prompt.js prompt_copy.js
sfoote@sfoote-mac:js $ ls
prompt.js   prompt_copy.js  kittenbook.html  values.js
```

rm (del)

Computer programmers don't like to type more than they have to, so the command to delete a file is `rm`, which is short for *remove*. The Windows name (`del`) is a bit easier to decode. This command deletes a file or directory (see Listing 3.16 and Listing 3.17, respectively). Use this command with caution, though, because there is no Undo button.

Listing 3.16   **Deleting a file with** `rm`

```
sfoote@sfoote-mac:js $ rm prompt_copy.js    # Delete prompt_copy.js
sfoote@sfoote-mac:js $ ls
prompt.js         kittenbook.html  values.js
```

Listing 3.17   **Deleting a Directory with** `rm`

```
sfoote@sfoote-mac:js $ cd ..
sfoote@sfoote-mac:kittenbook $ rm js_copy  # Delete the js_copy directory.
                                           # It won't work because js_copy is
                                           # a directory.
rm: js_copy/: is a directory
sfoote@sfoote-mac:kittenbook $ rm -rf js_copy   # Try again, adding 2 flags.
      # 'r' means recursive; delete this directory and any directories inside
      # this directory. 'f' means force; don't ask questions, just delete.
```

mkdir (md)

If you can delete directories, you have to be able to create them, too. `mkdir` creates a new directory with the given path. If you haven't actually been following along up to this point, you really need to now because we're going to start making changes that are important to how the kittenbook extension works. Listings 3.18 and 3.19 show how to create a new `release` directory using the command line.

Listing 3.18   **Creating a Directory with** `mkdir`

```
sfoote@sfoote-mac:kittenbook $ mkdir release  # create release directory
sfoote@sfoote-mac:kittenbook $ ls
js        manifest.json    release
```

Listing 3.19   **Creating a Directory with md**

```
C:\Users\sfoote\projects\kittenbook> md release
C:\Users\sfoote\projects\kittenbook> dir
Directory of C:\Users\sfoote\projects\kittenbook
04/24/2014  01:27 PM    <DIR>             js
04/24/2014  01:27 PM             324      manifest.json
04/24/2014  01:27 PM    <DIR>             release
           1 File(s)             324 bytes
           2 Dir(s)         XXX bytes free
```

cat (type or copy)

On Linux and Mac, cat is often used to concatenate files, but you also can use it to quickly view the contents of a single file. cat sends its output wherever you tell it to. If you don't tell it where, the output is printed to the screen. Nearly all command-line commands treat their output in this way. In fact, this is called "standard out," or STDOUT. The great thing is that you can take this output and put it wherever you want. You can use the output as the input of another command, or you can write the output to a file.

First, let's see the output of two files using cat in Listing 3.20.

Listing 3.20   **Use cat to See the Concatenated Output of Two Files**

```
sfoote@sfoote-mac:kittenbook $ cd js
sfoote@sfoote-mac:js $ cat values.js prompt.js
var projectName = 'kittenbook';
var versionNumber = '0.0.1';
var currentDate = new Date();    // Create Date object. More about objects and
                                 // Date objects in chapter 5. This object will
                                 // be used to build our date.
// currentTime will look like '2014-01-25 at 14:45:12'
var currentTime = currentDate.getFullYear() + '-' +  // Set year
                  currentDate.getMonth() + '-' +      // Set month
                  currentDate.getDate() + ' at ' +    // Set day of the month
                  currentDate.getHours() + ':' +      // Set hours (military time)
                  currentDate.getMinutes() + ':' +    // Set minutes
                  currentDate.getSeconds();           // Set seconds
var userName = prompt('Hello, what\'s your name?');
document.body.innerHTML = '<h1>Hello, ' + userName + '!</h1>' +
                  '<p>' + projectName + ' ' + versionNumber +
                  ' accessed on: ' + currentTime + '</p>';
```

Now let's redirect the output to a new file named main.js. Let's also put this new file in the release directory we just created. The way to redirect output to a file is by using a greater-than symbol (>) between the command and the name of the file where the output should go (see Listing 3.21). If the output file doesn't already exist, it will be created. Use caution, though, because if the file does already exist, its current contents will be completely overwritten by the output of the command—again, there is no Undo button.

Listing 3.21   **Use `cat` to Concatenate Two Files into One New File**

```
sfoote@sfoote-mac:js $ cat values.js prompt.js > ../release/main.js
sfoote@sfoote-mac:js $ cat ../release/main.js
var projectName = 'kittenbook';
var versionNumber = '0.0.1';
var currentDate = new Date();    // Create Date object. More about objects and
                                 // Date objects in chapter 5. This object will
                                 // be used to build our date.
// currentTime will look like '2014-01-25 at 14:45:12'
var currentTime = currentDate.getFullYear() + '-' +  // Set year
                (currentDate.getMonth() + 1) + '-' +     // Set month
                currentDate.getDate() + ' at ' +    // Set day of the month
                currentDate.getHours() + ':' +      // Set hours (military time)
                currentDate.getMinutes() + ':' +    // Set minutes
                currentDate.getSeconds();           // Set seconds
var userName = prompt('Hello, what\'s your name?');
document.body.innerHTML = '<h1>Hello, ' + userName + '!</h1>' +
                        '<p>' + projectName + ' ' + versionNumber +
                        ' accessed on: ' + currentTime + '</p>';
```

On Windows, either `type` or `copy` can do the job of concatenating files (see Listing 3.22).

Listing 3.22   **Use `type` and `copy` to Concatenate Files on Windows**

```
C:\Users\sfoote\projects\kittenbook> type values.js prompt.js > ..\release\main.js
C:\Users\sfoote\projects\kittenbook> copy /b values.js+prompt.js ..\release\main.js
```

grep (`findstr`)

If you need to find a file that contains some specific text, `grep` is the command for you. `grep` can search for specific text, such as `Steven`, and it can also search for patterns, as with `20XX` (for `2000`, `2001`, `2002`, and so on). See Listing 3.23.

Listing 3.23   **Use `grep` to Find Text Within kittenbook Files**

```
sfoote@sfoote-mac:js $ cd ..
sfoote@sfoote-mac:kittenbook $ grep -r "kittenbook" *  # Search for the text
                                                       # "kittenbook" in all files
                                                       # in the project directory
js/kittenbook.html:    <script type="text/javascript" src="kittenbook.js"></script>
js/values.js:var projectName = 'kittenbook';
manifest.json:    "name": "kittenbook",
```

Again, the best way to learn these commands is to practice them. As you start, it might be useful to open a command prompt and a graphical file explorer together so that you can see how what happens in one affects the other. Before long, you will see how much faster the command line can be.

Summing Up

In this chapter, you learned about:

- Your potential super powers when you learn to program
- The gory details of how computers work
- How your computer organizes data using the file system
- How to use the command line to interact with the file system

In the next chapter, you will learn about:

- Automated programming tasks
- Which tasks are well suited for automation
- How to automate tasks for kittenbook

Build Tools

The last two chapters were dense and difficult, but hopefully not boring. You learned a lot about how computers work and how software works. Those chapters had a lot of theory and not as many practical examples. You made it through, though, so congratulations are in order. Good work!

As with nearly every job, programming is full of repetitive tasks. Code needs to be compiled, files need to be moved from one directory to another, tests need to be run, test data needs to be created and refreshed, supporting code needs to be compiled and executed, and the list goes on. Each time a programmer performs one of these tasks, he or she must follow the same set of instructions. The programmer has some input (for example, which files to copy to another directory), follows some instructions, and produces some output (the files are successfully copied to the other directory). Hopefully, this all looks familiar from Chapter 2, "How Software Works"; the programmer is perform-ing the job of software.

Programmers have an advantage over other jobs, in that programmers build software, and software is exactly what is needed to eliminate (or at least minimize) these repetitive tasks. Build tools help auto-mate these tasks. Specifically, build tools build ready-to-execute software from the various source code files that make up that software. In complex software projects, building software means compiling the right software in the right order. A contractor building a house could build a perfect roof, perfect walls, a perfect foundation, and perfect kitchen cabinets, but if he tries to put on the roof before the walls and foundation are in place, he will not end up with a perfect house. Even if your source code has no errors, the software won't work if something is built out of order.

Automate (Almost) Everything

You don't need to memorize the order in which all your source code needs to be compiled because you can use build tools to handle that repetitive task. But why stop with compilation?

JavaScript doesn't even require a compilation step, but we will still be using build tools for our project because plenty of repetitive tasks can be automated. The more you are able to automate, the more time you will have to work on actually writing your code. Writing the code for build tools can take a little time, but so did building the railroad across the United States; both are good investments. Spending a bit of time and energy up front can save you a lot of time in the long run. You will reap the benefits every day for the life of your project.

Install Node

We will be using a piece of software called Grunt for our build tools. Grunt is a JavaScript framework that does the grunt work for you (get it?). You might recall from Chapter 2 that the execution environment for JavaScript is usually a website within a web browser. Grunt is not a website, and it runs from the command line, not inside a web browser. So even though you do have a way to run JavaScript on your computer, you probably can't run JavaScript from the command line yet.

You will need to install some software that can execute JavaScript in the environment of the command line. The software we will use is called Node.js. Installing Node.js is actually quite simple:

1. Go to http://nodejs.org/.

2. Click the big button that says Install (see Figure 4.1).

3. Click the downloaded file (see Figure 4.2).

4. Follow the steps in the installer (see Figure 4.3), accepting the default settings.

Figure 4.1   Click the big button that says Install.

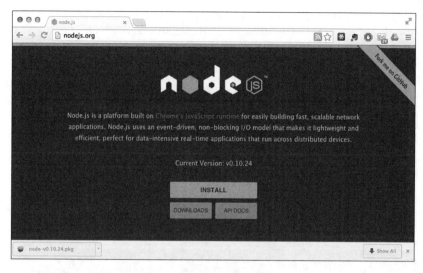

Figure 4.2   Click the downloaded file to start the installation.

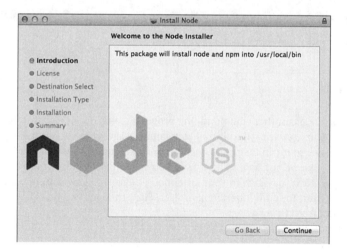

Figure 4.3   Follow the steps to install Node.js.

To check that the installation was successful, you need to open the command line. If you don't remember how to do that, look back at the last chapter. When you have the command line open, type **node** and press Enter. You should see something like Figure 4.4. This is the interactive mode of Node.js. You can type JavaScript commands one line at a time, and they will immediately be executed. The interactive mode can be really useful for experimenting with features of JavaScript as you first learn about them. Many other dynamic languages (including Python, Perl, Ruby, and R) have an interactive mode like this. You will use the interactive mode of Node.js (and a similar feature in Chrome) as you learn more about the features of programming languages. For now, the important thing to know is that if you can use the interactive mode, you successfully installed Node.js on your computer.

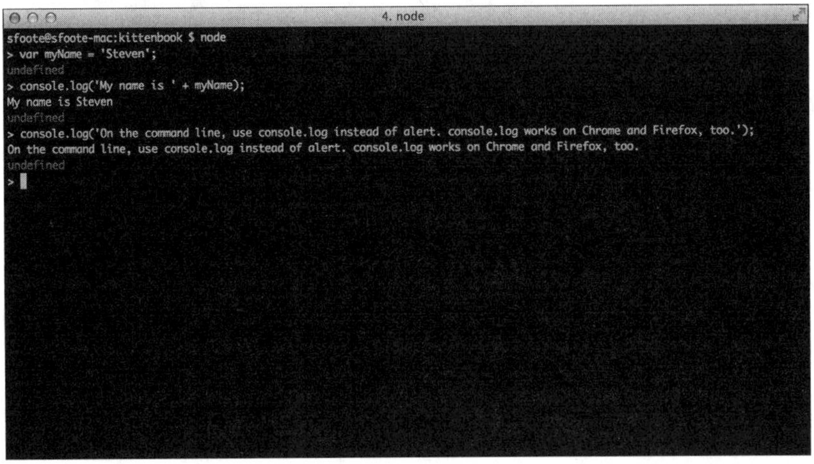

Figure 4.4   Interactive JavaScript on the command line!

Install Grunt

When you install Node, another command-line program called npm is also installed. npm, short for Node Package Manager, is used to install software packages that run on Node.js. Grunt is a Node.js package, so it can be installed using npm. First, make sure that npm is properly installed by typing **npm** on the command line. If you see something that looks like Figure 4.5, then you have npm. Next, navigate to your kittenbook directory using the command line. You will be installing Grunt for your kittenbook project. First, though, you need to install the Grunt command-line tool (see Listing 4.1).

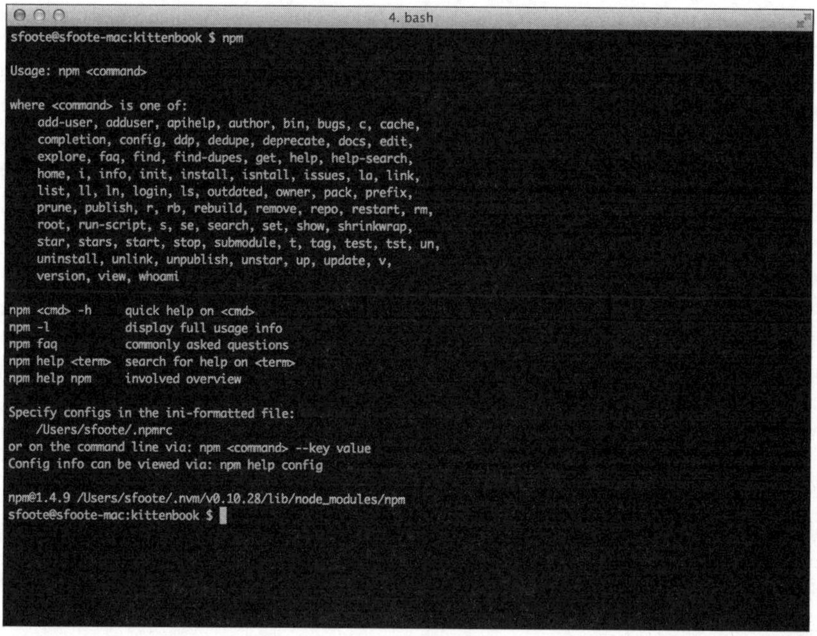

Figure 4.5   If npm is properly installed, you should see something like this when you run npm from the command line.

Listing 4.1   **Install the Grunt Command-Line Tool**

```
sfoote@sfoote-mac-laptop:~/projects/kittenbook/ $ npm install -g grunt-cli
```

> **Note**
>
> You might need to add `sudo` to the beginning of this command to get it to work:
>
> ```
> sfoote@sfoote-mac-laptop:~/projects/kittenbook/ $ sudo npm install -g grunt-cli
> ```

I don't really like using commands that I don't understand, so let's look at what is going on in this one. npm tells the computer that you want to use the Node Package Manager. install tells npm that you want to install a package. In this case, we want the package to be made available everywhere on the computer instead of just the directory where we are running the command, so we use the -g flag to indicate that we want to install "globally." The last part of the command is the name of the package, grunt-cli.

When grunt-cli is installed, you need to define what types of tasks you want Grunt to perform. For our project, we want to copy and concatenate JavaScript files and check JavaScript code quality using JSHint.

Think back to the `manifest.json` you created to make your code work as a Chrome extension. We need a similar file to make Grunt work for our project. This file is called `package.json`, and it is used to tell npm about our project and what packages our project needs. The packages our project needs are called dependencies. The `package.json` file, which you need to create in the kittenbook directory, needs the name of our project, the version number (use the same number you did for `manifest.json`), and a list of dependencies and their version numbers (see Listing 4.2).

Dependencies

If your software will work only if some other piece of software is available, that other software is called a dependency. Dependencies are great because they let you rely on the work of others instead of doing the work yourself. When your dependencies have dependencies, things can get a little tricky; the dependencies of your dependencies might have dependencies, *ad infinitum*. Package managers such as npm find every last dependency in this chain for you. The process of finding all the dependencies is called dependency resolution.

Listing 4.2   `package.json` **for kittenbook**

```
{
    "name": "kittenbook",
    "version": "0.0.1",
    "devDependencies": {
        "grunt": "~0.4.2",
        "grunt-contrib-concat": "~0.3.0",
        "grunt-contrib-jshint": "~0.6.3",
        "grunt-contrib-copy": "~0.5.0"
    }
}
```

When your `package.json` file is filled out with a name (`kittenbook`) and dependencies, you can run npm `install` from the project's root directory (`kittenbook`), and npm will download and install all your dependencies. See Figure 4.6.

Soon we will set up Grunt to handle our build tasks. For now, it is enough to know that Node and Grunt are successfully installed on our kittenbook project. If you had trouble at any point in the installation of Node, Grunt, or any of the Grunt dependencies, see http://gruntjs.com/getting-started for more detailed installation instructions. If that fails, search the Internet (for more on how to search for programming answers, see Chapter 13, "Learning to Fish: How to Acquire a Lifetime of Programming Knowledge").

Figure 4.6   Run `npm install` to install dependencies defined in `package.json`. npm resolves dependencies as it goes.

Software That Helps You Create Software

In theory, build tools are not absolutely necessary. Each task that a build tool automates could be performed manually by a human. However, some software projects get so large and complex that it would probably take a week to manually perform all the steps necessary to build the executable software package. Oh, and good luck performing all those tasks in the right order. If you mess up once, you might have to start all over. In cases like these, we can throw theory out the window. For practical purposes, you cannot work on large software projects without build tools.

Even on small projects, automating tasks can save you a great deal of time and pain. In the last chapter, you learned how to concatenate files using the `cat` command. As our JavaScript files are currently written, the files need to be concatenated in the correct order for `main.js` to work. Also, you need to run the `cat` command to concatenate the files again after each change you make to either of the files. That can add up to a lot of typing, and one wrong character can ruin everything. If we add another JavaScript file in the future (which we will), that's even more typing and more room for error. And what if you forget to include one of the files when typing the command? When we have Grunt all set up, you will be able to simply type `grunt`, and all your files will be properly concatenated for you, in the correct order.

Avoid Mistakes

I have to admit that I didn't learn about using build tools until long after I had learned the basics of programming. I knew there was such a thing as build tools, but I did not think I had enough time to learn about them. The build tools that I was aware of at the time were Ant and make. This excerpt is the first line from the Ant website:

> Apache Ant is a Java library and command-line tool whose mission is to drive processes described in build files as targets and extension points dependent upon each other.

I still can't figure out what that means, so I'm not surprised that I decided not to learn more about build tools at the time. I'm not surprised, but I lost a lot of time and productivity. I was building a web application, and every time I wanted to make an update, I had a long list of manual tasks that I had to perform. If I didn't perform each one just right, in the right order, I could take down the entire application for all my users (that happened more often than I would like to admit). Additionally, instead of concatenating JavaScript files, I wrote all my JavaScript in one monolithic, unmaintainable, error-prone file. Because I didn't understand build tools, I made design mistakes (one giant JavaScript file) and execution mistakes (copied the wrong file to the wrong place). I wish now that I would have taken the time to understand build tools from the beginning, and I really wish that simple build tools such as Grunt had been available then.

Work Faster

Even if you have perfect concentration and perfect memory (such that you never make a mistake while executing these long, complex tasks), you would still be wasting a lot of time by doing it manually. When a software project gets large and complex enough, build tools become a necessity. You will find yourself in a bad place if you wait until your project is that large before implementing automation. Take the time to learn now, and you will save yourself a great deal of time in the future.

In Chapters 9, "Programming Standards," and 15, "Advanced Topics," we discuss the ins and outs of building software with other people. Build tools become even more important when you work on a software project with other people. Each member of the team will work on a small piece of the whole project, and in order for everyone to test their individual piece, all the other pieces need to be built. Without build tools, every person on the team must have a thorough understanding of the work done by every other person on the team, enough to manually execute all the build steps correctly. You will be able to get a lot more done if you don't have to spend your time memorizing everyone else's build steps.

Tasks to Automate

Not everything can or should be automated. *You* have to write your code, *you* have to decide which button will go where, and *you* have to decide the color, size, and position of your text.

These parts of programming require a great deal of judgment, a quality that build tools do not possess. But some programming tasks are well suited for automation.

Compile

When you are working with a compiled programming language, compilation has to happen every time you change the source code. Just as source code is written in a file, compiled code is written to a different file. As changes are made to the source code, the two files can get out of sync. When such a conflict arises, your source code is the source of truth. The compiled code is really just a snapshot of what was in the source code at a given point in time (see Figure 4.7). These types of conflicts can be confusing and frustrating (my source code says to do the right thing, but my software isn't doing that thing!). Build tools can ease the pain by automatically compiling every time you save a source code file or by automatically compiling each time you try to run your software. Either way, you know that when your software runs, your source code and compiled code will be in sync.

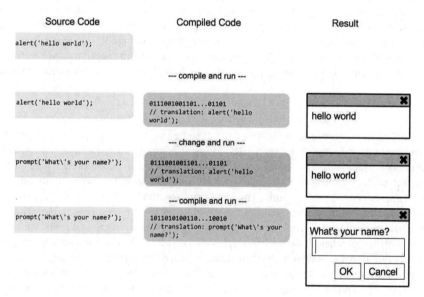

Figure 4.7   Confusion when source code and compiled code are not in sync

Test

In Chapter 12, "Testing and Debugging," you learn about writing code to test your code. Crazy, right? You can use build tools to run these tests automatically every time you change your code. If you break something, you can find out without having to do any manual testing. If you write good tests, you will know exactly what you broke. You can also set up your build tools to run your tests before packaging or deploying, and you can have them stop early if any tests fail.

Package

When writing software that is meant to be distributed to and executed on a user's computer, the software needs to be prepared for distribution. This is sometimes called packaging. Almost all software consisting of more than one file needs to be packaged in some way. Part of the packaging process might be compiling source code. Other parts include moving files from one place to another, concatenating files, renaming files, increasing version numbers, and creating and deleting files and folders. Just as a painter does not paint directly on a canvas that is already in a frame, you will rarely work on your project in the exact format that it is presented to your end user. Build tools allow you to automatically perform the packaging process quickly, without making any mistakes.

In the last chapter, we created the `release` directory for the kittenbook project. This directory is essentially our packaged Chrome extension. We performed all the steps manually using `cat` and `cp`. With just the simple packaging process for kittenbook, you can see how easy it would be to forget one of the steps or to have a typo in one of the commands. You can also see how time consuming it would be, especially if you need to repackage after every change to the source code. Just imagine a packaging process that includes hundreds or thousands of steps.

Deploy

When building server software, the software needs to be sent from development computers to test computers or production computers. Development computers are the computers where the programmers actually write the source code. Test computers are the computers where all the pieces of the packaged software are tested together. On small projects, development computers and test computers are often the same. The test computer should be the place where the code changes from all the different programmers come together to be tested. Once tested, the software can be deployed to the production computers, where it is served to real users. Packaging generally must happen before deploying. Deploying is kind of like updating an app on a smartphone: Software updates that were developed and packaged on another computer are used to update the software already installed on the computer accessed by a user. Without build tools, deploying can be a complex process; with build tools, it can be as simple as running a single command or pressing a button.

Build Your Own Build

Enough with the theory. Let's implement build tools for kittenbook and reap the benefits. The first step we take is deciding what we want to automate. JavaScript does not need to be compiled before being packaged, so we don't need to worry about that. We have not yet created any tests for our project, but we can still do some testing without having written any tests of our own. We definitely want to package our extension, to handle all the concatenating, moving, and renaming that we dealt with using the command line in the last chapter. We don't need to do any deploying for the extension, so we won't worry about that step. To summarize, we will use build tools to handle testing and packaging.

Gruntfile.js

To set up Grunt for your project, you need to create a new JavaScript file called Gruntfile.js in your kittenbook directory. Gruntfile.js is used to tell Grunt what to automate and how. The structure of Gruntfile.js is strict and well defined. We start with the basic structure in Listing 4.3 and then fill in the specifics.

Listing 4.3 **Basic Gruntfile.js Structure**

```
module.exports = funciton(grunt){
    // Project configuration
    grunt.initConfig({
      /*
       * We will configure our tasks here
       */
    });

    // We will load Grunt plugins here

    // We will register tasks here
};
```

The most important thing in our Gruntfile is grunt.initConfig. This is where you configure each of your tasks. Other parts of this file might be confusing (especially module.exports), but this is just the way a Gruntfile.js needs to be structured. Let's focus our attention instead on configuring, loading, and registering tasks.

Use Grunt Plug-ins

Without plug-ins, Grunt doesn't do anything. You need plug-ins to automate all your build tasks. We will be using grunt-contrib-concat, grunt-contrib-copy, and grunt-contrib-jshint (Grunt plug-ins with the grunt-contrib prefix are written and maintained by the same people who write and maintain Grunt), which we already added to our package.json and installed using npm install. Now we need to load them into Grunt and configure them (see Listing 4.4).

Listing 4.4 **Complete Gruntfile.js for kittenbook**

```
module.exports = function(grunt) {
    grunt.initConfig({
      concat: {
```

```
      release: {
        src: ['js/values.js', 'js/prompt.js'],
        dest: 'release/main.js'
      }
    },
    copy: {
      release: {
        src: 'manifest.json',
        dest: 'release/manifest.json'
      }
    },
    jshint: {
      files: ['js/values.js', 'js/prompt.js']
    }
  });

  // Load Grunt plugins
  grunt.loadNpmTasks('grunt-contrib-concat');
  grunt.loadNpmTasks('grunt-contrib-copy');
  grunt.loadNpmTasks('grunt-contrib-jshint');

  // Register tasks
  grunt.registerTask('default', ['jshint', 'concat', 'copy']);
};
```

Listing 4.4 has a lot of new, potentially confusing code. Let's go through it to make sure everything is clear. First, we have added a lot of { and } characters (called curly braces) and a few [and] characters (called brackets or square brackets). You learn a lot about curly braces, square brackets, and what they represent in the next chapter. You've already seen them in manifest. json and package.json. Suffice it to say that these characters are used to structure data in JavaScript. In Gruntfile.js, the structured data represents the task configuration. There is a configuration for each of our stated tasks: concat:, copy:, and jshint:. Finally, grunt.loadNpmTasks and grunt.registerTask are used to load plug-ins and register tasks, respectively.

Concatenate

Before we start trying to automate our tasks, it is a good idea to make sure we can describe the task in plain English. If you don't know exactly what you want to happen, how can you tell a computer to do it for you? The process of identifying and clarifying a problem is an important part of planning (which we discuss in Chapter 11, "Planning"). Before we can understand the concatenate task configuration (see Listing 4.5), we need to understand exactly what we want to happen.

1. Concatenate the contents of js/values.js and js/prompt.js, in that order.

2. Send the output of Step 1 to release/main.js.

Listing 4.5   `concat` **Task Configuration**

```
concat: {
  release: {
    src: ['js/values.js', 'js/prompt.js'],
    dest: 'release/main.js'
  }
},
```

Understanding precisely what steps we want performed should make understanding the configuration much easier. First, `concat`: is the type of task we are configuring. Next, `release`: is the name of the concat task we want to perform. We could potentially create several concat tasks, each with a different name. In our case, we have only one concat task, and we are calling it `release`. Within the `release` task, we see `src` and `dest`, which mean *source* and *destination*, respectively. Next to `src` is a list of file names. These are the source files that we want to concatenate, and they will be concatenated in the order they are listed. Next to `dest` is a single filename, which is the destination of the output of the concatenated source files. The `grunt-contrib-concat` plug-in is taking care of the actual concatenation and outputting behind the scenes.

Copy

Now that you've seen how the `concat` task works, the `copy` task should be relatively easy to understand. First, though, let's think about what steps we want the `copy` task to perform.

1. Copy the contents of `manifest.json` to `release/manifest.json`.

Okay, so there is just one step. That's pretty simple, so the configuration of the copy task should be pretty simple, too. See Listing 4.6.

Listing 4.6   `copy` **Task Configuration**

```
copy: {
  release: {
    src: 'manifest.json',
    dest: 'release/manifest.json'
  }
},
```

Based on what you already know from the `concat` task, you can probably figure out what is going on with the `copy` task. Again, we have a `copy` task called `release`, and we have an `src` and a `dest`.

JSHint

JavaScript is a powerful language, but it has certain features/bugs that allow low-quality code to still sort of work. One way to help you write better JavaScript is to use a tool such as JSHint.

JSHint checks a JavaScript file for common errors and mistakes (this process is called static analysis). Basically, it checks to make sure you are not using the language improperly and that you are not abusing any of the feature-bugs. Aside from helping improve the quality of your code, JSHint can also teach you a lot about how to write better JavaScript code. Similar tools are available for many other languages as well.

The configuration for the jshint task (see Listing 4.7) is quite a bit less complex than for concat and copy. All we need to do is add a list of files next to files:. JSHint checks each file in the list. One nice feature of grunt-contrib-jshint is that, if any errors are found, no further tasks are run and descriptions of the errors display in the terminal.

Listing 4.7   **jshint Task Configuration**

```
jshint: {
  files: ['js/values.js', 'js/prompt.js']
}
```

Load Grunt Plug-ins

Just because the plug-ins were downloaded and installed using npm install doesn't mean that Grunt actually knows about them; it only means that they are available for Grunt to use if we tell Grunt about them. We do that using grunt.loadNpmTasks (see Listing 4.8).

Listing 4.8   **Use grunt.loadNpmTasks to Load Our Plug-ins**

```
// Load Grunt plugins
grunt.loadNpmTasks('grunt-contrib-concat');
grunt.loadNpmTasks('grunt-contrib-copy');
grunt.loadNpmTasks('grunt-contrib-jshint');
```

Register Tasks

Finally, we need to register some tasks to be run. This step isn't entirely necessary, but it's like icing on the cake. You can already run the concat, copy, and jshint tasks individually. Open the command line, navigate to the kittenbook directory, and type **grunt jshint** (see Figure 4.8).

It works, and so do concat and copy, but we don't want to have to run each of them separately: That would only be a *little* better than no Grunt at all. Grunt allows you to register a task that will run a list of other tasks in order, using grunt.registerTask. We will register one task, called default, that runs jshint, then concat, and then copy. For Grunt, default is a special task name, and you can run it by just running grunt from the command line. See Listing 4.9 and Figure 4.9.

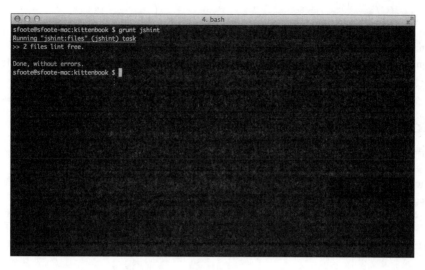

Figure 4.8   Run `grunt jshint`, and it works!

Listing 4.9   **Register New Tasks**

```
// Register tasks
grunt.registerTask('default', ['jshint', 'concat', 'copy']);
```

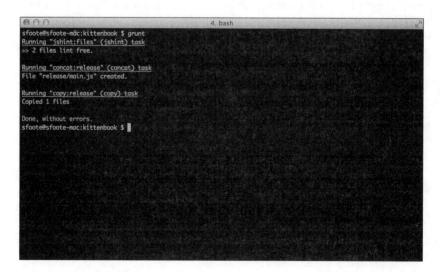

Figure 4.9   Now that everything is set up, just run `grunt`, and all our tasks are run in the right order.

Remember how the jshint task prevents all the subsequent tasks from running if it finds an error in the JavaScript code? We run the jshint task first so we can prevent the extension from being packaged if the JavaScript isn't up to snuff. Now we can package our extension with one command and be certain that we aren't forgetting any steps or doing anything out of order. This is a great step forward, but we can do even better.

Watch This!

What if we didn't have to run a command at all? I mean, we would have to run grunt every time we wanted to make a change to one of our files before we could test that change on Chrome. What if Grunt could just magically package our extension each time we made a change? Although it's not exactly magic, Grunt can do exactly that with a plug-in called grunt-contrib-watch. When we downloaded and installed our other plug-ins, we added them to package.json and then ran npm install. This time, we are going to download and install first, and then (automatically) add a new line to package.json. See Listing 4.10.

Listing 4.10   **Install grunt-contrib-watch, and Add It to package.json in One Command**

```
sfoote@sfoote-mac:kittenbook $ npm install grunt-contrib-watch --save-dev
```

To install, again we run npm install from the kittenbook directory, but this time we add a package name (grunt-contrib-watch) and a flag (--save-dev). The package name tells npm that we want to install only the package with the given name, and the flag tells npm that we want to add the package to our devDependencies inside package.json. Go ahead and open package.json before and after running this command. You will see that a new line has been added (see Listing 4.11).

Listing 4.11   **Updated devDependencies**

```
{
    "name": "kittenbook",
    "version": "0.0.1",
    "devDependencies": {
        "grunt": "~0.4.2",
        "grunt-contrib-concat": "~0.3.0",
        "grunt-contrib-jshint": "~0.6.3",
        "grunt-contrib-copy": "~0.5.0",
        "grunt-contrib-watch": "~0.5.3"
    }
}
```

Now we can set up a watch task in our Gruntfile.js. We want Grunt to watch for changes in manifest.json and all our JavaScript files, and then package our extension each time one of those files changes. Grunt will detect a change in the file only when the file is saved. First, we need to configure the watch task (see Listing 4.12). The watch configuration includes a list of files (such as jshint) and a list of tasks. Whenever one of the files in the files list changes, the tasks in the tasks list will run.

Listing 4.12 **Add the watch Configuration to grunt.initConfig**

```
grunt.initConfig({
    concat: {
      release: {
        src: ['js/values.js', 'js/prompt.js'],
        dest: 'release/main.js'
      }
    },
    copy: {
      release: {
        src: 'manifest.json',
        dest: 'release/manifest.json'
      }
    },
    jshint: {
      files: ['js/values.js', 'js/prompt.js']
    },
    watch: {
      files: ['<%= jshint.files %>', 'manifest.json'],
      tasks: ['default']
    }
});

// Load Grunt plugins
grunt.loadNpmTasks('grunt-contrib-concat');
grunt.loadNpmTasks('grunt-contrib-copy');
grunt.loadNpmTasks('grunt-contrib-jshint');
grunt.loadNpmTasks('grunt-contrib-watch');
```

Because we have already listed all our JavaScript files in the jshint file list, we don't have to list them again for the watch file list. Instead, we can reference the same list using a special Grunt-specific syntax: <%= jshint.files %>. We also want to package the extension if manifest.json is changed, so add that to the list as well. The only task we want to run is default, which runs our other three packaging tasks in the right order. To try it out, type grunt watch on the command line and then make a change to one of your JavaScript files. See Figure 4.10.

Grunt's watch task keeps running until you tell it to stop, and you might notice there is no Close or Cancel button to press. You can stop grunt watch (and almost any other command-line command) by pressing Ctrl+C. Alternatively, you can just close the terminal window, and any running task will be killed.

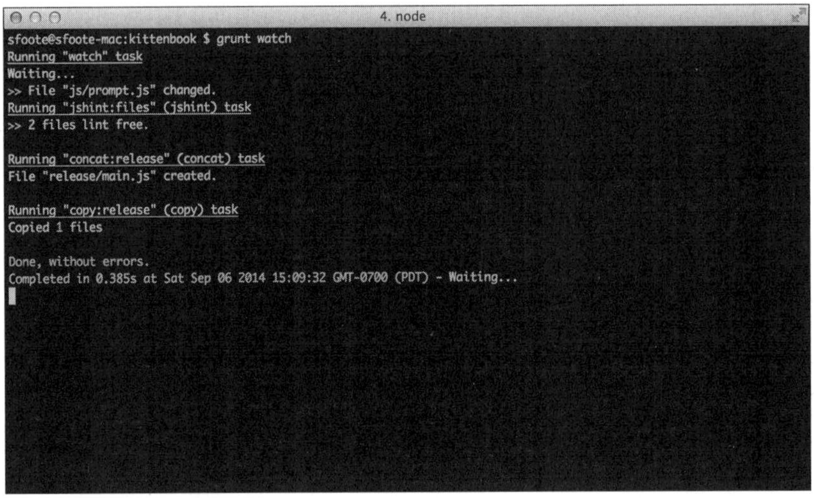

Figure 4.10 Run `grunt watch` one time, and your extension will automatically be packaged for you every time you make a change.

You have done some amazing work in this chapter. You have installed build tools and set them up to automatically package your extension every time you make a change. You have also laid the groundwork for automating new tasks in the future. We will be adding to and modifying `Gruntfile.js` throughout the rest of this book, and the work you did in this chapter is essential. Great work!

Summing Up

In this chapter, you learned about:

- How to avoid mistakes and work faster using build tools
- What types of programming tasks are well suited for automation
- How to set up your own build tools by installing `node.js` and Grunt
- How to configure Grunt for your project

Honestly, most programmers don't learn about build tools until they have been doing things the wrong way for a long time (myself included). The concepts and skills you learned in this chapter will make you a better, more valuable programmer, whether you want to work alone or work with a team.

In the next chapter, you will learn a lot about data, specifically:

- Different types of data
- What those { and [characters mean in your JavaScript and JSON files
- How to structure data, and why it matters
- What databases are and how they work

## 5

Data (Types), Data (Structures), Data(bases)

Note

Project: Use a JavaScript array to store data about the images in your Facebook feed.

To be an effective programmer, you need to know about data—and not just that more data is good, or that big data can lead to interesting insights. You need to know about the different types of data and how to use them correctly. You need to know how to store and retrieve data. Nearly every computer program has to deal with data in some way. You have already dealt with a few different types of data when building the kittenbook extension, and Gruntfile.js *includes a few more. You might not have understood that the strange symbols such as { and [are representations of different data types. Let's change that.*

Data Types

A lot of different types of data exist, and some types are made of other types put together. Some types of data you already know well:

- Number
- Character
- String
- Date

Others you might be familiar with:

- Boolean
- Set
- Array

And others you've probably never heard of:

- Float
- Long
- Hash

Why Different Data Types Exist

Different data types exist because the computer has to store and manipulate different types of data in different ways. The computer needs to reserve a lot less space to store the number 4 than it needs for a very long string (this entire book could be one big string). Sometimes different types of data don't play well together. For example, Listing 5.1 shows how you can add numbers to get numbers, you can add strings to get concatenated strings, and you can add numbers and strings to get ... strings? Getting '22' when you add 2 and '2' is a little nonsensical, but would 4 make any more sense? The difference between the string '2' and the number 2 is very significant to a computer, and confusing them can lead to strange and unintended consequences in your programs. In fact, some languages give you an error if you try to add a number and a string (see the section in this chapter on statically and dynamically typed languages).

Listing 5.1   **Mixing Data Types**

```
var numbers = 2 + 2;        // 4
var strings = '2' + '2';    // '22'
var numberStrings = 2 + '2'; // '22'
```

Primitive Data Types

Primitive data types refer to a single piece of data (such as an integer or a character). Primitive data types are sometimes called atomic because they can't be broken down any further.

Boolean

Perhaps the most important data type is the Boolean. The Boolean (named after George Boole, an English mathematician) is the simplest type of data: 1 or 0, on or off, yes or no, true or false. All the logic that happens within a computer program depends on the Boolean data type. In Chapter 7, "If, For, While, and When," you learn all about if statements and while statements and how to use Booleans to control how your program works. Try out the code in Listing 5.2 to see Booleans in action. For more on how to try out code, take a look at the sidebar.

Listing 5.2 **true or false**

```
if (true) {
  // console.log prints a message to the console.
  // It's like alert, but without the annoying window.
  console.log('It is true!');
}

if (false) {
  console.log('This line will never be executed.');
}
```

Experimenting with Chrome Dev Tools

I love programming the Web. You can see the source code of every website you visit if you know where to look. That is exciting to me because it means I can learn how to solve my problems by looking at how similar problems were solved on other websites. This implicit pooling of knowledge is one of the reasons web technology moves forward at breakneck speed. If you are trying to solve a problem and you find a web page that has already solved it, you can just look at the source code to see what it did. Of course, there is a difference between finding inspiration and copy-pasting other people's code. The former is an acceptable and important part of the Web; the latter should not be done without permission.

The key to all of this power is knowing where to look. Most browsers have tools that developers can use to view the source code. Internet Explorer has Developer Tools (push F12 to see them), Firefox has Firefox Developer Tools, and Chrome has Dev Tools. We are writing a Chrome extension, so we focus on the Chrome Dev Tools, but if you're serious about building websites, you should able to use the developer tools of every browser.

To open Chrome Dev Tools, you can right-click any web page and then click Inspect Element from the menu (see Figure 5.1). Or you can use the keyboard shortcut (my favorite): Ctrl+Shift+I on Windows and Linux, or Command+Option+I on a Mac. Alternatively, you can click the Chrome menu button, then Tools, and then Developer Tools (see Figure 5.2). You will see a box appear at the bottom of the web page, and you will probably see some HTML on the left side (see Figure 5.3). A lot is going on in this box—you will learn more in the "Debugging" section of Chapter 12, "Testing and Debugging." For now, we just want to use the Console tab.

You can use Chrome Dev Tools to explore the code that is being used on the website you are currently visiting, but for now, we just want to use Chrome Dev Tools to quickly try out code and experiment with new concepts, so it doesn't matter what site we are on. Remember the interactive mode of Node.js that you learned about in the last chapter? We can do something similar in the Chrome Dev Tools console (see Figure 5.4). You can open the console by pressing the Esc key or clicking Console in the top bar. Now try typing the code in Listing 5.2.

Hint: Every time you press Enter, whatever you have entered before that point is executed. To add a new line without executing the code, press Shift+Enter.

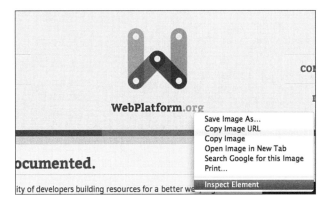

Figure 5.1   Opening the Chrome Dev Tools by clicking Inspect Element

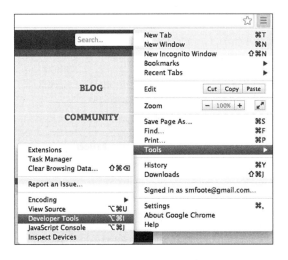

Figure 5.2   Opening the Chrome Dev Tools by using the Chrome menu

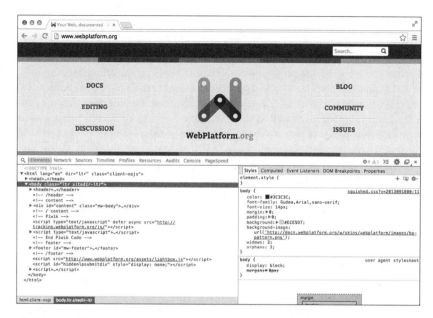

Figure 5.3   Your first look at the Chrome Dev Tools. In time, you will come to appreciate the beauty.

Figure 5.4   Running Listing 5.2 in the Chrome Dev Tools

Character

The character data type is just a character. For normal, English-language characters (the characters you see on your keyboard), this is quite simple. However, there are a lot of characters beyond what you see available on your keyboard, and that's where characters can be complicated. ASCII (American Standard Code for Information Interchange) is the simple way of encoding characters. ASCII defines 128 characters, including most of the characters commonly used in the English language, as well as some obsolete "control characters" that were once used to control how text was processed. Removing the obsolete control characters, ASCII has only 95 useful characters, including the space. ASCII has enough characters for simple situations (including ASCII art), but it can't handle most languages in the world. Other encoding schemes, such as UTF-8, can handle nearly every character in existence. Some programs use simple ASCII, but many use UTF-8. You can see how this can get confusing: You need to know not only what character you want to use, but how it is encoded. Fortunately, the environment you use usually abstracts away this problem for you.

Number: Integer, Float, Long, and So On

Numbers can be quite small and require not much space for storage, or they can be really, really large and require a lot more space for storage. Instead of just assuming that all numbers are really big and waste storage space or, conversely, assuming that all numbers are small and not have space for really big numbers, you must realize that there are different types of numbers that require more or less storage space.

For the purposes of programming, short integers are small numbers with no decimal points. The range of values that can be stored as an integer is from around –32,000 to 32,000. If you need a number outside that range, you need to store the value as a long integer instead. A long is like a short, but with a much larger range (in the billions or more, depending on the language). If you need to store numbers with decimal points, you need to use a float. The name *float* comes from the fact that the decimal point floats somewhere in the middle of the number. In some languages, you have to be explicit about what type of number you are using. JavaScript, however, figures out what type of number is best for the situation.

What the Hex?

You now know about the different types of numbers, but you might not realize that you have several ways to store a number. Most of the time, you will work with base 10 (decimal) numbers (this is the format you are used to), but sometimes you need to be able to work with other types, such as base 2 (binary) or base 16 (hexadecimal). One of the times you will most likely have to deal with hexadecimal numbers is in defining colors (especially for a web page). Hexadecimal uses 0–9 and A–F:

- 0 = 0
- 1 = 1
- 2 = 2
- 3 = 3
- 4 = 4

- 5 = 5
- 6 = 6
- 7 = 7
- 8 = 8
- 9 = 9
- A = 10
- B = 11
- C = 12
- D = 13
- E = 14
- F = 15
- 10 = 16
- 11 = 17
- ...
- FF = 255

This stuff can get a bit confusing, but you can find tools that convert from decimal to hexadecimal for you, so you don't need to know how to do it. I bring up this topic because you might start seeing letters in what you think ought to be numbers; when that happens, you know it's probably hexadecimal.

Composite Data Types

Some types of data are really compositions of other types of data. They might be made up of primitives, other composites, or a combination of both.

String

A string is perhaps the simplest composite data type; it is just a composition of characters. I consider strings to be important because they tend to be the easiest type of data to understand. They are basically just text, and most people understand text. Strings are used all over in computer programs. You already used strings in prompt.js in two ways. First, you stored the user's name as a string in the variable userName. Second, you constructed a message to be displayed to the user by concatenating several strings (including the strings stored in variables in values.js). It was a revelation to me when I realized that every message I see on a computer was at some point typed by a human.

Strings are used for things other than displaying messages, though. In fact, a source code file is just one big string. When the source code is sent to the compiler or the interpreter, it is sent as a string. It is the job of the compiler to figure out what that string means. Strings can also be used to send messages between programs, to identify resources, and to provide user identification numbers. Although user IDs are often numbers, they are usually stored as strings. You cannot perform mathematical operations (add, subtract, multiply, divide, and so on) on a string, and because the user ID is used to identify the user, you probably won't want to perform a math operation it.

Regular Expression

A regular expression is a tool that detects patterns in strings. A regular expression looks a lot like a string, but each character has meaning. Regular expressions are like a terse, cryptic programming language that lives within other programming languages. A regular expression is an interesting kind of data because it is data that does something.

In most languages, regular expressions are a group of characters between two forward slashes: /regular expression/. Because we have an entire chapter (Chapter 6, "Regular Expressions") on regular expressions, I won't go any further here. Just know this: Regular expressions can be confusing, but they can also be powerful.

Date

Many common programming languages (including JavaScript, Java, Perl, Python, Ruby, and C) use a system called Unix time for keep tracking of time. In Unix time, a date is represented as the number of seconds since "the beginning of the epoch." The epoch began January 1, 1970, at 00:00:00 UTC. That moment in time is represented as 0 in Unix time. The number increases by 1 for every second since that moment.

In many languages, a "date" is not just a number with special meaning. Instead, a date is stored as an object (see Dictionary—a.k.a. Map, Hash, Object, Associative Array—below), with special properties and methods that allow you to manipulate the number. You already saw this in values.js; we created a new Date, and then we were able to use methods such as getFullYear on that Date to get human-readable information about the date.

Another Y2K

Unix time is stored as a 32-bit signed integer (a signed integer can be positive or negative). As you learned earlier, a number cannot get any bigger than the space provided. A signed 32-bit integer can get as large as 2^{31}, or 2,147,483,648, and if you try to add one more, the number flips around to –2,147,483,648 (the lowest number that can be stored by 32 bits). January 19, 2038, at 3:14:07 AM UTC (the "wraparound date") will be 2,147,483,648 seconds since the beginning of the epoch. The next second, January 19, 2038, at 3:14:08 AM, all computer systems using Unix time will think the current date is December 13, 1901. That's going to be a problem. One solution is to use 64-bit signed integers instead of 32-bit ones. There would still be a wraparound date using 64-bit integers, but the wraparound date would be 20 times greater than the estimated age of the universe, approximately 292 billion years from now. I think we can live with that.

Array

An array is an ordered list of items. The concept of arrays exists in almost every programming language, but what they are called and how they work can be quite different. When you create an array in some programming languages, you have to declare what type and how many items your array will hold. Using this information, the computer can find a continuous stretch of memory in RAM to store the array. Other languages (JavaScript included) are more lax—you don't need to know beforehand the type or quantity of items to be stored in the array because the array can hold any data type. A single array can hold items of several different data types.

You can think of an array as a long row of numbered boxes, with the numbers starting at 0 (see Figure 5.5). (In programming, you almost always start with 0 when you are counting. I thought this was really weird at first, but I've gotten used to it.) The strict languages make you declare how many boxes you need and how big the boxes need to be (for example, I need a box big enough to fit a string). This allows the computer to find a place in RAM to fit all those boxes together in a line. The more flexible, lax languages still have numbered boxes, but the boxes might not be grouped together in a line (see Figure 5.6). The strict version allows for faster lookups because the array's items are all grouped together in order. The flexible version is a bit slower because it takes a little longer to find the right box.

Figure 5.5   An array is like a long row of numbered boxes.

Figure 5.6   Finding the right box can take more time when the array isn't strictly defined.

Let's do some experimenting with arrays. You can either open the Chrome Dev Tools console or open the interactive mode of Node.js from the command line. First, let's create an array of month names. In JavaScript, the best way to create an array is by using a comma-separated list of items surrounded by a pair of square brackets (see Listing 5.3).

Listing 5.3   **An Array of Month Names**

```
var months = ['January', 'February', 'March', 'April', 'May', 'June', 'July',
              'August', 'September', 'October', 'November', 'December'];
```

You can access a single item in an array by referring to that item's index (the index is like the box number). Remember that the index starts with 0, so if you are looking for the third item in the array, the index is actually 2. In JavaScript, the correct syntax for accessing an array is using the array's variable name and then square brackets surrounding the item's index (see Listing 5.4 and Figure 5.7).

Listing 5.4   **Accessing an Item in the months Array**

```
months[11];    // This displays 'December' (not 'November')
```

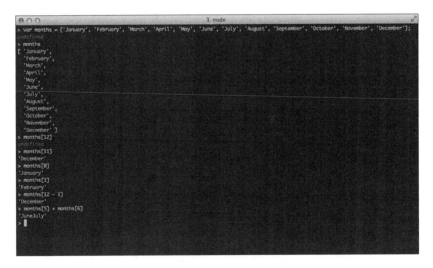

Figure 5.7   Experimenting with arrays using interactive Node.js

Languages such as JavaScript, where arrays can be any size, with items of any type, usually have methods to add and remove items from the array. In most cases, you want to add or remove items from the end of the array. In JavaScript, this is accomplished with push and pop, respectively. Running push adds an item to the array and then gives you the length of the array after the new item has been added. Running `pop` removes and returns the last item from an array (see Figure 5.8). You can also check the length of the array using `length` (`length` is a property, not a method, which means it doesn't need to be called, so you don't need to add the `()`).

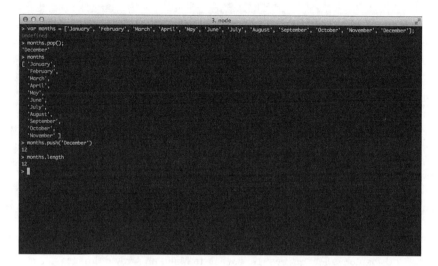

Figure 5.8   Adding and removing items from the end of an array using `push` and `pop`

Before moving on, take some time to experiment with arrays. You can create an array with days of the week, the members of your family, or a list of your favorite movies. Try popping and pushing items. What happens if you try to pop from an array that has zero items? Can you create an array with strings, numbers, and dates? Can you set the value of a single item in the array (remember, you can use `=` to set values)? This type of experimentation is really important as you learn new concepts in programming. You won't really get it until you try to use it.

Arrays become especially useful when you can iterate, or loop through, each item in an array (you learn to do that in Chapter 7). For our kittenbook project, we use an array to store references to all the images on a Facebook page, and then we will loop through that array and change each image. We can start that process now by creating an array of all the images on a Facebook page. On Facebook.com, right-click an image in the newsfeed and click Inspect Element to show the element in the Chrome Dev Tools (see Figure 5.9).

We don't want to replace *all* the images, only the images in the newsfeed, so we need to find something in the HTML that identifies an image as being a part of the newsfeed. In Figure 5.9, you can see the top line of HTML:

```
<div class="clearfix userContentWrapper _5pcr">
```

```
▼<div class="clearfix userContentWrapper _5pcr">
  ▼<a class="_5pb8" href="https://www.facebook.com/sample.user" data-ft="{"tn":"m"}" data-hovercard=",
      <img class="_s0 _5xib _rw img" src="https://fbcdn-profile-a.akamaihd.net/hprofile-ak-ash1/t5/5555
  </a>
  ▼<div class="_5pax">
    ▶<h5 class="_5pbw" data-ft="{"tn":"C"}">_</h5>
      <div class="mbs _5pbx userContent" data-ft="{"tn":"K"}">Sample Comment</div>
    ▼<div class="_5ys3" data-ft="{"tn":"H"}">
      ▼<div class="_5pb0" data-ft="{"tn":"H"}">
        ▼<div id="u_jsonp_2_o">
          ▼<a class="_5pb3 _5dec" aria-label="The 22 Easiest Ways To Destroy Any Friendship" href="htt
            easiest-ways-to-destroy-any-friendship");" onclick="LinkshimAsyncLink.referrer_log(this, "htt
            destroy-any-friendship&h=BAQEPSFn3&render_verification=0&enc=AZMwGtUzXFHba0e7a6_DCq6ofm4kE2ge
            ▼<div class="_5pao _5qeh">
              <img class="_5pcd img" src="https://fbexternal-a.akamaihd.net/safe_image.php?d=AQATUrDG—
              <i class="_5par"></i>
            </div>
          </a>
        </div>
```

Figure 5.9   The Chrome Dev Tools show the HTML for Facebook.com.

It turns out that every image we want to add to our array can be found within a `div` tag that has the class `userContentWrapper`. (Note that Facebook might change its HTML at any point in time. If you don't see `userContentWrapper`, find another class that identifies an image in the newsfeed.) We can create our array with a single command, using what is called a `querySelector`. In the Chrome Dev Tools, press Esc; you should see the console open. Now you can use `document.querySelectorAll` to find all the images (`img`) within `div`s with the class `userContentWrapper` (see Listing 5.5).

Listing 5.5   **Using `document.querySelectorAll` to Make an Array of Images**

```
var images = document.querySelectorAll('div.userContentWrapper img');
```

> **Note**
>
> `document.querySelectorAll` returns a `NodeList`, which is a lot like an array, but a `NodeList` does not have `push` and `pop` methods.

Try out the code from Listing 5.5 in the Chrome Dev Tools. Your new variable `images` should now contain a big array of images. Each item in the array is actually an "object" that describes the actual image in the HTML. We will need that array later, so go ahead and add the code from Listing 5.5 to a new file in the `js` directory called `getImages.js`. Now update `Gruntfile.js` so the new file is included when Grunt builds your extension.

Dictionary (a.k.a. Map, Hash, Object, Associative Array)

A dictionary goes by many names, but I think the name *dictionary* is the most descriptive of them. A dictionary is a group of values, where each of the values has a unique identifier (this concept is often referred to as *key-value pairs*). *Webster's Dictionary* is a group of values (definitions), where each value has a unique identifier (words). Some of the other names for a dictionary (object, map, hash, associative array) begin to make more sense as you become more familiar with other computer science concepts. In JavaScript, they are called objects, so we mostly use that name, but it is important to be aware of the other names as well.

You have already used several objects while building kittenbook. Remember that JSON is JavaScript *Object* Notation, so `manifest.json` and `package.json` are actually just JavaScript objects. You also used objects in `Gruntfile.js`. JavaScript objects are defined with an open curly brace of {, some key value pairs, and a closing curly brace of }, as shown in Listing 5.6.

Listing 5.6   **An Example JavaScript Object (Describing Me)**

```
var author = {
  firstName: 'Steven',
  lastName: 'Foot',
  age: 27,
  favoriteFoods: ['waffles', 'Thai curry']
};
```

Open a JavaScript console (`Node.js` or Chrome) and try making a `reader` object that describes you. When writing a JavaScript object, you need to place a comma between each of the key-value pairs, but you shouldn't put a comma after the last pair.

Now that you've created an object, you will want to be able to access the values of that object. You get the values of an object by using the object name, then a dot, and then the key. For instance, `author.firstName` returns 'Steven'. You can also change attribute values and create new attributes using this syntax. For instance, to change the spelling error in `author.lastName` and add 'grilled chicken' to the `favoriteFoods` array, I can use the code in Listing 5.7. The items in an object are not stored in any particular order; the computer stores them in whatever order makes the items easiest to look up later. Unlike arrays, items in an object cannot be accessed by numbered indexes.

Listing 5.7   **Modify Attributes of an Object**

```
author.lastName = 'Foote';
author.favoriteFoods.push('grilled chicken');
```

Now let's put objects to work for us in kittenbook. Your assignment is to create an object in `values.js` that contains all the values that are used in `prompt.js`. Up to this point, I have walked you through exactly how to write your code. From now on, I'm going to leave out some things so you can figure out the details on your own. The first thing I'm going to leave out is how to create an object in `values.js`. You will also need to modify `prompt.js` to use the object, so it should look something like Listing 5.8. Remember to run `grunt watch` from the command line so your changes get picked up as you save.

Listing 5.8   `prompt.js` **Using the** `pbValues` **Object**

```
var userName = prompt('Hello, what\'s your name?');
document.body.innerHTML = '<h1>Hello, ' + userName + '!</h1>' +
                  '<p>' + kbValues.projectName + ' ' + kbValues.versionNumber +
                  ' viewed on: ' + kbValues.currentTime + '</p>';
```

Dynamically and Statically Typed Languages

From the JavaScript you have written, you have seen that when you create a new variable, you don't have to tell JavaScript what type of data that variable is going to store. JavaScript just figures it out because JavaScript is a dynamically typed language; data types are assigned dynamically when the program runs. As you are writing your code, you don't have to think about what data types to use because the runtime figures that out for you. Shoot first, ask questions later. This Wild West approach lets you do crazy things such as add a string and a number together to get a string (see Listing 5.1).

On the other hand, statically typed languages require that you declare a data type as you declare new variables. Statically typed languages have some great benefits. You always know what type of data you are dealing with, so you don't have to deal with surprises, such as when 2 + '2' = '22', because you're not even allowed to add variables of different types. Honestly, I found statically typed languages to be hard to understand at first. I didn't really understand the advantages of using a statically typed language. All I could see was a more confusing syntax that would take longer to type. For instance, Listings 5.9 and 5.10 compare creating a string in Java (statically typed) and JavaScript (dynamically typed). For me, Listing 5.9 is just harder to understand.

Listing 5.9   **Create a String in Java**

```
String greeting = new String("Hello, world!");
```

Listing 5.10   **Create a String in JavaScript**

```
var greeting = 'Hello, world!';
```

Dynamic and static typing are just different philosophies for accomplishing the same job. Dynamic typing gives you the freedom to work quickly without having to think about the data types you are using because the runtime figures it out for you. Static typing gives you structure that helps you avoid a lot of strange, painful bugs that come up in dynamically typed languages and are difficult to track down. Each has its place, and understanding the motivations for each will help you better decide when you should use each one.

Data Structures

The data in software is often used to model some aspect of the real world, and as with any model, it is not a perfect representation of the real world. Consider the `reader` object you just created: It might contain certain attributes that correctly describe you, but there are certainly aspects of who you are that are not captured (I know there is more to me than name, age, and favorite foods). It is not possible or practical to create a full representation of yourself (or anything) in software. You must decide what is important for the purposes of your software and leave out the rest; then you must structure the important parts of the model so that the right information is easy to access and in a logical place.

To illustrate this point, let's consider three different ways to structure the `author` data. Our first option is to use a single string that contains all the values (see Listing 5.11). Our second option is to use an array with values but no keys (see Listing 5.13). Our third option is to use an object with keys and values (look back at Listing 5.6).

Listing 5.11 **`author` Data As a String**

```
var author = 'firstName=Steven&lastName=Foote&age=27&favoriteFoods=waffles,Thai
curry';
```

You can see that all the `author` data from Listing 5.6 is present in Listing 5.11, but it is harder to read. The string contains key-value pairs separated by ampersands (&). The key is on the left side of the = and the value is on the right. Values in an array are separated by commas. There is no way to distinguish strings from numbers, from arrays. Adding new key-value pairs is difficult, and modifying existing values is even more difficult. Look at all the code in Listing 5.12 that is necessary to update the `age` attribute.

Listing 5.12   **Update the `age` Value When `author` Data Is Stored As a String**

```
// Find the place in the string where the 'age' key appears
var ageLocation = author.indexOf('age=');

// Find the next '&' after the 'age' key
var nextAmpersand = author.indexOf('&', ageLocation);

// Extract the current age, which is the substring that starts 4 characters
// after the ageLocation, and ends at the nextAmpersand location.
var currentAge = author.substring(ageLocation + 4, nextAmpersand);

// Convert currentAge into an integer (using base-10)
currentAge = parseInt(currentAge, 10);

// and add 1 because it's my birthday!
currentAge = currentAge  + 1;

// Put the new value of currentAge back into the author string by concatenating
// 1. Everything up to the old age value
// 2. The new age value
// 3. Everything from the ampersand after the age to the end of the string.
author = author.substring(0, ageLocation + 4) +
         currentAge +
         author.substring(nextAmpersand);
```

With all its downsides, storing key-value pairs in a string is actually extremely common. Consider the URL in Figure 5.10: The part after the ? is using almost the exact format used in Listing 5.11 to structure key-value pairs. URLs use strings to store key-value pairs all the time. One of the reasons strings are used to store data is that strings are extremely portable (a string created in one programming language can easily be used in other programming languages), whereas other data structures are much less portable (an object created in JavaScript cannot be directly used in any other language).

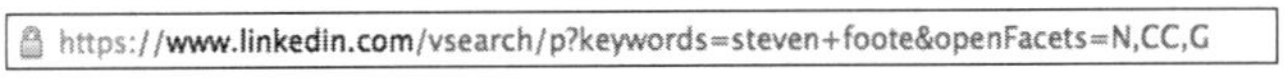

```
https://www.linkedin.com/vsearch/p?keywords=steven+foote&openFacets=N,CC,G
```

Figure 5.10   URLs are strings that often contain key-value pairs.

With the data structured as an array (see Listing 5.14), we have solved the major problems we ran into using strings—and created a new problem. The difference between strings, numbers, arrays, and other data types is clear when an array is used. Also, adding and modifying values is straightforward. In Listing 5.14, we do the same thing we did in Listing 5.12 (increase age by 1), but we do it in a single line of code.

Listing 5.13   author Data As an Array

```
var author = ['Steven', 'Foote', 27, ['waffles', 'Thai curry']];
```

Listing 5.14   Update the age Value When author Data Is Stored As an Array

```
author[2] = author[2] + 1;
```

The code in Listing 5.14 is much simpler than the code in Listing 5.12 because data structured in an array is much easier to access and update than data structured in a string. But we do have a new problem. What does that 2 mean? I know that the item in index 2 describes my age because I just wrote the array, but nothing about the 2 spot is intrinsically age-y. Arrays are useful for a list of items (such as the list of my favorite foods) but not as useful for describing something. Objects are much more useful for that.

As shown in Listing 5.15, modifying the age attribute of author structured as an object takes only one line of code, just like the array. However, because we use the name of the attribute instead of just the index, the object code is much easier to understand and much less error prone.

Listing 5.15   Update the age Value When author Data Is Stored As an Object

```
author.age = author.age + 1;
```

Strings, objects, and arrays can be used together to create even more complex data structures. Although occasionally you will do well to make up a completely new data structure, usually you are better served by using an established pattern, such as sets, stacks, trees, and graphs.

Set

You might already be familiar with the mathematical concept of sets. I didn't know I was aware of sets until I found out that sets are what make up Venn diagrams, and I totally get Venn diagrams. A set is basically an array in which duplicates are not allowed (see Listing 5.16). If you want to know all the people who have called you in the last week, you want your phone to show you the set. You don't care how many times someone called you (duplicates)—you just want to know whether they called you at all. In many programming languages (although not yet JavaScript), sets are built-in composite data types. An entire branch of mathematics is dedicated to sets and the applications thereof. If you come across a programming problem for which you need a list with duplicates removed, do yourself a favor and read up on set theory.

Listing 5.16 **Comparison of a Set and an Array**

```
// A call history, as an array with duplicates
var callsArray = ['George', 'George', 'Elaine', 'George', 'Newman', 'George',
'George', 'George', 'Elaine', 'Kramer', 'George'];

// The same call history as a set (duplicates removed)
var callsSet = ['George', 'Elaine', 'Newman', 'Kramer'];
```

Stack

A stack is an array in which you can add, remove, or view only the single item on the top. Think of it as a stack of papers; you can place a paper on top of the stack or pull a piece of paper from the top of the stack, but if you try to add or pull from the middle, things get messy. Stacks are useful in keeping track of history. For instance, your browser history works like a stack. When you load a new website, that site is added to the top of the stack. When you click the Back button, the page on the top of the stack is removed and the previous page is loaded. Listing 5.17 shows what the browser history stack might look like in JavaScript.

Listing 5.17 **What a Browser History Stack Could Look Like If Written in JavaScript**

```
// Start with an empty array, because no pages have been visited yet.
var browserHistory = [];

// Visit 'https://www.google.com'
browserHistory.push('https://www.google.com');
/*
    ['https://www.google.com']
*/
```

```
// Search for "droids"
browserHistory.push('https://www.google.com/#q=droids');
/*
    ['https://www.google.com',
     'https://www.google.com/#q=droids']
*/

// Click on a result
browserHistory.push('https://en.wikipedia.org/wiki/Star_Wars:_Droids');
/*
    ['https://www.google.com',
     'https://www.google.com/#q=droids',
     'https://en.wikipedia.org/wiki/Star_Wars:_Droids']
*/

// Interesting, but not the droids you're looking for. Hit the back button.
browserHistory.pop();
/*
    ['https://www.google.com',
     'https://www.google.com/#q=droids']
*/
```

Tree

A tree is perhaps the most common data structure used in computer science, and you are already more familiar with it than you probably realize. The tree is actually based on the tree that grows in the ground, complete with a trunk, branches, and leaves. You have seen trees in the `kittenbook` directory and in `kittenbook.html`. The `kittenbook` directory is the trunk (everything in the tree grows out of the trunk), the other directories are branches (branches can contain leaves), and the individual files are leaves. In `kittenbook.html`, the `<html>` tag is the trunk, tags that contain other tags are branches, and the remaining tags are leaves. Tags within tags are *nested* (more like Russian nesting dolls, less like the place where a bird lays its eggs).

Family trees are especially well suited for representation as a tree because they're already structured as a tree (see Listings 5.18 and 5.19). In fact, a number of terms from family trees are also applied to trees in computers. The terms *parent, child, ancestor,* and *sibling* are all present in the tree data structure. Trees do an excellent job of representing hierarchical relationships.

Listing 5.18 **A Family Tree Represented As an Array of Arrays**

```
var familyTree = ['Abraham J. Simpson', 'Mona Simpson', [
        ['Homer Jay Simpson', 'Marjorie Jacqueline Simpson',
            ['Bartholomew Jo-Jo Simpson',
            'Lisa Marie Simpson',
```

```
                'Margaret Evelyn Simpson']
         ]
      ]
];
```

Listing 5.19   **A Family Tree Represented As an Object**

```
var familyTree = {
  father: 'Abraham J. Simpson',
  mother: 'Mona Simpson',
  children: [
    {
      child: 'Homer Jay Simpson',
      spouse: 'Marjorie Jacqueline Simpson',
      children: [
        {
          child: 'Bartholomew Jo-Jo Simpson'
        },
        {
          child: 'Lisa Marie Simpson'
        },
        {
          child: 'Margaret Evelyn Simpson'
        }
      ]
    }
  ]
};
```

Graph

A graph is a group of interconnected items, such as a group of cities connected by roads or a group of friends connected by relationships. The items in the graph are called nodes, and the connections are called edges. An interesting aspect of a graph is that the connections are just as important as the nodes. The road between two cities can be as important as the cities themselves. Graphs are heavily used in social networks, defining connections between people, places, companies, and so on. The Internet itself is one large graph of pages connected by links. Figure 5.11 shows a simplified road map of cities in Nevada, and Listing 5.20 shows how those connected cities could be represented as a graph.

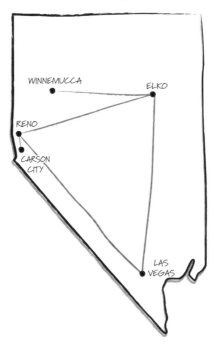

Figure 5.11   A simplified map of Nevada

Listing 5.20   **Cities in Nevada Represented As a Graph**

```
var nevadaCities = [
  {
    city: "Carson City",
    neighbors: [
      {
        city: "Reno",
        distance: 32
      }
    ]
  },
  {
    city: "Elko",
    neighbors: [
      {
        city: "Las Vegas",
```

```
        distance: 435
      },
      {
        city: "Reno",
        distance: 289
      },
      {
        city: "Winnemucca",
        distance: 124
      }
    ]
  },
  {
    city: "Las Vegas",
    neighbors: [
      {
        city: "Reno",
        distance: 452
      },
      {
        city: "Elko",
        distance: 435
      }
    ]
  },
  {
    city: "Reno",
    neighbors: [
      {
        city: "Carson City",
        distance: 32
      },
      {
        city: "Las Vegas",
        distance: 452
      },
      {
        city: "Elko",
        distance: 289
      }
    ]
  },
  {
    city: "Winnemucca",
    neighbors: [
      {
        city: "Elko",
```

```
        distance: 124
      }
    ]
  }
];
```

How to Choose an Effective Data Structure

The data structure you choose can have a huge effect on the complexity of the code you have to write. We saw this firsthand when we tried to update the age attribute of author. When you choose the wrong data structure, you end up fighting it in your code, but if you choose an effective data structure, it makes your code simpler and more concise. So how do you choose an effective data structure? It is a skill that you will develop over time, and you will learn through trial and error. An important first step is knowing that you are choosing a data structure and knowing what data structures you can choose from. On the first website I built, I used strings for nearly all my data structures because I didn't know there was a better way. One day I discovered JSON and the power of objects; that day, my life became much easier and my code became much cleaner and easier to understand.

Databases

The data you use within your programs is temporary, stored in RAM, and lasts only as long as your programming is running. When you need your data to stick around longer than that, a database is an excellent option.

Long-Term (Persistent) Storage

You have many ways to store data more permanently. The method you choose depends on the programming environment you are using and the nature of the data you need to store. For small amounts of simple data, your program can create a new file on the computer's hard drive and write the data to that file. As data grows in size and complexity, it becomes necessary to use a more robust solution, such as a database. When your programming environment is a web page within a web browser, your options are more limited. Very small amounts of data can be stored as cookies, but most data that requires long-term storage must be sent back to the server.

Relational Databases

The relational database is one of the most common methods of storing large amounts of complex data. Beyond just storing data, a relational database organizes data and creates a structured way of retrieving the portion of the data you need. Relational databases are not terribly flexible, so you need to spend time planning and designing your database before you dive into building it. To make these abstract concepts more concrete, let's go through an exercise in which we design a database for a library.

Tables

As with the data structures we used before, a database is used to model something in the real world. We will be modeling a library here, so we need to consider what entities in a library we should include in our model. What types of things will we want our database to know about and keep track of? Here is an incomplete list of things a library database should track, but there certainly could be more:

- Books
- Authors
- Patrons
- Checkouts
- Employees

Each of these types of things will be represented by a table in the database. The book table contains one row (called a record) for each of the books in the library. The columns of a table are called fields, and each field describes an attribute. The Books table might contain fields for book ID, publisher, publication date, genre, and number of pages.

Relationships

The power of a relational database lies in the relationships that exist between the tables. Three types of relationships are important in relational databases (see Figure 5.12):

- **One-to-one:** A single item in table A is related to exactly one item in table B. One-to-one relationships are somewhat rare because the two tables are describing the same thing, so they might as well be one table.
- **One-to-many:** An item in table A can be related to one or more items in table B. The Patrons table has a one-to-many relationship with the Checkouts table because a single checkout belongs to one and only one patron, but a single patron can have many checkouts.
- **Many-to-many:** An item in table A can be related to one or more items in table B, and an item in table B can be related to one or more items in table A. The Authors table and the Books table have a many-to-many relationship because a book might have many authors and an author might have written many books.

The relationship between records in different tables is created when a record in one table references the identifier of a record in another table. For example, the Patrons table has a one-to-many relationship with the Checkouts table, so the Checkouts table will have a field for `PatronID`, which describes which Patron from the Patrons table owns a particular Checkout. Instead of repeating all the information from the Patrons table within the Checkouts table, the Checkouts table needs only the `PatronID`, which points to the right record in the Patrons table.

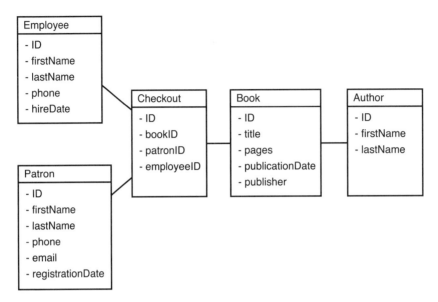

Figure 5.12   The library database architecture

Oh, CRUD!

For persistent storage systems (such as databases) to be complete, they need four basic functions: create, read, update, and delete (CRUD). If data is duplicated throughout the system, CRUD becomes nearly impossible. For example, imagine that a patron's phone number is recorded in the Patrons table, and also recorded in the Checkouts table for each checkout owned by a given patron. Now if a patron tries to update his or her phone number in the database, the database will have to update the phone number once in the Patrons table and many times in the Checkouts table. For the sake of CRUD, design your database so that data is not duplicated.

A Brief Introduction to SQL

Relational databases have a specialized language, called SQL (Structured Query Language), that is used for creating, reading, updating, and deleting records. The basics of SQL are straightforward and, in my opinion, pretty fun. SQL consists of structured queries (hence the name), and the structure is well defined. To read from the database, your query must start with the word SELECT, must declare which fields you want to read (use * if you want all fields), and must contain the name of the table you want to read from. Listing 5.21 fetches all fields from the Author table.

> **Note**
>
> The following code examples will work only if you are interacting with a real database. If you want practice writing SQL queries that will interact with a real database, try an interactive online tutorial such as http://sqlzoo.net.

Listing 5.21   SQL Query Reading All Data from the Authors Table

```
SELECT * FROM Author
```

A query can also contain conditions that determine which records will be retrieved using the WHERE statement. Listing 5.22 fetches all fields from the `Patron` table, but only for records where the value of firstName is 'Gary'.

Listing 5.22   SQL Query Reading All Patrons Whose First Name Is `Gary`

```
SELECT * FROM Patron WHERE firstName = 'Gary'
```

Two tables can be "joined" together based on their relationship. For instance, if I want all the information about the checkout with ID 42, I would need data from the Checkout table and the Patron table (see Listing 5.23). Data from related tables can be joined using the ... wait for it ... JOIN statement.

Listing 5.23   SQL Query Reading the `firstName` and `lastName` of the Patron Who Owns Checkout 42

```
SELECT firstName, lastName
       FROM Patron
       JOIN Checkout ON (Patron.id = Checkout.patronId)
       WHERE Checkout.id = '42'
```

SQL can do a lot more than what we discussed here, and crafting an effective SQL statement to find just the data you are looking for can be a fun puzzle to solve. If you are interested in learning more about SQL, you can find a lot of interactive tutorials online. A lot of what I know about SQL came from the tutorials on http://sqlzoo.net.

Summing Up

This chapter introduced a lot of concepts that are crucial pieces of a solid foundation in programming. The way you choose to store, structure, and use your data is a determining factor of how efficient and effective your software will be.

In this chapter, you learned about:

- What makes different types of data different
- How the way you structure data matters
- How data can be saved to a database for long-term storage

In the next chapter, you will learn about:

- How to find patterns with regular expressions

6

Regular Expressions

| Note

Project: Validate a phone number using regular expressions.

Most introductory programming books don't include an entire chapter on regular expressions because regular expressions can be intimidating. As a result, many programmers choose to never learn regular expressions. Although other tools can do much of what regular expressions can do, they don't do the job as well. You can drive nails with the backside of a screwdriver, for example, but using a hammer is so much easier. For certain jobs, nothing but regular expressions work. Becoming comfortable with regular expressions early will benefit you as long as you program.

Having said that, I should mention that regular expressions are hard. They are terse and can be quite confusing. They are difficult to document and difficult to read, and making mistakes is easy. Still, they are remarkably useful.

Ctrl+F on Steroids: Looking for Patterns

The last chapter briefly introduced you to regular expressions, but you are probably still wondering what they are and how they are used. Regular expressions are a lot like the Find (keyboard shortcut: Ctrl+F) feature in Word, Chrome, and Sublime Text. Regular expressions search a string for a given set of characters, but they are far more powerful. Imagine that you have a 300-page document and you want to find all the places where a year is mentioned (for example, 2014). With Find, you have to search for every single year individually—first you'd search for 1900, then 1901, then 1902, and so on before you'd give up as it would take way too long. With regular expressions, you can search for patterns, and a year is a very simple pattern: a sequence of four digits from 0 to 9. See Listing 6.1.

Listing 6.1   **Searching for Years with Regular Expressions**

```
var yearPattern = /[0-9]{4}/;
```

As you can see, the syntax for regular expressions is a bit strange, but if you look closely, you can see all the relevant pieces. The digits from 0 to 9 are represented by [0-9], and the requirement that there are four of them is represented by {4}. So yearPattern is really saying, "Any number from 0 to 9, repeated four times." A perfect regular expression will match everything you want to find in a string and not match anything you don't want to find. For example, yearPattern will match any four-digit sequence of numbers, so it will match all the four-digit years (good), but it will also match phone numbers like 800-555-3456 (bad) because there is a sequence of four digits in phone numbers. In this chapter, you learn the tools you need to turn yearPattern into a much better regular expression.

Using Regular Expressions in JavaScript

Regular expressions do nothing without a string to test them on. Let's start with a simple string and a simple regular expression. Open the Chrome Dev Tools on any page, and create a string with your name in it; then create a regular expression with your name in it. See Listing 6.2.

Listing 6.2   **My Name As a Regular Expression**

```
> var myName = 'Steven Foote';
  "Steven Foote"
> var namePattern = /Steven/;
  /Steven/
```

Now you need to test whether the string matches the regular expression. You can do this in a few different ways, each with a slightly different purpose and output.

- test returns a Boolean, true if the string matches and false if it doesn't.

- exec either returns an array of the first part of the string that matches or else returns nothing.

- match either returns the part (or parts) of the string that match in an array or else returns nothing. match is different because it is a method on the string and the regular expression is the argument (see Listing 6.3).

Listing 6.3   **Testing Our Regular Expression/String Combo All Three Ways (in the Console)**

```
> namePattern.test(myName);
  true
> namePattern.exec(myName);
  ["Steven"]
> myName.match(namePattern);
  ["Steven"]
```

Repetition

The regular expression namePattern isn't much of a pattern at all; it's no different than using Find. What if I want to match Steven or Steve? Listing 6.4 shows how inflexible namePattern is.

Listing 6.4   **Trying to Match steve**

```
> var myNickname = 'Steve Foote';
  "Steve Foote"
> namePattern.test(myNickname);
  false
```

Dang. My regular expression isn't flexible enough for even my nickname. We can fix that—but be warned, this is where regular expressions start to look weird.

?

Leave behind any preconceptions you might have about what the question mark means. In the land of regular expressions, unassuming characters can leave behind the roles they play in normal life and take on new, meaningful powers. The simple ? has the power to solve our nickname problem. See Listing 6.5.

Listing 6.5   **The Powerful ?**

```
> namePattern = /Steven?/;
  /Steven?/
> namePattern.test(myNickname);
  true
> namePattern.text(myName);
  true
```

Magic! The ? tells the regular expression that the character before the ? should appear once or not at all. In other words, the new namePattern says that the n is optional.

+

Right now you're probably thinking "Wooooooooooow! Regular expressions are amazing!" Well, maybe you're not quite that excited about it, but guess what? Regular expressions can handle it, no matter how excited you are. In Regular Expression Land, the + tells the regular expression to match the preceding character one or more times. See Listing 6.6.

Listing 6.6   **Regular Expressions Can Handle All Levels of Excitement**

```
> var excitementPattern = /Wo+w/;
  /Wo+w/
> var notYetExcited = 'Wow... Regular Expressions are weird :/';
  "Wow... Regular Expressions are weird :/"
> excitementPattern.exec(notYetExcited);
  ["Wow"]
> var startingToGetExcited = 'Wooow. Regular Expressions are... pretty cool.';
  "Wooow. Regular Expressions are... hard."
> excitementPattern.exec(startingToGetExcited);
  ["Wooow"]
> var totallyLovingRegEx = 'Wooooooooooww! Regular Expressions are awesome!!!';
  "Wooooooooooww! Regular Expressions are awesome!!!"
> excitementPattern.exec(totallyLovingRegEx);
  ["Wooooooooooww"]
> var excitedButBadAtSpelling = 'Www! Relugar Expresions, I <3 u!';
  "Wwwwww! Relugar Expresions, I <3 u!"
> excitementPattern.exec(excitedButBadAtSpelling);
  null
```

*

The star (sometimes called the Kleene star, after its creator, Stephen Kleene) tells the regular expression to match the preceding character zero or more times. It's truly a regular expression rock star. We can make our `excitementPattern` regular expression flexible enough to even handle bad spelling. See Listing 6.7.

Listing 6.7   **A Regular Expression Rock Star**

```
> excitementPattern = /Wo*w/;
  /Wo*w/
> var excitedButBadAtSpelling = 'Www! Relugar Expresions, I <3 u!';
  "Wwwwww! Relugar Expresions, I <3 u!"
> excitementPattern.test(excitedButBadAtSpelling);
  true
```

Special Characters and Escaping

Now that you've met some of the super-powerful characters of Regular Expression Land, you might want to create a regular expression that matches strings that contain those amazing characters, just to show what a huge fan you are. Give it a shot and check out Listing 6.8.

Listing 6.8 **Looking for Stars, Plus More**

```
> var starPattern = /*/;
  SyntaxError: Unexpected token ILLEGAL
> var plusPattern = /+/;
  SyntaxError: Invalid regular expression: /+/: Nothing to repeat
```

Well, that didn't go well. The first SyntaxError is pretty mysterious, but the second error is a bit more helpful. Our plusPattern regular expression is invalid because the + has no preceding character that should be repeated. But we're trying to match the +, not repeat some other character. We need to tell the regular expression that we want to match a literal + instead of giving + super powers. Do you remember when we ran into this problem in Chapter 1, "Hello World! Writing Your First Program," with the apostrophe inside a string? We needed an escape character then, as we do now. Regular expressions also use the backslash for escaping. See Listing 6.9.

Listing 6.9 **Looking for Stars and Actually Finding Them**

```
> var starPattern = /\*/;
  /\*/
> var aStar = 'Kleene, you\'re a *';
  "Kleene, you're a *."
> starPattern.test(aStar);
  true
```

$\{1,10\}$: Make Your Own Super Powers

The special characters you just learned about are some of the most commonly used characters in regular expressions, but there's more. If ?, +, and * aren't specific enough, you can define your own lengths using curly braces. Remember the yearPattern example that matches a sequence of exactly four digits? You can use the curly braces in three ways:

- $\{n\}$ matches the preceding character exactly *n* times.
- $\{n,\}$ matches the preceding character at least *n* times.
- $\{m,n\}$ matches the preceding character at least *m* times, but no more than *n* times.

You can actually use the curly brace syntax to get the same result as ?, +, and *. ? is the same as $\{0,1\}$, + is the same as $\{1,\}$, and * is the same as $\{0,\}$. We will be using the curly braces extensively in the project in this chapter.

Match Anything, Period

Sometimes you want a pattern that matches anything. For instance, we could make our excitementPattern match only strings that contain some form of Wow *and* contain an exclamation point (!), but there may be some stuff between the Wow and the ! that we don't really care about. Regular expressions have another super-powerful special character to handle that situation: The period, usually called the dot (as in *dot-com*), matches any character. It's like the regular expression wildcard. You can combine the dot and the star to match zero or more characters, regardless of what those characters are. See Listing 6.10.

Listing 6.10   **Matching Anything**

```
> excitementPattern = /Wo*w.*!/;
  /Wo*w.*!/
> excitementPattern.test(notYetExcited);
  false
> excitementPattern.test(excitedButBadAtSpelling);
  true
```

As our patterns get more complex, it can be useful to visualize what is happening. www. regexper.com/ is an amazing online tool that creates a visualization for any regular expression. Figure 6.1 is the visualization for the excitementPattern, in the "railroad" diagram format. Your train starts at the dot on the left, and each of the squares is like a train station. Each time the train stops at a station, exactly one character from the string has to get off the train, and the characters have to get off the train in the correct order. The label on the station describes what kind of character is allowed to get off the train. If the train stops at a station and the next character in line is not allowed to get off, the train derails, which means the string does not fit the pattern defined in the regular expression.

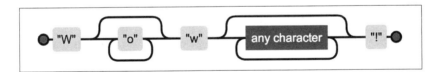

Figure 6.1   A visualization of /Wo*w.*!/

Don't Be Greedy

Regular expressions are greedy—not the *Wall Street*/Gordon Gekko kind of greed, but they are greedy all the same. The regular expression greed means that a regular expression wants to match as much of a string as it can. For example, given the string 'Www! Regular Expressions, I <3 u!', the excitementPattern (/Wo*w.*!/) will match the entire string instead of just the Www! part. This is because the .*! tells the regular expression to match everything (including the !) until it finds the *last* !. Sometimes greed is good, but if you want your regular expression not to be greedy, there is hope. Add a ? (wow, ? sure has a lot of super powers) after the * or +, and its greed will go away.

Understanding Brackets from [A-Za-z]

The powerful . is great when you want to match anything and everything, but sometimes "anything" is too broad. Using brackets, you can define exactly which characters you want to match. If I want to match my name whether or not the S is capitalized, I can use brackets to match either S or s. See Listing 6.11.

Listing 6.11   **Use Brackets to Handle Lowercase Names**

```
> lowerCaseName = 'steven foote';
  "steven foote"
> namePattern      // remember what the name pattern looks like
  /Steven?/
> namePattern.test(lowerCaseName);
  false
> namePattern = /[Ss]teven?/;
  /[Ss]teven?/
> namePattern.test(lowerCaseName);
  true
```

Lists of Characters

The simplest way to use brackets is to list all the acceptable characters within the brackets. In the updated namePattern, the acceptable characters are S and s, so those two characters go inside the brackets. If you wanted to match double or single quotes, you could use ["']. If you wanted to match any lowercase letter in the English alphabet, you could use [abcdefghijklmnopqrstuvwxyz], and if you wanted to match any lowercase or uppercase letter in the English alphabet, you could use [abcdefghijklmnopqrstuvwxyzABCDEFGHIJKLMNOPQRSTUVWXYZ]. Wow, that is ugly. There must be a better way.

Ranges

There *is* a better way! With the yearPattern, we matched any digit from 0 to 9 using [0-9], which is way easier than typing out [0123456789], although they both do the same thing. Within brackets, a dash between two characters is called a range. Ranges are most commonly used for ranges of numbers and letters. Ranges on other characters can be quite confusing, and I don't recommend using them. You can match any upper- or lowercase letter in the English alphabet using [a-zA-Z]. That is much better (and you don't have to worry that you missed one of the letters). Ranges don't have to start with 0 or A, and they don't have to end with 9 or z. If you want to match only letters in the second half of the alphabet, you can use [n-z], for instance. You can also use a combination of individual characters and ranges: [12357a-z].

A time might come when you want to include a dash as one of the characters in your list, but the dash has super powers within the brackets, so you need to use … that's right, you need to use an escape character. The pattern /[a-z\-]/ matches a dash or any lowercase letter. You can also use brackets and repetition together. The `yearPattern` uses brackets to say that it wants to match digits 0 to 9; then it uses repetition to say that it wants to match those digits exactly four times.

Negation

If you want to match anything but a group of characters, regular expressions have got you covered with another character with super powers. Add a caret (^) at the beginning of the group to match anything but the characters in the group. Let's say that I am adamant about being called Steve instead of Steven. In fact, I would take any character at the end of my name, as long as it's not n (I actually prefer to be called Steven, but for the sake of the example, let's pretend). My new `namePattern` could look like Listing 6.12.

Listing 6.12   **Don't Call Me Steven**

```
> namePattern = /Steve[^n]/;
  /Steve[^n]/
> namePattern.test('Steve Foote');
  true
> namePattern.test('Steveq Foote');
  true
> namePattern.test('Steven Foote');
  false
```

A Pattern for Phone Numbers

At this point, you have learned enough to get started on the project of validating phone numbers. First, we need to think of the different valid phone number formats. Here are a few possibilities:

- 1-555-867-5309
- 555-867-5309
- (555)867-5309

We can quickly experiment with these three formats using an online regular expression tool called regexpal: http://regexpal.com/. In the upper box, we enter our regular expression (no need for the / when using this tool), and in the lower box, we enter the strings we want to match, one per line. Add each of the three formats to the lower box. You should also add some strings that should not match the pattern, such as `'Regular Expressions are great'` and `'-0-1-2-3-4-5-6'`. These are clearly not phone numbers, so if our pattern matches them, we need to do some work.

In each of these formats, we see some digits and some dashes. In one of these formats, we see parentheses. The formats have between 12 and 14 characters. We can turn that into a rudimentary regular expression using brackets and repetition. Listing 6.13 shows the regular expression, and Figure 6.2 shows a visual representation of the regular expression.

Listing 6.13   **Phone Number Regex, Round 1**

```
var phoneNumberPattern = /[0-9\-\(\)]{12,14}/;
```

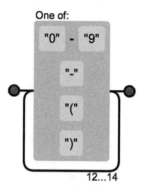

Figure 6.2   A visualization of `phoneNumberPattern`

Our first attempt is great; it matches all three formats. But it also matches one of the non–phone number strings (see Figure 6.3). It's good, but we can do better.

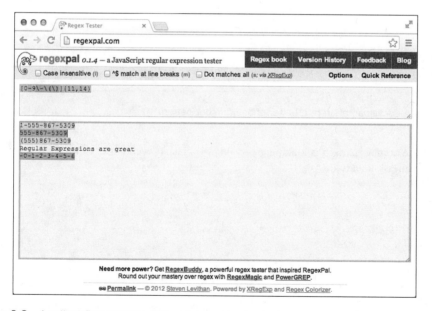

Figure 6.3   A valiant first attempt, but we have a way to go.

To make our pattern even better, we need to break down the phone number into its parts: 1) An optional prefix: `1-`. 2) An optional opening parentheses. 3) A three-digit area code. 4) Either a dash or a closing parentheses. 5) Three digits. 6) A dash. 7) Four digits. Each of these parts is a relatively simple pattern:

1. `1?-?`

2. `\(?`

3. `[0-9]{3}`

4. `[\-\)]`

5. `[0-9]{3}`

6. `-`

7. `[0-9]{4}`

Putting them all together (see Listing 6.14), we get a not-so-simple pattern, but we know what each part does, so it's not impossible to understand. With the help of the railroad diagram in Figure 6.4, things get even easier. The real test, though, is whether our new pattern matches everything it should match and rejects everything it should not match (see Figure 6.5).

Listing 6.14   **Phone Number Regex, Round 2**

```
var phoneNumberPattern = /1?-?\(?[0-9]{3}[\-\)][0-9]{3}-[0-9]{4}/;
```

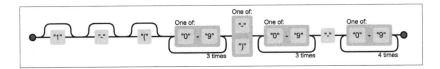

Figure 6.4   A visualization of a better phone number pattern

The phone number pattern is looking great. We will make it even better as we learn more about regular expression features.

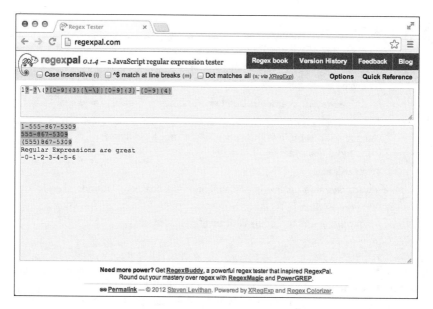

Figure 6.5   A much better phone number pattern

I Need My \s

We have improved our patterns a lot from the first regular expression we wrote (/Steven/), and we haven't even gotten into one of the most prolific features regular expressions have to offer: the backslash. So far, we've used the backslash as an escape character, a way to take the super powers away from a special character. But the backslash doesn't just take; the backslash can give super powers to ordinary characters, too.

Shortcuts for Brackets

Most commonly, the backslash turns letters into groups. For instance, \s matches any type of whitespace character, such as a space, a tab, and a newline (among others). The backslash can also represent a character that cannot be used literally in a regular expression. For instance, a regular expression generally has to be all on one line, so to represent a new line, you need to use \n because you can't just press Enter. The following table describes all the characters that take on special meaning with the backslash.

Symbol	Meaning
\b	A word boundary. This matches a place where a word character (see \w) is next to a nonword character (see \W).
\B	A nonword boundary. This matches a place where two word characters are next to each other or two nonword characters are next to each other.

Symbol	Meaning
\d	A digit. \d is shorthand for [0-9].
\D	Anything but a digit. \D is shorthand for [^0-9].
\n	A newline character.
\r	A carriage return character. Used on Windows to create a new line.
\s	A whitespace character. Whitespace characters include a space (the character you get when you press the spacebar), a tab, a newline (\n), a carriage return (\r), and a few others.
\t	A tab character.
\w	A word character, which is any alphanumeric character or underscore. \w is shorthand for [0-9a-zA-Z_].
\W	A nonword character, equivalent to [^0-9a-zA-Z_].

With this knowledge, we can make our phone number pattern a little more readable. Our pattern currently repeats [0-9] three times. We can replace [0-9] with \d for a slightly more concise regular expression without changing what it does (see Listing 6.15).

Listing 6.15   **Phone Number Pattern, Round 3**

```
var phoneNumberPattern = /1?-?\(?(?\d{3}[\-\)]\d{3}-\d{4}/;
```

Let's add some code to our kittenbook project. In prompt.js, we'll ask users for their phone numbers instead of their names. Then we'll validate the phone numbers using our regular expression (see Listing 6.16). As you learned in Chapter 2, "How Software Works," we could send an SMS to that number to further our validation. However, that is beyond the scope of this book. Let's just stick to validation via regular expressions for now.

Listing 6.16   `prompt.js` **Now Asks for and Validates Phone Numbers**

```
// Get the user's name.
var userName = prompt('Hello, what\'s your name?');
// Get the user's phone number.
var phoneNumber = prompt('Hello ' + userName + ', what\'s your phone number?');
// Create the phone number pattern.
var phoneNumberPattern = /1?-?\(?(?\d{3}[\-\)]\d{3}-\d{4}/;
// Create a variable to store the output.
var output = '<h1>Hello, ' + userName + '!</h1>';

// Is the phone number valid?
if (phoneNumberPattern.test(phoneNumber)) {

    // Yes, the phone number is valid! Add the success message to the output.
```

```
output = output + '<p>' + kbValues.projectName + ' ' + kbValues.versionNumber +
         ' viewed on: ' + kbValues.currentTime + '</p>';

} else {
  // No, the phone number is not valid. Tell the user about the problem.
  output = output + '<h2>That phone number is invalid: ' + phoneNumber;
}
// Insert the output into the web page.
document.body.innerHTML = output;
```

Limitations

Some of these normal characters endowed with super powers are absolutely necessary because they represent a single character (such as \n and \t) that cannot be represented in any other way in a regular expression. However, some of these characters are just shortcuts to allow you to write less code (such as \w and \s). The shortcuts are useful, as long as you recognize their limitations. The \w matches only the letters from the English alphabet. Throw in just a little bit of Spanish flair to your string (as with olé), and your regular expression will fail. Also, \s matches a lot of space characters that you might not actually want to match. In both cases, writing out the exact set of characters you want to match (within brackets) is sometimes necessary. The shortcuts are useful—until they're not.

(?:Groups)

I will admit that, up to this point, regular expressions might seem a little boring. Although I do think it's pretty cool to be able to create a pattern that can match any phone number in a whole bunch of different formats, groups (and especially capturing groups) is what made me really love regular expressions. Groups are like subpatterns within the larger regular expression, and the super characters can operate on the entire group together. A few examples should help make this clearer. Let's you have a dog named fifi, and you want to create a regular expression that matches any string with your dog's name in it. To complicate matters, let's say you sometimes call your dog "fi" for short. You need a group, which is a set of characters surrounded by parentheses. A noncapturing group, which is the type we want to use to find fifi, starts with ?:. See Listing 6.17.

Listing 6.17   **Finding** fifi

```
> var fifiPattern = /(?:fi){1,2}/;
  /(?:fi){1,2}/
> var fifi = 'I have a dog named fifi';
  "I have a dog named fifi"
> var fi = 'Sometimes I call my dog fi';
  fi = "Sometimes I call my dog fi"
> fifiPattern.test(fifi);
  true
```

```
> fifiPattern.test(fi);
  true
```

What about the `namePattern` to match `'Steven'` and `'Steve'`—what if we want to match `'Stephen'`, too? We can make it happen with a group, but we'll also need to introduce another super character: `|`. The `|`, or pipe (found on the Backslash key, between the Backspace and Enter keys), means "or" in regular expressions. The pipe splits the regular expression and matches either what is on the left or what is on the right. For example, `/apple|broccoli/` matches `'apple juice'` and `'baked broccoli'`, but not `'carrot cake'`. We can use a pipe inside a group to match either v for `'Steven'` or ph for `'Stephen'`. See Listing 6.18.

Listing 6.18   **Searching for `'Stephen'`**

```
> var namePattern = /Ste(?:v|ph)en?/;
  /Ste(?:v|ph)en?/
> var myName = 'Stephen';
  "Stephen"
> namePattern.test(myName);
  true
> myName = 'Steven';
  "Steven"
> namePattern.test(myName);
  true
```

As a final example, let's consider the prefix in our `phoneNumberPattern`. It's almost right, but it has a slight problem. When we divided the phone number into parts, the first part was an optional prefix of 1-, which we achieved with `1?-?`. The problem is that `1?-?` matches phone numbers that look like `-877-555-1234` because the pattern matches the 1 zero or one times, and then matches the - zero or one times. We really want to match them together zero or one times, and we can do that with a group. See Listing 6.19.

Listing 6.19   **Fixing the Prefix**

```
var phoneNumberPattern = /(?:1-)?\(?\d{3}[\-\)]\d{3}-\d{4}/;
```

That's much better. Another point to note in the `phoneNumberPattern` is the backslashes in front of the nongroup parentheses. Now that you know that parentheses are special characters, those backslashes should make a little more sense.

(Capture)

Capturing groups are (for me, anyway) the most interesting and useful feature of regular expressions. They allow you to extract data from your matched string. For instance, we can use capturing on the `phoneNumberPattern` to extract just the area code from the string. Capturing groups are surrounded by just parentheses (with no special characters such as `?:` at the beginning). You need to use `match` or `exec` to be able to access what the group captured. See Listing 6.20.

Listing 6.20 **Capture the Area Code**

```
var phoneNumberPattern = /(?:1-)?\(?(\d{3})[\-\)]\d{3}-\d{4}/;
```

Now that we have access to the area code, we can create a more personalized message for our users. We'll assume that the user lives in the location related to the area code (cellphones have kind of ruined this assumption, but we'll go with it anyway). You can add an `areaCodes` object to the `kbValues` object in `values.js`. See Listing 6.21.

Listing 6.21 **Add an `areaCodes` Object to `kbValues`**

```
var kbValues = {
  projectName: 'kittenbook',
  versionNumber: '0.0.1',
  areaCodes: {
    '408': 'Silicon Valley',
    '702': 'Las Vegas',
    '801': 'Northern Utah',
    '765': 'West Lafayette',
    '901': 'Memphis',
    '507': 'Rochester, MN'
  }
};
```

You can add as many area codes as you want to the `areaCodes` object. Now you can update `prompt.js` to use the area code from the user's phone number to create a more personalized greeting. The first step is to update the regular expression to include the capturing group for the area code (see Listing 6.20). Then you need to capture the matches using `exec` or `match`, which will return an array with the area code in index position 1. See Listing 6.22.

Listing 6.22 **Capture the Area Code**

```
// Create the phone number pattern.
var phoneNumberPattern = /(?:1-)?\(?(\d{3})[\-\)]\d{3}-\d{4}/;
// Get matches from phoneNumber
var phoneMatches = phoneNumberPattern.exec(phoneNumber);
// If the phone number is 901-555-5309, then phoneMatches will be
// ['901-555-5309', '901']
var areaCode = phoneMatches[1];
```

Finally, you need to add the personalized message to the output. This brings us to an interesting problem. You know how to access the different attributes of an object using the object name, then a dot, and then the attribute name, as in `kbValues.projectName`. So we can access the area codes object with `kbValues.areaCodes`, and we have the area code we want stored in the `areaCode` variable. But how can we access the value related to that area code? We could try `kbValues.areaCodes.areaCode`, but that would look for an attribute whose name is `areaCode` inside the `areaCodes` object. In JavaScript, you can use the bracket syntax to access attributes of an object (see Listing 6.23). It looks similar to the syntax for accessing items in an array. Listing 6.24 shows how to use the bracket syntax to get the location based on area code.

Listing 6.23   **Accessing Object Attributes with the Bracket Syntax**

```
> var states = {'AL': 'Alabama',
                'AK': 'Alaska',
                'AZ': 'Arizona',
                'AK': 'Arkansas'};
> states.AL;
  'Alabama'
> var stateName = 'AL';
  'AL'
> states.stateName;   // This won't work :(
  undefined
> states[stateName];
  'Alabama'
> states['AL'];
  'Alabama'
```

Listing 6.24   **Getting the Location Based on the `areaCode`**

```
// Get the location using bracket syntax
var userLocation = kbValues.areaCodes[areaCode];
```

Now you can add the `location` to the output in whatever way you want. Maybe you could ask how the weather in `location` is these days. Regardless, your users are going to be impressed that you figured out where they live based on their phone number. They would be even more impressed if they knew all the regular expression magic you had to do to figure out their location.

Capture the Tag

Now that you've seen a bit about how using regular expressions and capturing groups work, it's time to try some out on your own. Open the Chrome Dev Tools on any page (I recommend the Mozilla Developer Network, but any page will do). Find an HTML tag in the Elements tab, copy the HTML of that element (see Figure 6.6), and save the string to a variable in the console (I recommend an element that has no children so that you don't have to deal with newlines when saving the string to a variable). Now write a regular expression that will capture the tag name (for example, the tag name of <h2> is h2). You should be able to use the same regular expression to capture the tag name of any HTML tag you copy.

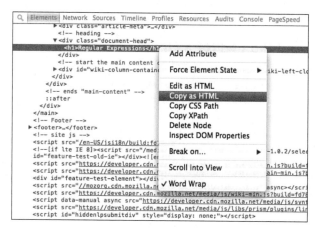

Figure 6.6   Copy the HTML of a given tag.

Advanced Find and Replace

To see another way capturing groups can be useful, let's think back to Listing 5.9 of the last chapter. That was the one where we updated the age attribute of the author string with the long, complex code. We can improve that long, complex code a lot by using a regular expression with a capturing group and also using advanced find and replace (see Listing 6.25).

Listing 6.25   **Improving the String Data Structure with a Capturing Group**

```
var author = 'firstName=Steven&lastName=Foote&age=27&favoriteFoods=waffles,Thai
curry';

// Use the String's built-in replace method.
author.replace(/(age=)(\d+)/, function(fullMatch, group1, group2) {
  /**
    * fullMatch contains "age=27"
    * group1 contains "age="
    * group2 contains "27"
    */

  // Whatever we return will replace the entire match in the original string
  // Add 1 to group2, then put the two groups back together.
  // parseInt turns the string "27" into the number 27, so we can add them together.
  // Without parseInt, "27" + 1 becomes "271", not 28.
  return group1 + (parseInt(group2, 10) + 1);
```

```
});
// author is now 'firstName=Steven&lastName=Foote&age=28&favoriteFoods=waffles,Thai
curry'
```

The Beginning and the End (of a Line)

Find and replace with regular expressions is pretty amazing, but one part of the previous regular expression is not quite right. The regular expression matches `'age='` and then some numbers. What if the author string also contained `'page=23'`? Then our regular expression would match `'age=27'` and `'page=23'`. We could change our regular expression to be `/ (&age=) (\d+) /`, but we would still have a problem: What if `'age'` is at the beginning of the string and there is no preceding `&`? Fortunately, regular expressions have a way of identifying the beginning (and end) of a line. The beginning of a line is represented by a `^` (remember, the `^` has a different meaning inside brackets—regular expressions sure can be confusing), and the end of the line is represented by a `$`. We can change our find-and-replace regular expression to match either `&` or the beginning of the line, then `'age'`: `/ ((?:^|&) age=) (\d+) /`.

Flags

Regular expressions have a few default behaviors that you can turn on or off using flags. These default behaviors usually work just fine, but when they don't, it's nice to be able to turn them off.

Global

By default, as soon as a regular expression finds a match within a string, it stops looking. The global flag tells the regular expression to find all matches in the string, not just the first. To set the global flag, you place a `g` outside the closing forward slash of your regular expression: `/ [0-9] {4} /g` finds all years in a string, not just the first one.

Ignore Case

Regular expressions are case sensitive by default, but sometimes you don't care whether text is upper or lower case. You can keep your regular expressions from being case sensitive using the ignore case flag (set with an `i`, so `/ste(?:ph|v)en/gi` finds every instance of `'Steven'`, `'steven'`, `'Stephen'`, and `'stephen'` in a string). Note how the global flag and the ignore case flag can be (but don't have to be) used together.

Multiline

By default, ^ and $ match only the beginning of the string and the end of the string, respectively. In other words, if your string contains multiple lines, the beginning and ends of the lines are not actually matched by ^ and $ unless you turn on the multiline flag. The multiline flag is set with an m. `/.*\.html$/gm` matches every line in a string that ends with `'.html'`.

When Will You Ever Use Regex?

By now you are probably thinking, "I never want to see another regular expression again. My head hurts." Or maybe you're thinking, "Wow! I <3 regular expressions!" I'm guessing it's not the latter. Either way, you've learned a lot about regular expressions, and you might be wondering about when and how you will actually use them. The following examples are a few of the ways that I have actually used regular expressions to make my work easier (for real, regular expressions can actually make life easier, not harder).

grep

In Chapter 3, "Getting to Know Your Computer," you learned about the command-line tool grep. At the time, I made grep seem like Find for searching multiple files at once. But grep is actually all about regular expressions (in fact, *grep* stands for global regular expression print). Using grep, you can search for patterns within multiple files at once. When working on a project that has a lot of files (LinkedIn has a *lot* of files), grep is a necessity. For example, I can search all my CSS files for places where I am using float: left; or float: right; using one grep command.

Code Refactoring

I am writing this book using HTML, and I have used regular expressions (and especially advanced find and replace) to help me work faster. As I start a new chapter, I copy the portion of my outline that relates to that chapter into a new HTML file. The items in the outline use HTML lists (<ul> and <li> tags), but these items become headers in the actual chapter (<h1>, <h2>, and so on). I could switch each of these tags by hand, but instead I write a couple regular expressions. As shown in Figure 6.7, Sublime Text, Vim, and many other editors support regular expressions (and capturing groups) in their find-and-replace features.

```
15        <ul>
16        <section class="container">
17            <h2>Operators</h2>
18            <ul>
19                <li>Comparison operators</li>
20                <li>Binary operators</li>
21            </ul>
22        </li>
23        <section class="container">
24            <h2>If</h2>
25            <ul>
26                <li>Booleans</li>
27                <li>Comparison Operators</li>
28                <li>"Truthy" and "Falsy"</li>
29            </ul>
30        </li>
31        <li>
32            For
33            <ul>
34                <li>Counting from 0</li>
35                <li>Looping Through an Array</li>
36                <li>Nested Loops</li>
37            </ul>
38        </li>
39        <li>
40            While
```

Find What: `^ {8}(<)li(>)\n?\s*(.*)$`

Replace With: `\1section class="container"\2\n        <h2>\3</h2>`

Figure 6.7   Change list items to headers with regular expressions

Validation

In this chapter, you have written a pretty good phone number validation (for U.S. phone numbers). Nearly every time I have to do validation, I use regular expressions. Emails are especially difficult to validate; do a search for "email regular expression," and you will see what I mean. Again, just because a phone number or email address matches a regular expression does not mean that it is valid, but regular expressions can tell you whether the string at least *looks* reasonable.

Data Extraction

My very first programming project was to use regular expressions to extract data about books from a very large (1MB) text file. That project could be the reason I am particularly fond of capturing groups. When I saw regular expressions turn an unusable 30,000-page report into a useful spreadsheet, I was hooked.

Summing Up

You have learned a lot in this chapter. What once looked like random characters (ahem, `/(?:1-)?\(?(\d{3})[\-\)]\d{3}-\d{4}/`, ahem) now makes sense to you. Sure, it might take some time to figure out what it means (and I think it always will), but you can figure it out. Regular expressions are a great tool, but remember that just because you're holding a hammer doesn't make everything a nail. In this chapter, you learned about:

- The regular expression syntax

- Quantifiers such as `?`, `+`, and `*`

- Character sets in brackets

- Groups and capturing groups

- Advanced find and replace and other applications of regular expressions

In the next chapter, you will learn about:

- Operators

- Programming with flow control

- How to use `if`, `for`, `while`, and `switch` to control flow

- Another way to code defensively with `try`

- Triggers and events

if, for, while, **and When**

This is the chapter you have been waiting for. Up to this point, you have mostly been learning about how to program, but not as much about how to code. You have been learning the skills necessary to create an actual working program, but you haven't done too much coding. This chapter is all about learning how to code. Specifically, you learn how to control the flow of your program's execution. Flow control tools allow your program to make decisions about which instructions to execute, how many times the instructions should be executed, and when they should be executed. Learning to code is a fundamental part of learning to program, and flow control is an essential part of learning to code. So pay attention.

Operators

Thanks to elementary school math, you are probably already familiar with operators. Addition, subtraction, multiplication, and division are all operators. An operator performs a given action on its operands. In the equation `20 + 22`, 20 and 22 are operands, + is the operator, and addition is the action performed. You have already seen a few operators in the code we have written. Several types of operators exist.

Comparison Operators

A comparison operator compares the values of its two operands and returns a Boolean (`true` or `false`). Six comparison operators exist, and you probably learned about all of them but one in elementary school.

1. "Equals" checks that the two operands are the same. In most languages, the operator is `==`. In JavaScript, it is best to use `===`, for reasons that are explained in the section on coercion. So `'abc' === 123` returns `false` and `42 === 42` returns `true`.

2. "Not equals" checks that the two operands are not the same. Whatever the equals operator would return for two operands, not equals will return the opposite. In many languages, the not equals operator is `!=`, but again, JavaScript is different and uses `!==`. Now `'abc' !== 123` would return `true` and `42 !== 42` would return `false`. The not equals operator was not discussed in my elementary school class.

3. "Greater than" checks that the operand on the left is greater than the operand on the right, and the operands have to be numbers. The greater than operator uses the familiar `>` (even in JavaScript). `100 > 10` returns `true` and `-1 > 1` returns `false`.

4. "Greater than or equal to" works the same as the greater than operator, but it also returns `true` if the operands are equal: `42 >= 42` returns `true`.

5. "Less than" is the opposite of the greater than operator: `-1 < 1` returns `true`.

6. "Less than or equal to" at this point requires no explanation: `-1 <= 1` returns `true` and `42 <= 42` returns `true`.

Logical Operators

As you begin to use the three logical operators (and, or, and not), you will change the way you think and the way you talk—at least, I did. For me, the word *and* put off its role as an absent-minded connector of thoughts because *and* has a very specific meaning. For example, let's say that you are standing in the rain waiting for a bus, and let's say you are standing in front of a little store. The owner of the stores comes to the door and says to you, "You're welcome to wait inside if you are cold and wet." (*Warning:* You are about to begin to understand why programmers have a stereotype of being rude and antisocial.) What the store owner probably meant to say is, "You're welcome to wait inside if you are wet *or* cold." Certainly, the store owner (we'll call her Sue) would be willing to have you wait inside if either condition is true. Certainly, she wouldn't stop you at the door and say, "Wait a minute, you're just wet. You don't look cold at all. Out in the rain with you." But a programmer is used to the very precise meaning of *and*, so a programmer might be tempted to take Sue literally or even correct her. Fortunately, in my experience, few programmers actually act on the urge to take things so literally.

The and operator (`&&` in JavaScript) has two operands and tests that both are true. If either is false, the and operator returns `false`. The and operator evaluates the operand on the left first and evaluates the operand on the right only if the operand on the left is true. If the operand on the left is false, the and operator already knows that the total statement is false, regardless of the value of the operand on the right, so there is no need to evaluate the operand on the right. See Listing 7.1.

Figure 7.1   The stereotypical programmer struggles not to think like a computer. (Cartoon courtesy of Dennis Hengeveld, happysimpleton.com)

Listing 7.1   **The and Operator**

```
> true && true;
  true
> true && false;
  false
> false && true;
  false
> ('a' === 'b') && (3 > 2); // (3 > 2) is never evaluated
  false
```

The or operator (|| in JavaScript) also has two operands and returns true if either is true. Like the and operator, the or operator evaluates the operand on the left first. The operand on the right is evaluated only if the operand on the left is false. If the operand on the left is true, the or operator already knows that the entire statement is true. See Listing 7.2.

Listing 7.2   **The or Operator**

```
> true || true;
  true
> true || false;
  true
> false || false;
  false
> ('a' === 'a') || (3 === 2); // (3 === 2) is never evaluated
  true
```

The not operator (! in JavaScript) has a single operand and returns the opposite. If the operand is true, the not operator returns `false`, and vice versa. See Listing 7.3.

Listing 7.3   **The not Operator**

```
> !true;
  false
> !false;
  true
> !('a' === 'b')   // this is confusing. 'a' !== 'b' does the same thing and
                   // makes more sense.
  true
```

Unary Operators

A unary operator is an operator that performs an action on a single operand. You've already seen a unary operator in the not operator. Another example of a unary operator is an increment. The operand of an increment is a number, and the increment operator increases the value of the number by one (see Listing 7.4). The increment operator is how the programming language C++ got its name (C++ is like C, but 1 better).

Listing 7.4   **Using the increment Operator**

```
> num = 2;
  2
> num++;   // same as num = num + 1;
  3
> num;
  3
> num--;   // You can decrement, too.
  2
```

Binary Operators

By far the most commonly used operators are binary operators. A binary operator is *not* an operator that performs actions only on 0's and 1's, but rather an operator that has two operands. All the comparison operators are binary operators.

Coercion

Some languages (including JavaScript) sometimes coerce type when working with operands of different types. This means that the data type of one of the operands is changed so that the operator can perform its action. You have seen JavaScript coercing type when we tried to add

'2' + 2. The number 2 was coerced to become a string, so the output was '22'. Type coercion can be really useful if you know what you are doing, but it can be quite dangerous in some situations. If you try '2' + 2 in Perl, you will get 4, not '22', because Perl changes the string to a number instead of changing the number to a string. If you try '2' * 4 in JavaScript, you get an error, not '2222'.

One notorious feature of JavaScript is the capability to use type coercion in an equality check. If you use == (instead of ===) to check equality, JavaScript coerces type. Listing 7.5 shows how strange == can be.

Listing 7.5   **Type Coercion on a Comparison Operator Can Be Confusing**

```
> '' == '0'    // No coercion necessary. Equivalent to '' === '0'
  false
> '' == 0      // coercing '' to a number yields 0, so this is
               // equivalent to 0 === 0
  true
> 0 == '0'     // '0' is coerced to a number 0, so this is
               // equivalent to 0 === 0
  true
```

Order of Operations

Just as it is in math, the order in which operations occur is well defined (and very important) in programming. The good news is that the order of operations is the same for all the math operators (multiplication comes before addition), but in programming you have a few more operators to learn. Just as in math, you can use parentheses to force the correct operands and operators to be grouped together. Honestly, I haven't run into this problem much, but when I do, using parentheses is usually the solution.

Assignment

Assigning a value to a variable is actually an operation—and a unique one, at that. Most binary operations evaluate the operand on the left before evaluating the operand on the right, but the assignment operation starts on the right. If you have multiple assignments in a single statement, you start from the right and work your way to the left. See Listing 7.6.

Listing 7.6   **Multiple Assignments**

```
var x = 1;
var y = 2;
var z = x = y = x + y;
// x, y, and z are all 3 (1 + 2)
```

Math Operators

The basic math operations are binary operations. The addition operator is +, subtraction is -, multiplication is *, and division is /. Some languages include an operator for exponentiation (** in Python and Perl, ^ in Visual Basic), but JavaScript does not. Beyond exponents, many math operations are not related to a special symbol (such as square root, log, and sine). Most languages support these operations with built-in functions. If you need to use one, just Google it using a query such as "JavaScript math square root."

Mod

When I started programming, all the math operators except modulo were already familiar to me from my elementary school math classes. Modulo has a strange name and a strange symbol, but it is actually not that strange of a concept. The modulo operator gives you the remainder when the left operand is divided by the right operand. That means 2 % 2 (pronounced "two mod two") is 0, and 3 % 2 is 1. The modulo operator is especially useful when dealing with numbers that are cyclical in nature, such as with time. For example, let's say that today is Thursday and your program wants to create an event 85 days from now. What day of the week is 85 days from now? Thursday is the fifth day of the week, and there are seven days total, so (5 + 85) % 7 gives us six, Friday. The modulo operator is also useful in determining whether a number is even or odd (see Listing 7.7).

Listing 7.7   **Even or Odd**

```
// Ask for a number
var favoriteNumber = prompt('What\'s your favorite number?');

// Turn the string into a number.
favoriteNumber = parseInt(favoriteNumber, 10);

// Check if the number is even or odd using modulo operator
if (favoriteNumber % 2 === 0) {
  alert('Your favorite number is even');
} else {
  alert('That\'s an odd number, literally');
}
```

Ternary Operators

While we're on the topic of operators, we might as well throw in the ternary operator. As you might have guessed, the ternary operator has three operands. Not all languages have ternary operators because a ternary is really just a more concise way of writing a simple if/else statement (see `else if` section). The syntax for a ternary is `operandA ? operandB : oper-andC`. If `operandA` is true, then evaluate `operandB`; otherwise, evaluate `operandC`. Let's see it in action in Listing 7.8.

Listing 7.8   **Ternary Fun**

```
// Ask for a number
var favoriteNumber = prompt('What\'s your favorite number?');

// Turn the string into a number.
favoriteNumber = parseInt(favoriteNumber, 10);

var oddOrEven = ( (favoriteNumber % 2 === 0) ? 'even' : 'odd' );
alert('You\'re favorite number is ' + oddOrEven);
```

When you understand what it's doing, you have to admit that ternary operators are pretty convenient. However, they can be confusing and should not be overused.

if

Our somewhat lengthy discussion of operators was leading up to this moment. The `if` statement is the keystone of flow control in code. The flow of a program is often represented in a flowchart similar to the one in Figure 7.2. Each of the diamonds contains a "yes" or "no" question, and the program takes a different path depending on the answer. An `if` uses a "yes" or "no" question called a conditional to decide what code to execute. Listing 7.9 shows the syntax of a simple `if` statement. If the answer to the question is true, the instructions in the `if` block are executed. If you want, you can add an `else` statement, as you saw in Listing 7.7. The instructions in the `else` block are executed only if the answer to the question is false.

Listing 7.9   **Simple if Statement Syntax**

```
if (yesOrNoQuestion) {
  // if block

  // Instructions in here are executed if the answer to yesOrNoQuestion is "yes"
  // or "true"
}
```

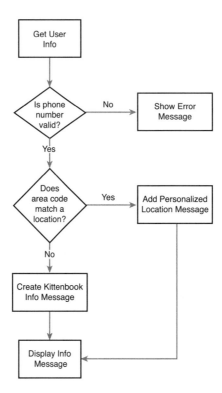

Figure 7.2   A flowchart representing the code in `prompt.js`

else if

If the answer to your first question is "no," it might be useful to ask a second question. Using `else if`, you can ask that second question (and a third, a fourth, and so on). When it comes to flow control, `else if` is a hugely important feature. See Listing 7.10 for an example.

Listing 7.10   **What Sport You Should Play, Based on Height, Using `else if`**

```
if (heightInFeet > 7) {
  // You are pretty tall, so basketball might be a good career for you.
  learnToPlayBasketball();
} else if (heightInFeet < 5) {
  // You could be a great jockey.
  learnToRaceHorses();
} else {
  // You're not exceptionally tall or short. Try baseball.
  learnToPlayBaseball();
}
```

"Truthy" and "Falsy"

The idea that an `if` statement expects a "yes" or "no" question as its argument is only partially correct. What would happen if you use something other than a "yes" or "no" question, as in Listing 7.11? Try it out in the console.

Listing 7.11   **When `if` Meets a String**

```
> if ('true') {
    console.log('"true" is true');
  }
  "true" is true
> if ('false') {
    console.log('"false" is true(?)');
  }
  "false" is true(?)
```

How did `'false'` become true? Many programming languages have a notion of "truthiness," which means a value in any data type is either "truthy" or "falsy." The truthiness of a value is determined by what is returned when that value is coerced to a Boolean, either `true` or `false`. Each programming language decides for itself what is "truthy" and what is "falsy." In general, 0 is "falsy" and all other numbers are "truthy," and `''` (empty string) is "falsy" and all other strings are "truthy." Thus, the string `'false'` is "truthy" and is coerced to `true`. Truthiness allows you to use something other than a Boolean as the condition in your `if` statements. We can use truthiness in `prompt.js` to check whether our user has entered a name (see Listing 7.12).

Listing 7.12   **Using Truthiness to Improve `prompt.js`**

```
// Get the user's name.
var userName = prompt('Hello, what\'s your name?');

// If no user name was entered, ask again.
if (!userName) {
  userName = prompt('You didn\'t enter a name. Really, what\'s your name?');
}
```

switch

While we're on the topic of kittenbook, suppose you want kittenbook to give a special welcome to anyone named Tyler. You could use the `if` statement that you just learned about to add that personalized message. Now suppose that you also want to add a special welcome for people named Jeremy, Kimberly, Lisa, and Jason. You could do that with a bunch of `if-else` statements, but your code would get pretty lengthy and you would be asking basically the same yes/no question in each `else if`. Instead, you can use a `switch` statement. A `switch` statement is given a value and compares that value to each of a set of other predefined values (called cases). See Listing 7.13.

Listing 7.13 **Special Welcomes Using `switch`**

```
var userName = prompt('Hi, what\'s your name?');
switch (userName) {
  case 'Tyler':
    greeting = 'Howdy!';
    break;
  case 'Jeremy':
    greeting = 'Cheers!';
    break;
  case 'Kimberly':
    greeting = 'Maayong aga';
    break;
  case 'Lisa':
    greeting = 'Bonjour';
    break;
  case 'Jason':
    greeting = 'Ola';
    break;
  default:
    greeting = 'Hello';
    break;
}
```

The `switch` compares the given value (in this case, `userName`) with the values in each of the cases, in order, from top to bottom. If the values match, the code following that case is executed. If none of the values match, the code under `default` is executed. Note the `break` statement at the end of each `case`; if you don't include a `break` statement, the code in the next `case` will be executed, even though the value doesn't match the `case`. In a sense, this is a feature because you can have multiple cases execute the same code. However, this "feature" can cause a lot of bugs if you're not careful.

"Syntactic Sugar"

The `switch` statement does exactly what a bunch of `if-else` statements would do, but in a more concise way. In programming, you can often perform the same task in several different ways. When a programming language gives you an easy, concise way of performing a specific type of task, this is often called syntactic sugar (perhaps because the concise syntax "tastes" better?). There is almost always another way to write whatever code you have written. The alternative might execute faster, might be easier to understand, might be more secure, or might just be different. Regardless, your way is probably not the only way, so keep an open mind.

for

Another way to control your program's flow is to use a loop. A loop executes a given set of instructions over and over again until you tell it to stop. One of the most common types of loops is the `for` loop, which allows you to define exactly how many times the loop's instructions will be executed. The syntax of a `for` loop is made up of four parts: the assignment, the condition, the increment, and the body. A `for` loop also has an iterator, which basically keeps track of how many times the loop has been executed. See Listing 7.14.

Listing 7.14   **`for` Loop Syntax in JavaScript**

```
for ( /* assignment */ ; /* condition */ ; /* increment */ ) {

    /* body */

}
```

The assignment is where the iterator gets its initial value. The assignment is executed only once, before the first iteration of the `for` loop. The iterator is a variable, and the variable name is almost always i. Is it i for *iterator*? i for *index*? i because of programming's roots in mathematics? The Internet doesn't have a clear answer for this one, but using i for iterators is a well-established pattern that you should follow.

The condition is a yes/no question, just like the condition in an `if` statement, although the condition in `for` loops is almost always a greater than or less than. (You'll see why in a moment.) The condition is executed before each iteration of the loop. If the condition is false, the loop ends.

The increment is used to change the value of the iterator. The increment is executed after each iteration of the loop. The increment usually increases the value of the iterator by 1, but it can increase or decrease the iterator by any amount you choose.

The body contains the set of instructions that are executed on each iteration of the loop. Any valid instruction is allowed inside the body, including assignments, `if` statements, and even `for` loops.

The loop in Listing 7.15 is executed 11 times. The iterator i starts with a value of 0, the condition checks that 0 is less than or equal to 10 (yep), the body executes, and then the increment increases the iterator by 1. The loop repeats until i is 11; 11 <= 10 returns `false`, so the `console.log` is not executed. Remember that array indexes start with 0? It turns out that counting almost always starts with 0 in computer science, and `for` loops are no exception.

Listing 7.15   **A Working `for` Loop**

```
for ( var i = 0; i <= 10; i++ ) {
  console.log('The loop has executed ' + (i + 1) + ' times.');
}
```

Looping Through an Array

for loops are particularly useful for looking at each item in an array. Suppose we want to print all my favorite foods from the author object. The for loop is perfect for the job (see Listing 7.16).

Listing 7.16   **Looping Through an Array**

```
for ( var i = 0; i < author.favoriteFoods.length; i++ ) {
  console.log(author.favoriteFoods[i]);
}
```

When looping through an array, the iterator i starts with 0 (the index of the first item of the array) and increases by 1 until the iterator is 1 less than the length of the array. Why stop at 1 less? Because you start with 1 (not 0) when counting the number of items in an array (the length). Confusing, right? If we used <= instead of < in the condition, we would get a list of favorite foods with the last item being undefined because we are trying to access an item that doesn't exist in the array. In some languages we would get an error for trying to access an item outside the bounds of an array. This mistake is common enough (and confusing enough) that it has its own name: the off-by-one error.

Looping Through Images

In Chapter 5, "Data (Types), Data (Structures), Data(bases)," you created an array of the images on Facebook in getImages.js. Your challenge for this chapter is to loop through each item in the images array and print the image's URL (the src attribute) to the console using console.log. (*Hint*: To get this to work, you should comment out the last line of prompt.js, as shown in Listing 7.17.)

Listing 7.17   **Comment Out the Last Line of** prompt.js

```
// Insert the output into the web page.
// document.body.innerHTML = output;
```

You have already learned everything you need to know to complete this challenge, so I'm not going to show you how to do it. Use Listing 7.16 as an example, and do some research online if you are having trouble. If you are completely stuck, a possible solution is posted on the book's website in the Chapter 7 section. You will have a much better understanding of these concepts if you figure out this challenge on your own, so look at the posted solution only as a last resort. When you're done, you should see something like Figure 7.3 in the Chrome Dev Tools console.

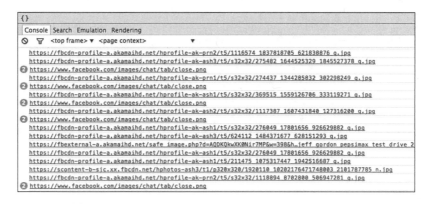

Figure 7.3   Looping through all the images gives you a lot of image URLs.

Nested Loops

The body of a `for` loop can contain any code, including another `for` loop. Nested `for` loops can be useful when used prudently, but they also have the potential to drastically slow down your program. To see why, imagine that you want to loop through a list of your Facebook friends, and for each of your friends, you want to loop through all their Facebook posts looking for a certain word ("Have any of my friends ever posted about `for` loops?"). Suppose that the average Facebook user has 100 posts. If you have just one friend, you need to execute the inner `for` loop only about 100 times, but if you have two friends, you have to execute the inner `for` loop about 200 times. The number of times the inner `for` loop is executed increases much faster than the number of friends you have. If you have 10,000 really active friends, your program could take a long time to execute. If you find yourself using a nested `for` loop, be aware of how quickly the costs can add up. Sometimes structuring your data in a different way can help alleviate this problem.

You Need a Break

In some situations, you want to terminate a `for` loop before the condition becomes false. For example, let's say you that want to check whether spaghetti is one of my favorite foods. The `author.favoriteFoods` array is pretty small in our example code, but let's say that it's hundreds of items long (which is probably a better reflection of reality). You can loop through all the items in the array, checking whether each one is `'spaghetti'`, but you might not need to loop through *all* the items. If the second item in the array is `'spaghetti'`, it would be wasteful to loop through all the other items because you already know that "spaghetti" is in the array. In this case, you can use a break (see Listing 7.18).

Listing 7.18   **Using a Break in a `for` Loop**

```
for (var i=0; i < author.favoriteFoods.length; i++) {
  if (author.favoriteFoods[i] === 'spaghetti') {
    console.log('I like spaghetti too');

    // As soon as "spaghetti" is found, stop looping.
    break;
  }
}
```

forEach

That `for` loop syntax sure can be confusing, especially if all you want to do is loop through each item of an array. Fortunately, however, there is a better way to loop through arrays (as long as you are not using a version of Internet Explorer less than IE9). Arrays have looping functionality built right in with the `forEach` method (see Listing 7.19). If you try to use `forEach` on the `images` array from `getImages.js`, you will run into problems. That's because `images` is actually an array-like collection of HTML elements, not an actual array. As such, `images` doesn't have all the array methods, including `forEach`. JavaScript is weird that way.

Listing 7.19   **Looping Through an Array with `forEach`**

```
> var lettersArray = ['a', 'b', 'c'];
  ["a", "b", "c"]
> lettersArray.forEach( function(letter) {
    console.log(letter);
  } );
  "a"    "b"    "c"
```

Many languages provide a convenient way to loop through items in an array because it is a common task. The syntax is a bit different in each language, but the idea is the same: For each item in an array, execute some code. Python has a simple syntax that is a good comparison to JavaScript (see Listing 7.20).

Listing 7.20   **Looping Through a List (in Python, Arrays are Called Lists) with Python**

```
lettersList = ['a', 'b', 'c']
for letter in lettersList:
    print letter
```

Arrays aren't the only collection we've seen so far. What if we want to loop through each item in an object? JavaScript can loop through items in an object using a `for-in` loop, very similar to the Python loop you just saw. On each iteration of a `for-in` loop, you get the key of the next item, not the value. See Listing 7.21.

Listing 7.21   **Loop Through an Object Using a `for-in` Loop**

```
> var lettersObject = {
    aKey: 'a',
    bKey: 'b',
    cKey: 'c'
  };
  Object {aKey: "a", bKey: "b", cKey: "c"}
> for (key in lettersObject) {
    console.log('The key is: ' + key);

    // If you want to get the value of the current item, you have to use
    // the lettersObject
    console.log('And the value is: ' + lettersObject[key]);
  }
  The key is: aKey
  And the value is: a
  The key is: bKey
  And the value is: b
  The key is: cKey
  And the value is: c
```

while

The `while` loop is a bit like an `if` statement and a bit like a `for` loop. The `while` is like an `if` statement because it has a condition, and the body of the `while` loop executes only if the condition is true. The `while` loop is like a `for` loop without the assignment and the increment. The body executes over and over again until the condition is false. See Listing 7.22.

Listing 7.22   **The Basic Syntax of a `while` Loop**

```
while ( /* condition */ ) {

    /* body */

}
```

Infinite Loops

A traditional `for` loop executes only a finite number of times because the increment changes one of the values in the condition until the condition is false. The `while` loop doesn't have an increment, so the condition might never be false, and if the condition never becomes false, the loop will keep executing forever (theoretically—most runtime environments won't actually let this happen). (See Listing 7.23.) An infinite loop is a bad thing; you don't want the same code to keep executing forever, right?

Listing 7.23   **An Infinite Loop**

```
while (true) {

    // true will never be false; loop forever

}
```

To prevent an infinite loop, you need instructions in the body of the loop to modify the value of the condition. Suppose that you want to loop through an array and pop items off the top of the array each time you go through the loop. `for` loops do strange things if you modify the array you are looping through in the loop body, but `while` loops handle this problem well. You can use the array's length as the condition and pop an item from the array in the body. See Listing 7.24.

Listing 7.24   **Pop All Items off the Top of an Array Using a `while` Loop**

```
var browserHistory = ['https://www.google.com',
                      'https://www.google.com/#q=droids',
                      'https://en.wikipedia.org/wiki/Star_Wars:_Droids'];
 while (browserHistory.length) {
   console.log(browserHistory.pop());
}
```

When all the items have been popped out of the array, the array's length will be `0`, and `0` is "falsy," so the `while` loop is done.

Take Another Break

Another way to avoid an infinite loop is to use a `break` statement. The `break` statement in a `while` loop works just like a `break` statement in a `for` loop. In most cases, it is better to rely on the condition becoming false, but the `break` statement is a nice option to have.

When You Don't Know When to Stop

The `while` loop is particularly useful when you don't know how many times the loop needs to execute. Suppose that you are programming a robot whose job is to clean up the toys in your toddler's room (as a parent, I can attest that such a robot would be really useful). The robot's job is to keep picking up toys until there are no more toys to pick up. But your toddler might walk into the room while the robot is cleaning and get out some more toys. A `while` loop is perfect for this situation. Your robot's code could look something like Listing 7.25.

Listing 7.25   **The Robot Keeps Picking up Toys Until There Are No More Toys to Pick Up**

```
var thereAreToysOnTheGround = inspectRoomForToysOnTheGround();
var nearestToy;
while (thereAreToysOnTheGround) {
  nearestToy = locateNearestToy();
  pickUpToy(nearestToy);
  thereAreToysOnTheGround = inspectRoomForToysOnTheGround();
}
```

The `while` loop will keep executing as long as there are toys on the ground, even if your toddler gets out more toys while the robot is putting away one of the toys. Aren't `while` loops great?

When

One of the great features of user interfaces is that they react to our actions. When I click the Send button in my email client, the email gets sent. When I rotate my phone, the screen orientation flips. Sometimes we want the computer to do something at a certain time. My calendar gives me a reminder 15 minutes before a meeting starts. My phone starts making sound at 5:00 AM to let me know it's time to wake up (okay, we might not necessarily *want* the phone to wake us up). Other times, we want the computer to do something after a certain amount of time has passed. Gmail deletes a spam message 30 days after it arrives in my inbox. In each of these cases, the computer executes code "when" something happens.

Events

One way to execute code when something happens is to use events. You can think of an event like the music of an ice cream truck. Everyone can hear the music, but not everyone cares. If you do care, you will react in some way when you hear the ice cream truck music (run for your wallet, then run to the truck, then pretend you're buying ice cream for a kid and not for yourself). If you don't care, you can just ignore the music.

Listeners

For your program to care about events, you need to create a listener. A listener basically has two parts:

1. The type of event the listener cares about (see /* `event type` */ in Listing 7.26)

2. What the listener will do when the event occurs (see the `function` in Listing 7.26)

Listing 7.26   **JavaScript Event Listener Syntax**

```
el.addEventListener(/* event type */ 'click', function () {
  /* instructions to be executed when the event is triggered */
});
```

You might want to listen when a user clicks a button, presses a key, or taps a picture (in a mobile app). Each of these actions causes an event to be triggered. As an example, let's create an event listener for `kittenbook.html` (see Listing 7.27). To make it easier for our JavaScript to hook into our HTML, we will add an ID to the `<p>` tag that contains the greeting, so `<p>Hello, World!</p>` will become `<p id="greeting">Hello, World</p>`. We will create a new JavaScript file called `events.js`, where we will add our event listener. Remember to reference this new file in `kittenbook.html`, just as you did with `kittenbook.js`.

Listing 7.27   **Add a Click Event Listener**

```
// get the greeting element using the id we just added in kittenbook.html
var greeting = document.getElementById('greeting');

// Create a listener for clicks on the greeting element
greeting.addEventListener('click', function() {
  if (greeting.innerHTML.match(/World/)) {
    greeting.innerHTML = 'Ola, mundo!';
  } else {
    greeting.innerHTML = 'Hello, World!';
  }
});
```

Now open the `kittenbook.html` page in your browser and try clicking on the greeting. Cool, huh? We use a regular expression and an `if` statement to change the greeting from English to Portuguese and back again.

Cron Jobs

Another way to execute code based on time is to use a cron job. A cron job is code that executes at a specified time. One of the most common uses of cron jobs is in backing up files. You can create a cron job that backs up all the files that you modified during the day and set that cron job to run every night at 10:00 PM. After you've set your cron job, your computer will never forget to do the backup, and you don't have to think about it. Creating cron jobs is outside the scope of this book, but if they sound interesting to you, a quick Google search will help you get started.

Timeouts

When you send an email using Gmail, you get a notification saying your email that has been sent and giving you the option to "undo" the sending. After a few moments, the undo option goes away, and the notification just says that your message has been sent. See Figure 7.4.

Figure 7.4   For a few moments, you have the power to unsend your email, but then that power goes away.

The truth is, after an email has been sent, it is not possible to undo. Gmail doesn't actually send your email until the undo option goes away, and if you click Undo, the email is never sent. JavaScript has a feature called setTimeout that enables you to execute some code only after a given amount of time has passed. If Gmail is using setTimeout, the code for the undo feature might look something like Listing 7.28.

Listing 7.28   **Unsending an Email Using setTimeout**

```
var emailForm = document.getElementById('email-form');

// Create an event listener for when the email is sent
// using a form submit event
emailForm.addEventListener('submit', function() {
  showUndoNotification();

  // Use setTimeout to wait 5 seconds before actually sending the email
  // 5 seconds is 5000 milliseconds, and setTimeout uses milliseconds
  setTimeout(function() {

    // Check if the undo button was clicked.
    if (undoWasNotClicked) {

      // Actually send the email and update the notification.
      sendEmail();
      showMessageSentNotification();
    }
  }, 5000);
  // The first argument for setTimeout is the code we want to execute (wrapped in a
  function).
  // The second argument is how many miliseconds to wait before executing that code.
});
```

try

Computer programs have expectations, and sometimes those expectations are not met. Computers aren't good at handling disappointment gracefully—your mobile apps crash, your word processor shuts down just as you were about to save, or the blue screen of death appears. Computer programs might just quit unless you tell them how to handle their problems. One method of handling problems is called try/catch: Try to execute some code where problems might occur, and catch the problems. See Listing 7.29.

Listing 7.29 **try/catch Syntax in JavaScript**

```
try {
  // code that may cause an error
} catch (error) {
  // if an error occurs in the try block, execute this code instead
}
```

Catch When Things Go Wrong

You might be wondering why you would want to be writing risky instructions in the first place. What makes an instruction risky? Remember in Chapter 2, "How Software Works," we wrote some fake code to open a Microsoft Word document? See Listing 7.30 for a refresher. That code is actually quite risky.

Listing 7.30 **Open a Microsoft Word Document (Example from Chapter 2)**

```
function openWordFile(filePath) {
  var wordWindow = openWordWindow();
  var fileContents = loadFile(filePath);
  displayFile(wordWindow, fileContents);
}
```

The risky part of that code is loadFile(filePath). What if the file path isn't valid? What if the file was deleted? What if the file path points to an external hard drive that isn't currently connected? A lot of things can go wrong when trying to load a file, but because we recognize that those instructions are risky, we can wrap them in a try/catch and handle problems gracefully. See Listing 7.31.

Listing 7.31 **Handle File Loading Errors Gracefully with try/catch**

```
function openWordFile(filePath) {
  var wordWindow = openWordWindow();

  // try to execute the risky code.
  try {
```

```
    var fileContents = loadFile(filePath);
    displayFile(wordWindow, fileContents);
  } catch (error) {
    // Show an appropriate error message if the file could not be loaded.
    displayMessage('Sorry, the file ' + filePath + ' could not be loaded');
    displayMessage('due to the following error: ' + error);
  }
}
```

Writing Robust Code

As you write your code, take time to think about what could go wrong. Under what circumstances will your code break? If your code breaks, how will that affect the user's experience? With questions like these in mind, you can use tools such as validation and `try`/`catch` to write code that can handle whatever crazy stuff gets thrown at it. That is the kind of code that makes good programs, and that is the kind of code you want to write.

Summing Up

You learned a lot about how to write code in this chapter. The tools in this chapter are some of the most important concepts for writing code. You also wrote code to loop through all the images in your Facebook feed, which is one of the most important steps for creating our kittenbook extension.

In this chapter, you learned about:

- Operators
- Flow control
- `if` statements
- `switch` statements
- `for` loops
- `while` loops
- Events, timeouts, and cron jobs
- `try`/`catch` blocks

Each of these concepts was demonstrated with examples JavaScript code. Take some time to experiment with each of them so you can better understand how to use them. One good way to understand the concepts better is to learn how they work in a language other than JavaScript. Before you begin the next chapter, try to figure out how to write an `if`, `for`, and `while` in Python or Ruby (or both, if you're feeling ambitious). For a good online resource to try out different languages, check out http://repl.it/. As you learn the different syntax for each language, the essence of what these tools are actually doing will become more clear.

In the next chapter, you will learn about:

- Functions and methods
- Code encapsulation
- Code reuse
- Scope

Functions and Methods

Your kittenbook code is a mess. I'm sorry to say so, but it's a complete mess. All your variables are global (see the later section, "Scope"), and it is unclear which instructions are meant to achieve what job. I suppose the mess is really my fault because I told you to write the code the way it is written, but it's a mess nonetheless. You might be questioning my methods. If I'm supposed to be teaching you how to program, why would I tell you to write bad, messy code? I have my reasons, I promise. First, you can't appreciate the value of clean code until you have worked with messy code. Second, to understand the tools you need to write clean code, you need to have already written some code. It is better to have written messy code than no code at all.

Functions are one of the best tools for organizing your code. A function is a group of instructions that perform a specific task, like a mini program within your program. Depending on the language, functions might also be called procedures, subroutines, or methods. A function should have a single task, and all instructions related to completing that task should be contained within the function.

Function Structure

The syntax of a function is actually quite simple (much simpler than a `for` loop), as shown in Listing 8.1. The syntax is different for each language, but the building blocks are mostly the same. A function is declared to be a function using a specific keyword, such as `function`, `def`, or `sub`. A function is given a name, which should describe the task the function performs. The function's parameters are stated and given names. Finally, a function has a group of instructions called a function body. If the function returns a value, the body contains a `return` statement.

Listing 8.1   **The Function Syntax in JavaScript**

```javascript
function countToTen( /* parameters go here */ ) {
  /* code goes here, in the function body */

  for (var i=1; i<=10; i++) {
    console.log(i);
  }
}
```

Definition

The example in Listing 8.1 is a function definition. With a function definition, you are saying that you intend to use the code in the function body eventually, and perhaps multiple times, but not yet. When code is being executed, the runtime executes the first instruction in the file and then moves on to the second, then the third, and so forth. However, when the runtime encounters a function definition, it registers the function and then skips over the function body. To see what I mean, try out the code in Listing 8.2.

Listing 8.2   **A Function**

```javascript
console.log('Instruction 1');
console.log('Instruction 2');
function instructionThree () {
  console.log('Instruction 3');
}
console.log('Instruction 4');

/*
 Output:

 Instruction 1
 Instruction 2
 Instruction 4

*/
```

Invocation

The body of a function is not executed until the function is invoked (or called). Function invocation looks much the same in most languages: the function's name followed by a pair of parentheses. The parentheses might or might not have some arguments inside. To invoke the countToTen function, you simply use countToTen();. Give it a try in the console. You have invoked many a function already: console.log('Instruction 1'); is a function, as is phoneNumberPattern.exec(phoneNumber); (from prompt.js). These examples include arguments between the opening and closing parentheses (see the next section), but they are function invocations all the same.

Arguments

Functions can be set up so that they accept arguments (the stuff between the parentheses). Arguments are values passed into a function that help determine the behavior of the function. For instance, the argument for `console.log` is whatever text you want displayed in the console. A regular expression's `exec` function accepts a string argument and tries to find matches for the regular expression in the string.

Arguments let you make your functions more flexible. For instance, our `countToTen` example is not flexible at all. What if we want to count to only 7, or all the way to 15? We can let `countToTen` count to any number by using an argument (although we'd better change the name of the function because it will be capable of counting to numbers other than 10). See Listing 8.3.

Listing 8.3   **Count to Any Number**

```
function countTo(num) {
  /* code goes here, in the function body */

  for (var i=1; i<=num; i++) {
    console.log(i);
  }
}

countTo(3);
```

Parameters

The idea of arguments is related to the idea of parameters, and the two terms are used almost interchangeably. However, there is a subtle difference between the two, and understanding that difference will help you understand functions a bit better. A parameter is a special kind of variable created within a function that represents the value of an argument. In Listing 8.3, the `num` variable is a parameter (`function countTo(num) {`) and 3 is the argument (`countTo(3);`). The function handles the assignment of the argument (3) to the parameter (`num`) behind the scenes. If your function accepts multiple arguments, the arguments are assigned to the parameters in the order they appear.

In Listing 8.4, the function assigns the argument 1 to the parameter a, the argument 2 to the parameter b, and the argument 3 to the parameter c.

Listing 8.4   **Multiple Parameters**

```
function manyParams(a, b, c) {
  console.log('a: ' + a);
```

```
    console.log('b: ' + b);
    console.log('c: ' + c);
}

manyParams(1, 2, 3);
```

Too Many Arguments

No limit governs the number of arguments that a function can have, but that doesn't mean you should write a function that accepts 200 arguments. Remember, arguments are assigned to parameters in order; if you have 200 arguments, putting one of them in the wrong place would be easy, and the problem would then be hard to identify. Additionally, if your function accepts too many arguments, that's a good indicator that the function is trying to do too much. As a rule of thumb, functions shouldn't accept more than three or four arguments; if a function needs more, it should probably be broken into multiple functions.

return

In Chapter 2, "How Software Works," you learned about input and output in software. When it comes to functions, arguments are the input, and return values are a form of output. The purpose of some functions is to *get* something rather than *do* something. The `prompt` function is a great example of a function that gets something (the output of `prompt` is whatever the user types into the prompt window). Now the first line in `prompt.js` should make a bit more sense; we call the `prompt` function and assign its output to `userName`. See Listing 8.5.

Listing 8.5 `prompt` **Returns a Value**

```
var userName = prompt('Hello, what\'s your name?');
```

For a function to return a value, the function body must have a `return` statement. If the function body has no `return` statement, the function returns `undefined` (`console.log` doesn't have a return value, and that is why you see `undefined` in the console whenever you run `console.log`). Listing 8.6 shows an example `sum` function that uses the `return` statement to return the sum of two numbers. For practice, try to write a `product` function that returns the product of two numbers.

Listing 8.6 **Return the Sum of Two Numbers**

```
function sum (x, y) {
    return x + y;
}
```

The `return` statement is always the last instruction to be executed in a function body, even if there are other instructions after the `return` statement. The `return` statement is the function's way of saying, "I have done everything I need to do, and here is the result." You can use this "early exit" feature of the `return` statement to your advantage. For example, you could use a `return` statement instead of a `break` statement to exit a loop. Consider the `for` loop in Chapter 7, "If, For, While, and When," that we used to determine whether `'spaghetti'` was in an array of favorite foods. Listing 8.7 shows this loop written in a function using a `return` statement instead of `break`.

Listing 8.7   **Use `return` to Exit a Loop Early**

```
function doesStevenLikeSpaghetti(favoriteFoods) {
  for (var i=0; i < favoriteFoods.length; i++) {
    if (favoriteFoods[i] === 'spaghetti') {
      // As soon as "spaghetti" is found, stop looping.
      return true;
    }
  }

  // if the loop completes, that means spaghetti was not found, so return false
  return false;
}
```

Try rewriting the function in Listing 8.7 so that it can check for any food instead of just spaghetti. Make sure you give your function a new name that reflects its new functionality.

Call Stack

Functions can call other functions, which can call other functions. The list of what function called what function is known as the call stack. When a function is called, that function is added to the top of the call stack. When a function finishes executing, that function is removed from the call stack. Listing 8.8 gives an example of functions calling functions, and Figure 8.1 shows what the call stack looks like when `third` is being executed.

Listing 8.8   **Functions Calling Functions**

```
function first() {
  console.log('Executing first function');
  console.log('Calling second function');
  second();
}

function second() {
  console.log('Executing second function');
  console.log('Calling third function');
  third();
}

function third() {
```

```
  console.log('Executing third function');
}

first();
```

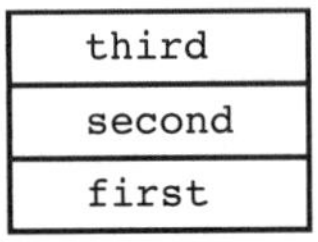

```
┌──────────┐
│  third   │
├──────────┤
│  second  │
├──────────┤
│  first   │
└──────────┘
```

Figure 8.1   The call stack for Listing 8.8, at the point when the `third` function is being executed.

Code Encapsulation

One of the primary purposes for functions is organizing your code. A function neatly packages (or encapsulates) many instructions so that they can be called using a single instruction. For the sake of code organization, all the instructions in a function should be related.

Do One Thing Well

A function should have one job to do, and it should do that job really well. Every task required to do that one job should be performed by the function, and any task that is not related to that job should not be included in the function. Unrelated tasks can create bizarre side effects. Listing 8.9 demonstrates the type of strange behavior that might happen when unrelated tasks are included in a function.

Listing 8.9   **Make the Bed (and Some Other Stuff)**

```
function makeTheBed(bed) {
  // Put the pillows on the bed
  bed.pillowsOnBed = true;

  // Put the sheets on the bed
  bed.sheetsOnBed = true;

  // Straighten the sheets
  bed.sheetsStraightened = true;

  // Put the blankets on the bed
  bed.blanketsOnBed = true;

  // Straighten the blankets
```

```
bed.blanketsStraightened = true;

    // Brush my teeth, because I always brush my teeth after I make my bed
    brushTeeth();
}

// I'm visiting my grandma today
goToGrandmasHouse();

// I want to help my grandma with some chores
makeTheBed(grandmasFeatherBed);

// Gross, I just brushed my teeth with my grandma's toothbrush
```

The `brushTeeth` task might *seem* related to the other tasks in the `makeTheBed` function because I always brush my teeth after I make the bed, but come on—do I really need to brush my teeth for the bed to be made? In Listing 8.9, I go to my grandma's house and make the bed, and I end up brushing my teeth (with Grandma's toothbrush) because the `makeTheBed` function dictates that I *must* brush my teeth for the bed-making task to be complete. Admittedly, this example is a bit contrived, but this is a real problem when it comes to code organization.

> ### Naming Functions
>
> If you can't figure out what name to give your function, that's a sign that your function doesn't have a clear purpose. What job is your function meant to perform? The answer to that question should be the name of your function. When you have a good name for your function, you can easily determine whether a given task belongs in your function. `makeTheBed` is a good function name because the purpose and scope of the function are clear. Brushing teeth clearly doesn't belong in the `makeTheBed` function.

Divide and Conquer

As you begin to think about the individual jobs that your software needs to perform, the task of building an entire computer program becomes less daunting, and your code becomes much cleaner and more organized. Along those lines, let's think about the jobs we want kittenbook to perform:

- Get the user's name
- Get the user's phone number
- Determine the user's location based on the phone number
- Get a list of images on the user's Facebook feed
- Replace all the images in the list with images of puppies or kittens, based on the user's location

Right now, the code for executing these different jobs is all mixed together, making it hard to tell which code is related to which job. Let's make a function for each of these jobs. Your task is to first come up with good names for each of the functions and then divide up the code into each of the functions. First, you need to create a new file called main.js that will be used as the entry point for your program. After you have created your functions, remember that you have to call them, or the code won't run.

To get you started, Listing 8.10 shows the new main.js file. Listing 8.11 shows an example of what prompt.js might look like, and Listing 8.12 has the code for a new replaceImages.js file. You'll also need to create a getImages function in the getImages.js file and a getAreaCodes function in the values.js file. If you get stuck, you can find example code for all the other files on the book's website.

Listing 8.10   `main.js` **kittenbook Control Center**

```
function main() {
  var userName = getUserName();
  var phoneNumber = getPhoneNumber(userName);
  var location = getLocation(phoneNumber);
  var images = getImages();

  // setInterval is like setTimeout, except it repeats its code instead of
  // executing it just once. Use setInterval to replace new images that are
  // loaded as you scroll down the page.
  setInterval(function() {
    images = getImages();
    replaceImages(images, location);
  }, 3000);
}

main();
```

Listing 8.11   `prompt.js` **Encapsulated**

```
// Get the user's name.
function getUserName() {
  var userName = prompt('Hello, what\'s your name?');

  if (!userName) {
    userName = prompt('You didn\'t enter a name. Really, what\'s your name?');
  }
  return userName;
}

// Get the user's phone number.
function getPhoneNumber(userName) {
```

```
  var phoneNumber = prompt('Hello ' + userName +', what\'s your phone number?');
  if (!validatePhoneNumber(phoneNumber)) {
    phoneNumber = prompt('Please enter a valid phone number.');
  }
  return phoneNumber;
}


// Validate a phone number
function validatePhoneNumber(phoneNumber) {
  return phoneNumber.match(/(?:1-)?\(?(?(\d{3})[\-\)][\-\)]\d{3}-\d{4}/);
}


// Determine location based on phone number
function getLocation(phoneNumber) {
  // Create the phone number pattern.
  var phoneNumberPattern = /(?:1-)?\(?(?(\d{3})[\-\)][\-\)]\d{3}-\d{4}/;
  // Get matches from phoneNumber
  var phoneMatches = phoneNumberPattern.exec(phoneNumber);
  var areaCodes, areaCode, locationName;
  if (phoneMatches) {
    areaCode = phoneMatches[1];
    areaCodes = getAreaCodes();
    locationName = areaCodes[areaCode];
  }

  // Look, it's a ternary operator.
  // Return the locationName if it exists, else return 'somewhere'
  return locationName ? locationName : 'somewhere';
}
```

The code to replace the images in the Facebook feed, shown in Listing 8.12, can be broken into four parts:

1. Decide what kind of image will be used in the replacement, based on the `location` parameter. The `baseImageUrl` variable will be used to get the images. http://placepuppy.it/ gives us images of puppies, and http://placekitten.com/g/ gives us images of kittens. You can add dimensions to the end of these URLs to get an image with the specified dimension. For example, http://placepuppy.it/300/500 will give you an image of a puppy that is 300 pixels wide and 500 pixels high. I prefer placekitten over placepuppy because placekitten is more reliable and the images load faster, but you can try both.

2. Loop through the images from the `images` parameter.

3. Get the dimensions for each image in the loop. We want the new image to be the same size as the original image.

4. Set the image's `src` attribute using the `baseImageUrl` from Step 1 and the dimensions from Step 3. The `src` (short for *source*) attribute tells the browser where to look for the

image. All the images you see on the Web have a source, and those sources are URLs. As we update the source attribute of our images, we are basically telling the browser to go get a new image and show it in place of the old image.

Listing 8.12   **Replace All Images with Pictures of Puppies or Kittens**

```
function getImageHeight(image) {
  return image.height;
}

function getImageWidth(image) {
  return image.width;
}

function replaceImages(images, location) {
  var baseImageUrl, height, width, image;
  switch (location) {
  case 'Memphis':
    // Use puppies for Memphis
    baseImageUrl = 'http://placepuppy.it/';
    break;
  default:
    // Use kittens everywhere else
    baseImageUrl = 'http://placekitten.com/g/';
    break;
  }
  for (var i=0,len=images.length; i<len; i++) {
    image = images[i];
    height = getImageHeight(image);
    width = getImageWidth(image);
    image.src = baseImageUrl + width + '/' + height;
  }
}
```

A Place for Everything and Everything in Its Place

You might have noticed as you went through the kittenbook code that some of the instructions are not really related to any of the jobs we listed. Every line of code in our project should be helping to accomplish the goals of our program. The unnecessary code was a lot harder to identify before we added functions, but now we can clearly see that we can get rid of some code. The practice of deleting unneeded code can be rewarding. If you have code that is not helping you accomplish the goal of your program, throw it out.

Code Reuse

So far, we have used functions for the purposes of organizing code, but functions can do more. One of the great parts of functions is that they can be called as many times as you want to call them, from wherever you want to call them.

Solve the General Problem

One of the keys to writing reusable code is to change the way you think about the problem you are solving. Don't just think about the problem in front of you, but consider the type of problem you are solving and then create a solution that works for any problem of that type— not just your problem. Changing the way you think is no easy task, and it takes practice and experience. At the beginning of the chapter, I introduced the countToTen function, which solves a specific problem of "count from 1 to 10." Then we built countTo, a function with parameters that can count from 1 to any number we want, which solves a much more general problem.

Do More with Less

Now, supposing that we want to count from 10 to 15, we can't use countToTen or countTo because they both start counting at 1. We could write a new function, countFromTenTo, but that's not much better. What if we want to start at 11 or 9? What we really want is a function that can count from any number to any number. We'll call our function countFromXtoY. See Listing 8.13.

Listing 8.13 **A Generalized Function for Counting from Any Number to Any Number**

```
function countFromXtoY(x, y) {
  for (var i=x; i<=y; i++) {
    console.log(i);
  }
}
```

Now that is reusable. Now I can use countFromXtoY(10, 15) to count from 10 to 15, or countFromXtoY(300,5000) to count from 300 to 5,000, or countFromXtoY(10, 1) to count down from 10 to 1. Wait a minute! That last one doesn't work. Try it—and you will see that countFromXtoY works only if x is greater than y. We can make the function truly reusable and flexible, but it will get pretty complicated. See Listing 8.14.

Listing 8.14 **A Truly Resuable countFromXtoY**

```
function countFromXtoY(x, y) {

  if (x > y) {
```

```
  // x is greater than y, which means we are counting down
  var incrementor = function(idx) {

    // reduce the value of the index by 1
    return idx - 1;
  }
  var comparison = function(idx, num) {

    // until the index is no longer greater than or equal to the ending number
    return idx >= num;
  }
} else {

  // y is greater than x, so we're counting up.
  incrementor = function(idx) {

    // increase the value of the index by 1
    return idx + 1;
  }
  comparison = function(idx, num) {

    // until the index is no longer less than or equal to the ending number
    return idx <= num;
  }
}

// The starting number is x
// Use the comparison function to know if we should keep looping
// Use the incrementor function to know which direction to count
for (var i=x; comparison(i, y); i = incrementor(i)) {
  console.log(i);
}
}
```

This version of countFromXtoY will count up or down from any integer to any other integer (although it is a bit confusing). In the last chapter, you learned that the for loop has an assignment, a comparison, and an increment. The function in Listing 8.15 uses internal functions for the comparison and the increment, and the behavior of those functions depends on whether x is greater than y.

Assigned Functions

Listing 8.14 introduces a new feature of functions: In JavaScript, you can assign a function to a variable. For countFromXtoY, we have to assign the functions to variables instead of defining the functions the normal way because of an interesting feature in JavaScript called hoisting. Hoisting is beyond the scope of this book, but you can look it up if you are interested in learning more.

Don't Repeat Yourself (DRY)

The DRY concept comes up a lot in programming (you already saw it in database design—don't repeat data in multiple tables), and it is especially important in organizing your code. If you have two different functions that do almost the same thing, you will end up writing the same instructions twice, which is a waste of time. What's worse, though, is that when you find a bug in one of your functions (and, believe me, you will find a bug), you will have to fix it in both functions. Even worse still is when you fix the bug in one function but forget to fix it in the other function, and you end up thinking, "What is going on? I already fixed this bug."

The first big project I worked on was a somewhat complex website for my university. One of the most important features of the website was a typeahead (see Figure 8.2—I didn't know that these were called typeaheads when I was building the website). In the process of building the website, I probably made 15 typeaheads, and I had to repeat a whole bunch of code for each one. I did a lot of copy-and-pasting, and every time I found a bug, I had to fix it in 15 different places. Every time I found a better way of handling the typeahead, I had to update 15 different functions. Don't repeat yourself—because you are just creating more work for yourself.

Figure 8.2   Typeaheads are so useful—and even better when you have to write the code only once.

Let's get back to the counting to 10 example. If we do a lot of counting from 1 to 10, we might still want a `countToTen` function. But instead of repeating a bunch of code, we can just use the `countrFromXtoY` function inside of `countToTen` (see Listing 8.15). No repeated code. Awesome!

Listing 8.15   `countToTen` Using `countFromXtoY`

```
function countToTen() {
  countFromXtoY(1, 10);
}
```

Anonymous Functions and Callbacks

Most functions have names. Almost every function you have seen in the code examples in this book has had a name. You execute a function by calling it by name. But some functions are anonymous; they have no name. How can you execute a function if you don't know the name to call it? Why would anyone ever want an anonymous function? That's crazy talk. Well, think back to the `forEach` example from the last chapter. `forEach` is a special function for accessing each item in an array, and `forEach` accepts an anonymous function as an argument. See Listings 8.16 and 8.17.

Listing 8.16   forEach Revisited

```
> var lettersArray = ['a', 'b', 'c'];
  ["a", "b", "c"]
> lettersArray.forEach( function(letter) {
    console.log(letter);
  } );
  "a"
  "b"
  "c"
```

Listing 8.17   forEach's Anonymous Function

```
function(letter) {
  console.log(letter);
}
```

That function has no name. A function that is passed as an argument to another function is often called a callback. A callback is a block of code to be executed by the other function. The callback function is just a container of instructions, so it doesn't need a name. Now that is some crazy stuff.

Scope

Now that you have a pretty good understanding of functions, let's go back and think about variables. A variable is a reference to some value, maybe a string, a Boolean, or an object. When a variable is encountered while a program is executed, the program's runtime looks up the value related to the variable's name. In this context, scope determines where the runtime is allowed to look for the value. If a variable is defined within a function, the runtime is allowed to look only inside the scope of the function to find the value related to that variable's name. A variable defined in one function cannot be used in another function. That concept is confusing, but an example should make it a bit easier to understand. See Listing 8.18.

Listing 8.18   Variables and Scope

```
var myName = 'Steven';

function sayAName() {
  // Inside the function create a new variable with the same name (myName) as
  // a variable outside the function.
  var myName = 'Mike';
  console.log('myName inside sayAName is: ' + myName);
```

```
}

function sayMyName() {
  var myLastName = 'Foote';
  console.log('myName inside sayMyName is: ' + myName);
  console.log('myLastName inside sayMyName is: ' + myLastName);
}

sayAName();
sayMyName();
console.log('myName outside the functions is: ' + myName);
console.log('myLastName outside the functions is: ' + myLastName);
```

You really need to try this code and observe firsthand what is going on. We have two variables with the same name (myName), one defined outside any function and one defined inside a function. The value of myName depends on where it is being referenced. When referenced outside the functions, myName has the value 'Steven'. When referenced inside of the sayAName function, myName has a value of 'Mike' because myName is declared within the sayAName. When referenced within the sayMyName function, myName has the value 'Steven' again. The runtime first looks within the function's scope for a definition of a variable and then looks at the outer scope. When referenced within sayMyName, the value of myLastName is 'Foote'. However, when myLastName is referenced outside the sayMyName function, an error occurs because myLastName exists only in the scope in which it was defined.

Global

Global variables are variables that are available everywhere. In general, a global variable is a variable that is declared outside any scope. Global variables can be convenient because they are available everywhere. You don't have to think about what scope you are in because a global variable is always in scope. That really is useful, but global variables have downsides as well. Extensive use of global variables leads to messy code that is difficult to understand and difficult to debug. For instance, the sayAName function in Listing 8.19 is almost identical to Listing 8.18, but the small difference causes a big problem.

Listing 8.19   **Be Careful with Global Variables**

```
var myName = 'Steven';

function sayAName() {
  myName = 'Mike';
  console.log('myName inside of sayAName is: ' + myName);
}

sayAName();
console.log('myName outside of sayAName is: ' + myName);
```

Now the value of myName is 'Mike' inside and outside the sayAName function, all because we left out the var statement in sayAName in Listing 8.19. var myName = 'Mike'; is a declaration of a new variable in the scope of the sayAName function and also an assignment. But myName = 'Mike'; is just an assignment to a variable that already exists in the global scope (the global myName).

Global variables are easily overwritten elsewhere in your code. All JavaScript files on a web page share the same global variables (which is how we were able to access kbValues in earlier versions of kittenbook). You might have a global variable whose value is important to the successful execution of your program, yet that variable's value can easily be changed or deleted by code in some other file, and you won't even know about it. For these reasons, I recommend that you avoid global variables as much as possible, even though they can be convenient. Your code will be much cleaner. This advice is not limited in scope to JavaScript; it is *global* advice!

Local

Local variables are available only within the function. When the function finishes executing, the local variable goes away. When creating variable names inside your function, you don't have to worry about whether those names already exist outside your function; the scope inside the function takes precedence. However, some global variables you don't want to overwrite. For instance, the function in Listing 8.20 creates a local variable called console and then tries to use console.log, but it fails because, within the scope of the function, the value of console is the string 'bash', and the string 'bash' has no log method.

Listing 8.20   **Choose Your Local Variable Names with Care**

```
function terminal() {
  var console = 'bash';
  console.log(console + ' is a cool tool to use in a terminal');
}

// Calling this function will produce an error
terminal();
```

How Variable Lookups Happen

When you use a variable in your code, the runtime has to look up the value of that variable. The past few examples should have given you an idea about how this process works, but a more direct definition is helpful. When looking for the value of a variable, the function first looks in the current scope for variables with the given name. If no variable with the given name is found in the current scope, the variable looks in the scope in which the current scope is defined. This process is repeated until either a variable with the given name is found or the runtime reaches the global scope. If a variable with the given name is not found in the global scope, an error occurs (a reference error because the runtime has no reference to the variable). The concepts of scope and variable lookups were really difficult for me to understand; you might find this section worth reading through a few times. To avoid being really confused when something such as Listing 8.20 happens, you need to understand scope.

To help you better understand scope and variable lookups, the code in Listing 8.21 is represented in Figure 8.3. The state outlines and the outline of the United States in Figure 8.3 represent scope. The globe represents the global scope. The arrows represent the direction variable lookups are allowed to happen. The arrows point only outward because an outer scope can never access a variable in an inner scope (for example, the global scope can never access variables defined inside the USA scope, and the USA scope can never access variables defined inside the North Dakota scope).

Listing 8.21 **Local and Global Scope**

```
var globalName = 'the world';
var name = globalName;

function USA() {
  var nationalName = 'United States of America';
  var name = nationalName;
  var capital = 'Washington D.C.';

  function nevada() {
    var name = 'Nevada';
    var capital = 'Carson City';
    console.log(capital + ' is the capital of ' + name + ' in ' + nationalName
              + ' in ' + globalName);
  }

  function northDakota() {
    var name = 'North Dakota';
    var capital = 'Bismark';
    console.log(capital + ' is the capital of ' + name + ' in ' + nationalName
              + ' in ' + globalName);
  }

  console.log(capital + ' is the capital of ' + name + ' in ' + globalName);
  nevada();
  northDakota();
}

USA();
```

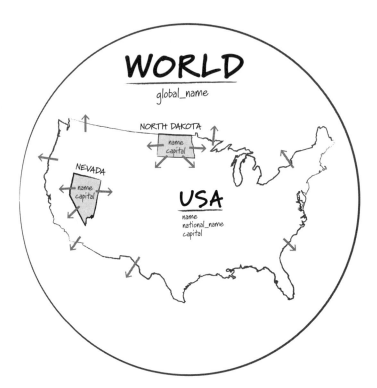

Figure 8.3   Variables check out, but they don't check in.

Functions for the Sake of Scope

What should you do if you want to make a variable available to all your functions, but you want to avoid the pitfalls of global scope? You can create a function whose single purpose is to restrict scope. You can create a named function and then immediately invoke that named function, as in Listing 8.22, but then the name of that function is available in the global scope. An even better solution is to create an anonymous function that is immediately invoked, as in Listing 8.23. In JavaScript, this is referred to as an IIFE (immediately invoked function expression), and the syntax is pretty strange. You surround the anonymous function in parentheses and then add another set of parentheses to call the anonymous function.

Listing 8.22   **A Named Function Whose Sole Purpose Is Restricting Scope**

```
function restrictedScope() {
  var name = 'world';

  function greeting() {
    console.log('Hello, ' + name + '!');
```

```
  }

  function sayHello() {
    greeting();
  }

  sayHello();
}

// Great, but restrictedScope is now part of the global scope
restrictedScope();
```

Listing 8.23   **An IIFE Whose Purpose Is Restricting Scope**

```
(function() {
  var name = 'world';

  function greeting() {
    console.log('Hello, ' + name + '!');
  }

  function sayHello() {
    greeting();
  }

  sayHello();
})();
```

Summing Up

Functions are pretty amazing, aren't they? You have learned a lot of skills to make your code more organized, more efficient, and more reusable. In this chapter, you learned about:

- The structure of functions
- How to organize code using functions
- Ways to make code reusable with functions
- Scope

In the next chapter, you will learn skills that will help you become a great programmer. Specifically, you will learn about:

- Formatting your code
- Writing good, maintainable code
- Following programming best practices

9

Programming Standards

Up to this point, the chapters have been technical in nature. You have learned a lot of the nuts and bolts of programming, and you have looked at and written a lot of code. But there is more to programming than the nuts and bolts. You learned a lot about the tools you need to write computer programs. In this chapter, you begin to learn the rules of writing computer programs, what makes really good code, and how to write code that you can be proud of.

"But wait," you think, "I don't care about the rules. As long as my program works, I'm happy." If all you want to do is write little programs that help you do some small aspect of your job better, do you really need to learn to write high-quality code? Well, yes. Programming is a powerful tool, and you need to learn to use it properly. At first your programs might be small and you might be the only user, but soon you will be adding new features and your little programs will start to grow. Soon your friends and coworkers will be asking to use them. If you learn the rules and write high-quality code from the beginning, those new features will be easier to add and the bugs your friends find will be easier to fix.

Learning the rules of a programming language is like having good technique when you are playing a sport. When playing basketball, you might occasionally make a basket with a granny shot from half court, but if every shot you take is a granny shot from half court, no one will want to play with you. Likewise, you can write code that works without following rules, standards, and conventions, but no one will want to work with you (including your future self).

Coding Conventions

Whatever programming language you are using, you should follow certain standards. Some of the standards are there to help you avoid bugs in your code. For example, in JavaScript, you should always use === (triple equals) instead of == (double equals) because == can have unintended consequences (see Chapter 7, "If, For, While, and When"). Other standards are really just conventions that help keep your code consistent and readable. Some conventions should be followed any time you are writing in a given language. For instance, JavaScript variable names should use camel case (myName), while Python variable names should use all lowercase letters with underscores to separate words (my_name). Underscoring works in JavaScript and camel case works in Python, but virtually everyone writing in these languages follows the convention.

Some conventions vary from project to project, even in the same language. For example, some JavaScript projects use single quotes ('a single quoted string'), whereas others use double quotes ("a double quoted string"). These conventions are a matter of preference, but everyone working on the project should agree and follow them.

Setting Standards

Speaking of agreeing on standards and conventions, you should make sure you are familiar with the standards and conventions of the language and project you are working on. If you want to start working on a Python project, do a quick Google search for something such as "Python coding standards," and you will find the resources you need to get to know the Python standards. Then you should set your own standards for the project. You probably don't know what standards to set at this point, and that's okay. If you have found the general standards for your language, you are already doing much better than I did for years. You can start with just one standard: "Avoid global variables." As you continue to program, you will find little things you do that keep causing problems. Write them down as part of your standards to help remind you to stop doing those things. You should always be at least a little embarrassed of the code you wrote 6 months ago. That is proof you are improving.

You already have a project, so you can practice setting standards right now. Remember way back in Chapter 4, "Build Tools," when you learned about build tools? Remember how we set up JSHint to check our JavaScript code quality? How about that—you already have standards on your first programming project, *and* those standards are being programmatically enforced by JSHint and Grunt.

To Hack or Not to Hack

For your own good, you want to write high-quality code. You will learn more, your code will run better, and your code will be easier to fix in the future. However, sometimes a durable, long-term solution is not necessary or desirable. Develop the ability to distinguish when a short-term hack is actually better than a long-term, robust solution.

Hacking

You have been taught that hacking is a malicious attempt to gain access to secure systems: "Hack into the bank and steal a bunch of money." Perhaps in popular culture, this is what hacking means. Among programmers, hacking does not generally carry that negative connotation. Many programmers call themselves hackers. Well-respected technology companies regularly hold events called "hack-a-thons," where "hackers" get together to build cool new apps and services. In this sense, hacking is the act of writing code. Hacking is good.

Hacking can also mean writing code that is the digital equivalent of duct tape and bailing wire. The solution might be ugly, fragile, and ridiculous, but it works. When I say "to hack or not to hack," I am referring to this meaning of *hack*.

Pay Now or Pay Later

If you quickly write hacky code now, you will pay the price with bugs and maintenance later. Usually it is worth the time to do the hard work now because fixing bugs can be exponentially more costly than writing good code in the first place. However, in some situations, quickly writing hacky code is actually the right thing to do. If you are playing with code to learn a new concept (for example, experimenting in the console), there is no reason to follow all your standards. Your code is thrown away as soon as it is executed. If you want to quickly build a prototype to prove that some idea can actually be implemented, a quick, hacky solution might be best. When you decide whether you will write quick-and-dirty code or high-quality code, you should realize that you are making the decision of whether you will pay now or pay later. Deciding to pay later is often called tech debt, and it's about as nice to have as credit card debt.

Writing Maintainable Code

One of the biggest motivations for creating and following coding standards has to do with the software development life cycle. The software development life cycle basically has just four steps:

1. Get an idea.

2. Plan how to turn your idea into reality.

3. Turn your idea into reality by writing the code.

4. Keep your idea-turned-reality alive and relevant by fixing bugs and adding features (maintenance).

These four steps do not all take the same amount of time. Getting an idea can take about 5 seconds while you are in the shower. Planning how to actually build your idea should take a lot longer than 5 seconds, but we're often so excited to get to Step 3 that we skip over this one (guilty). The process of turning your idea into reality takes a bit longer. Depending on the grandiosity of the idea, it might take days, months, or even years. The longest step by far, though, is maintenance. You will continue maintaining your project as long as the project survives. If you write high-quality, maintainable code, the maintenance step will be a joy. If you choose not to set standards and write maintainable code, the maintenance step will be painful.

What makes for maintainable code? This (incomplete) list should get you started:

- Well documented (good comments, diagrams, and so on)

- Well thought out and planned (did you think things through first, or did you just jump in and start coding?)

- Well tested and relatively free of bugs (have you thoroughly tested your program, or are you just guessing that it works?)

- Easy to understand (for someone who knows the programming language)

- Reusable (see Chapter 8, "Functions and Methods")

Code Formatting

Writing good code is more than just putting the right instructions in the right order. The way your code actually looks can make a huge difference in how successful your program is. Listing 9.1 shows `values.js` with super-compact formatting, Listing 9.2 shows `values.js` with better but inconsistent formatting, and Listing 9.3 shows `values.js` with good formatting. Which is easier to read? Which will be easier to work with?

Listing 9.1   `values.js` with **Super-Compact Formatting**

```
var kbValues = {projectName:'kittenbook',versionNumber:'0.0.1',areaCodes:{
'408':'Silicon Valley','702':'Las Vegas','801':'Utah','765':'West Lafayette',
'901':'Memphis'}};function getAreaCodes() {return kbValues.areaCodes;}
```

That ridiculously confusing code actually works exactly the same as the code in Listing 9.2 and Listing 9.3. The difference is that, to read the code in Listing 9.1, you must have a lot of patience and a high tolerance for pain.

Listing 9.2   `values.js` with **Inconsistent Formatting**

```
var kbValues =            {
  projectName: 'kittenbook',
versionNumber: '0.0.1',
  areaCodes:{
    '408': 'Silicon Valley',
  "702":          'Las Vegas',
    '801': 'Utah'      ,
    '765':"West Lafayette",
    '901':       'Memphis'
}
};

function getAreaCodes() {
  return kbValues.areaCodes;
  }
```

I literally felt a little sick writing that. It's hard for me to look at it. I hope I have made my point and we can move on, because I don't think I can look at that code again.

Listing 9.3   `values.js` with Good Formatting

```
var kbValues = {
  projectName: 'kittenbook',
  versionNumber: '0.0.1',
  areaCodes: {
    '408': 'Silicon Valley',
    '702': 'Las Vegas',
    '801': 'Utah',
    '765': 'West Lafayette',
    '901': 'Memphis'
  }
};

function getAreaCodes() {
  return kbValues.areaCodes;
}
```

Computers Don't Understand Programming Languages

As you consider how to format your code, remember that your computer doesn't understand your source code anyway. The source code has to be turned into binary before your computer understands it. Source code is for humans to read, so your formatting should be easy for humans to understand.

Keep It Consistent

The way you format your code is up to you (or the team you are working with). As you saw in the three code examples just now, the way you format your code doesn't affect the way your code runs (see "Python Style" for a caveat). You should decide how you are going to format your code and then consistently follow the conventions you have chosen. Staying consistent in your formatting will help make your code more readable (see Listing 9.2 for an anti-example), and it can also help you avoid bugs. In all the code examples in this book, I have used single quotes for strings, but I could have used double quotes. JavaScript understands both. However, if you start a string with a double quote, you must end it with a double quote, and vice versa. If you decide to use double quotes for some strings and single quotes for other strings, you might accidentally open a string with a double quote and try to close it with a single quote. That doesn't work—the JavaScript would get confused and all your code would break.

Whitespace

Consistently using whitespace is perhaps the most important code formatting convention that you can adopt in your code. The proper use of whitespace dramatically improves the readability of your code. Consider again the difference between Listing 9.1 and Listing 9.3. It is the exact same code, but Listing 9.1 has all spaces and new lines removed. A guiding principle for using whitespace is that the whitespace should be consistent with the logic of your code. The lines of code inside a function should be indented the same amount, and the lines of code inside a `for` loop should all be indented the same amount. That way, it is clear which lines are intended to be run in the function or `for` loop. Listing 9.2 shows how difficult it can be to read code when inconsistent indentation is applied.

When it comes to indentation, you can use either spaces or tabs. That decision might not seem that important to you right now, but the topic is hotly debated among programmers (seriously). Honestly, I don't think it makes much of a difference, but I prefer spaces. Most text editors allow you to turn on soft tabs, which insert a given number of spaces when you press the Tab key. Whatever you choose, stay consistent. Mixing spaces and tabs is one of the worst offenses when it comes to inconsistent code formatting.

> ### Python Style
>
> Consistent formatting can be a big problem. The Python programming language tries to alleviate the problem by enforcing certain whitespace conventions. Instead of using curly braces, Python uses indentation to indicate which instructions belong in a block of code. Listing 9.4 shows a `for` loop in Python. Some programmers really prefer giving whitespace meaning, as is the case in Python. Love it or hate it, though, you have to admit that it does help improve formatting consistency.

Listing 9.4   **A Python `for` Loop**

```
print 'Starting the for loop'

for i in range(10):
    print(i)

print 'Ending the for loop'
```

It Doesn't Happen on Its Own: Make Rules

After you have established your standards and conventions, make sure you write them down. When you have written your rules, you will be more likely to live by them. If you are working on a project with other people, having an agreed-upon, written set of standards will help keep your source code clean and consistent, and it will help you avoid conflicts ("DOUBLE QUOTES ARE BETTER!!!", 'NO, SINGLE QUOTES ARE BETTER!!!'). These written standards are sometimes called styleguides. One form of a styleguide is the options file for JSHint, `.jshintrc` (the `example.jshintrc` in Listing 9.5 should be saved in the `kittenbook` directory). This options file is one of the hidden "dot-files" we discussed in Chapter 3, "Getting to Know Your Computer." The contents of `.jshintrc` are a set of options in the form of a JSON object. To learn more about the available options, visit http://jshint.com/docs/options/.

Listing 9.5   **`.jshintrc` for kittenbook**

```
{
  "predef": {
    "kittenbook": true,
    "kbValues": true,
    "prompt": true
  },

  "bitwise": true,
  "camelcase": true,
  "curly": true,
  "eqeqeq": true,
  "immed": true,
  "indent": 2,
  "latedef": true,
  "quotmark": "single",
  "undef": true,
  "unused": true,
  "strict": false,
  "trailing": true,

  "browser": true
}
```

The most important options in our `.jshintrc` (for purposes of our discussion) are `"predef"`, with our list of variables in the global scope; `"indent"`, which says the proper indent is 2 spaces; `"quotmark"`, which says we will be using single quotes; and `"browser"`, which tells JSHint to expect to see things like `document` because our code is meant to be run in a browser (as opposed to `Node.js`). If you are interested in learning more about the other options, check out the JSHint website mentioned earlier.

To get the new `.jshintrc` options to work, you also need to update `Gruntfile.js` so that Grunt knows where to look for `.jshintrc` when it runs the `jshint` task (see Listing 9.6). You might also want to run the `concat` task before the `jshint` task and check only the concatenated file. The concatenated file is the one that we really want to check for errors anyway. We have to update `watch` as well because it was using `<%= jshint.files %>` to know which files to watch. Finally, switch the order of `'concat'` and `'jshint'` in `grunt.registerTask`, so that `release/main.js` is updated before the `jshint` task runs.

Listing 9.6   **Changes Made to `Gruntfile.js` to Use `.jshintrc`**

```
module.exports = function(grunt) {
  grunt.initConfig({

    ...

    jshint: {
      options: {
        jshintrc: '.jshintrc'
      },
      files: ['release/main.js']
    },
    watch: {
      files: ['js/*.js', 'manifest.json'],
      tasks: ['default']
    }
  });

  ...

  // Register tasks
  grunt.registerTask('default', ['concat', 'jshint', 'copy']);
};
```

Now that you have Grunt set up to use `.jshintrc`, open the command line, navigate to the kittenbook project directory, and run `grunt`. You will probably see a few errors from JSHint now. See if you can figure out what those errors mean and how to fix them. If you get stuck, you can take a look at the code for Chapter 9 on the book website.

Using the Work of Others

I wish I had learned to take advantage of the work of others much sooner than I did. I love to build things, so I was intentionally ignorant of the free software others were creating that I could have been using. What a terrible idea. I learned a lot by trying to build everything myself. Fortunately, I learned that other people do great work, too. Having said that, there is a balance between building things for yourself and freely plugging in open source projects.

Build Faster

Probably my most egregious example of not using the work of others was when I insisted on building a typeahead. I refused to believe that a typeahead could be made reusable enough that I could use a typeahead that someone else had built on my website (my refusal was partly due to my lack of understanding of callbacks). I didn't even believe I could make a typeahead that I could use in more than one place on my own site. I built 15 typeaheads, for crying out loud. What a waste of time. For the next project I worked on, I found an open source typeahead project that I could easily plug in every time I needed a typeahead. Using the open source project saved me many hours of work.

Whether the work is done by someone in the open source community or another member of your team, using the work of others can really speed up the time it takes for you to create a project. Remember, the purpose of my project was not to build a typeahead, but to build a functioning application that happened to include a typeahead. Including a typeahead built by someone else would not have cheapened my work or the value of the application as a whole. On the contrary, I could have spent more time making my application great.

Open Source Software

You have probably heard of or read about open source software; even pointy-haired bosses have some notion of what open source software is: a magical land where all your problems go away—for free! Or maybe a place where the ideals of free speech and free stuff come together to make the world a better place. Amazing!

Most commercial software is distributed as packaged, compiled code, but the source code is kept private. Open source software is software whose source code is made publicly available. Mozilla Firefox, Google Chrome, Android, Linux, JavaScript, and Python are all examples of large-scale open source projects. If you have the time and patience, you can dig through the Android source code to learn more about how Android notifications work; the source code is available.

There is a notion that anyone can contribute to an open source software project and that anyone can use an open source software project for any purpose. In reality, open source projects have varying degrees of freedom. Android is developed internally at Google, and the source code is made publicly available only when a new release is ready (closed development, open source). Most open source software projects include some sort of license with two basic ideas:

1. You can use and distribute this software freely.

2. If you make modifications to this software, those modifications must be made publicly available.

This type of licensing ensures that if any person or group improves the software, those improvements are made available to everyone. In that sense, open source software works a lot like Wikipedia: The quality of an active project tends to increase over time.

Built by the Community

One of the biggest advantages of using open source software is the very fact that anyone can contribute. If you want to use some open source software that properly formats dates for German users, you can nearly be certain that a German programmer who knows a lot about date formatting has contributed to that project. Programmers are drawn to the projects for which they have the most expertise, so the open source community generally has the right people working on the right projects. These experts have seen and fixed the weird bugs related to the software they are building so you don't have to. You don't have to understand all the intricacies that go into the solution because the expert programmers in the open source community have done that work for you.

You should be aware, however, that anyone can create and publish an open source software project. Just because you have found an open source project that seems to solve your problem doesn't mean you should use it. Do some investigation. Are other people using it? How many? Is anyone actively working on it? Are there lots of reported bugs? Using low-quality open source software is more costly than building the software yourself.

When to Build It Yourself

Sometimes your best choice is to ignore the open source alternatives and build something yourself. If you find an open source project that seems to solve your problem, there are still reasons to build it yourself. Maybe it doesn't quite solve the same problem you're trying to solve. Maybe the software licenses make you (or your legal department) uncomfortable. Maybe you have concerns about the security of the code. Maybe you just think you could do a better job. Just because someone has already built it doesn't mean you should not also build it. You'll find many web browsers, many operating systems, and many programming languages. Technology moves forward as different solutions to similar problems compete with and learn from each other.

Best Practices

Certain coding standards go beyond the actual writing of code. The standards I refer to are documentation, planning, and testing. These best practices will help you become a great programmer who writes great programs. As you learn to effectively use these three tools, your confidence in your programs will increase. When I built my first website, I did very little planning and testing, and I documented only occasionally. As a result, I had very little confidence in the website. I was nervous every time I made a change, major or minor. Would my new code break everything? If the website crashed, would I be able to fix it? It turns out that my fears were justified; I broke the website frequently, and sometimes I couldn't figure out how to fix it for days (my users were not happy with me). Using these best practices will help you avoid the fear and pain I felt.

Documentation

Documentation is so important that it is the subject of the next chapter. Throughout this book, you have seen one form of documentation in the form of comments. Documentation is crucial to you being confident in your code. If you don't document your code as you go, you might forget what your code is supposed to do. Although code is meant for humans to understand, that doesn't mean it reads like a novel. In theory, you can read through it all to get an idea of what is going on, but that can take a long time—and you still might not remember why you made certain decisions. If you document your decisions as you make them, you can have more confidence that you made the right decision. Documentation involves a lot more, too, as you will see in the next chapter.

Planning

Planning is so underrated. Too often a programmer gets an idea and just starts writing code, hoping all the pieces will fall into place (guilty). Planning gives you confidence as a programmer because you will have taken the time to think through your entire problem to find what you consider to be the best solution. As you start writing code, you might realize that your plan is a bit off. Adjusting your plan as you go is totally allowed. We discuss planning in more detail in Chapter 11, "Planning."

Testing

Of all these tools, testing will probably give you the most confidence that you have written good code. Testing lets you know that your code behaves in an expected way under given circumstances. In Chapter 12, "Testing and Debugging," you will learn how to write code that tests your code. Every time you make a change to your code, you can run your tests to make sure your code continues to behave as expected. I really could have used some tests like that when I was building my website. Live and learn, right?

Summing Up

This chapter has been less about the technical details of writing code (it included only six code examples) and more about how to write better code. We included a fair amount of theory, but we put that theory into practice by creating `.jshintrc` for kittenbook. In this chapter, you learned about:

- Coding standards
- Code formatting
- Open source software
- Programming best practices

In the next chapter, you will learn about:

- The different ways to document software
- How to write good documentation
- How to document for yourself
- How to document for others

## 10

Documentation

Note

Project: Use JSDoc and Grunt to create documentation for your kittenbook project.

I know what you're thinking at this point: "Is he really going to make me read an entire chapter about writing documentation? If there's anything more boring than writing documentation, it must be reading documentation, and if there's anything more boring than reading documentation, it must be reading about writing documentation. I already know how to write comments in my code—how much more can there be?" Although I understand the sentiment, I hope you will soon see that documentation is not the programming equivalent of a VCR manual. Programming documentation is actually really cool. You can write notes about what you are doing right where you are doing it. Imagine if Leonardo DaVinci could have made notes about his work directly on his work. Good documentation makes code less mysterious.

Figure 10.1   Mystery solved. Comments are great!

Document Intentions

Documenting your code is almost always a good thing, but bad documentation does more harm than good. Documentation that is vague, misleading, incorrect, or outdated causes confusion and frustration. Writing good documentation is hard because you not only have to correctly explain what your code is doing (which can be a challenge), but you have to do so in a way that is precise and will not get outdated. One of the best ways to do this is to document what your code is intended to do rather than what your code is actually doing.

Self-Documenting Code

One possible solution to not writing bad documentation is to write no documentation at all. Woo hoo! No documentation! Before you get too excited, let me explain. Modern programming languages can be quite descriptive, to the point that the code can read almost as clearly as plain English. If your code reads like plain English, what need have you for comments in plain English? None! I don't fully buy into this idea myself, but some programmers out there believe that descriptive, self-documenting code is enough—no comments necessary. They even say that this is better than code with comments; if the code is the documentation, the documentation is never outdated. This argument has a lot of merit, and the principles behind self-documenting code should be applied, even if you choose to use comments as well.

The most important part of writing self-documenting code is using descriptive names for variables and functions. Listing 10.1 is an extreme example of poorly named variables and functions. Listing 10.2 is the same code, but with descriptive names.

Listing 10.1   **This Code Isn't All That Complicated, but It's Pretty Hard to Understand**

```
function gL(pN) {
  var pNP = /(?:1-)?\(?(\d{3})[\-\)]\d{3}-\d{4}/;
  var pM = pNP.exec(pN);
  var aCs, aC, lN;
  if (pM) {
    aC = pM[1];
    aCs = gAC();
    lN = aCs[aC];
  }
  return lN ? lN : 'somewhere';
}
```

Listing 10.2   **This Is the Same Code As in Listing 10.1, but the Function and Variable Names Are Descriptive**

```
function getLocation(phoneNumber) {
  var phoneNumberPattern = /(?:1-)?\(?(\d{3})[\-\)]\d{3}-\d{4}/;
  var phoneMatches = phoneNumberPattern.exec(phoneNumber);
  var areaCodes, areaCode, locationName;
  if (phoneMatches) {
    areaCode = phoneMatches[1];
    areaCodes = getAreaCodes();
    locationName = areaCodes[areaCode];
  }
  return locationName ? locationName : 'somewhere';
}
```

You might recognize this code; it is the getLocation function from prompt.js. The code in Listing 10.1 is completely unreadable, but the code in Listing 10.2 is fairly easy to understand. I have removed the getLocation comments in Listing 10.2, and it is still pretty easy to understand (much more so now that you understand a bit about JavaScript). When you write descriptive code like this, you greatly diminish the need for comments. You can even get away with not adding a comment about the regular expression because phoneNumberPattern describes exactly what the regular expression is intended to match.

> ## Don't Be Sneaky
>
> As with most programming languages, JavaScript has a lot of tricks and shortcuts. Some are pretty fun and useful (see Listing 10.14 for one of my favorite JavaScript tricks), but some of them are plain confusing. Listing 10.3 shows a sneaky way of checking whether an item is in an array. Listing 10.4 shows a descriptive, understandable way to do the same thing. The ~ in Listing 10.3 is the bitwise NOT, which is beyond the scope of this book. The only place I've ever seen a bitwise NOT used in JavaScript code is to check whether an item is in an array or whether a character is in a string. The indexOf method returns the location of the item, or -1 if the item given as the argument is not found in the array or string. So a way to check whether an item is in an array or string is to check whether indexOf returns a number greater than -1. Most JavaScript developers don't really understand what the ~ does, so the code in Listing 10.3 is sneaky, but not in a good way. If your code is so sneaky that you need to add a comment to explain the sneakiness, you should probably rewrite your code so that it is more understandable.

Listing 10.3   **Checking Whether an Item Is in an Array Using ~**

```
var name = 'steven';
var searchForLetter = 'p';


if (~name.indexOf(searchForLetter)) {
  console.log('Apparently there is a "p" in "Steven"');
} else {
  console.log('The name is "Steven", not "Stephen"')
}
```

Listing 10.4   **Checking Whether an Item Is in an Array Using the Easily Understood > Method**

```
var name = 'steven';
var searchForLetter = 'p';


if (name.indexOf(searchForLetter) > -1) {
  console.log('Apparently there is a "p" in "Steven"');
} else {
  console.log('The name is "Steven", not "Stephen"')
}
```

Don't Document the Obvious

In Chapter 8, "Functions and Methods," you learned about DRY code. The "don't repeat yourself" concept extends to comments as well. Documentation that restates exactly what is happening in the code adds no value. Instead, it gets in the way by breaking up the flow of the code, and it gets outdated too quickly. Listing 10.5 contains the same code as in Listing 10.2, but Listing 10.5 is written with comments describing every line. Which is easier to read?

Listing 10.5   Repeating Your Code in the Form of Comments Is Not Helpful

```
/**
 * Get location
 */
function getLocation(phoneNumber) {
  // Create the phone number pattern
  var phoneNumberPattern = /(?:1-)?\(?(\d{3})[\-\)]\d{3}-\d{4}/;

  // Get phoneMatches using the phoneNumberPattern
  var phoneMatches = phoneNumberPattern.exec(phoneNumber);

  // Declare areaCodes, areaCode, and locationName variables
  var areaCodes, areaCode, locationName;

  // If phoneMatches is truthy
  if (phoneMatches) {
    // Set the areaCode variable using the item 1 in the phoneMatches array
    areaCode = phoneMatches[1];

    // set area codes using getAreaCodes function
    areaCodes = getAreaCodes();

    // set locationName using areaCode and areaCodes
    locationName = areaCodes[areaCode];
  }

  // return locationName or 'somewhere'
  return locationName ? locationName : 'somewhere';
}
```

The function names and variable names are descriptive enough that these explanations are not necessary. In fact, they are harmful. With so many comments, where is the real code? The flow of the actual code is broken up by useless comments, making Listing 10.5 much harder to read. Comments can also act as an indicator of code that needs special attention or that might take extra time to understand. A comment can be a good indication to a programmer to slow down and read a given section of code carefully. If comments appear everywhere, a programmer reading the code will have no idea what code needs extra attention. Comments are good, but comments that restate the obvious are bad.

The Danger of Outdated Documentation

Comments are good as long as they are current, but an outdated comment causes a lot of confusion. Comments become outdated when they get out of sync with the code they are supposed to be documenting. Is the comment correct or is the code correct? They are confusing, and if too many of them are outdated and incorrect, they will simply be ignored. Outdated comments can be quite dangerous. Whenever you update your code, you should try to remember to update your comments as well. It's easy to forget to update your comments because the code will still run correctly, even if your comments are inaccurate. Because you will sometimes forget, it's important to document your intentions. Even if the underlying code changes, your intentions are likely to stay the same.

The code and comments in Listing 10.6 are in sync. However, when we decide to refactor getLocation in Listing 10.7 (so that it does one thing, and does it well), the comment doesn't make sense anymore. In fact, the comment is misleading. If someone just reads the comment and not the code, he or she will believe that no arguments are necessary when calling getLocation, but that's not true anymore.

Listing 10.6   `getLocation` **Before Refactoring**

```
/**
 * getLocation asks a user for a phone number, then returns a location based on
 * that phone number. NO ARGUMENTS NECESSARY!
 */
function getLocation() {
  var phoneNumber = prompt('What is your phone number?');
  var phoneNumberPattern = /(?:1-)?\(?(\d{3})[\-\)]\d{3}-\d{4}/;
  var phoneMatches = phoneNumberPattern.exec(phoneNumber);
  var areaCodes, areaCode, locationName;
  if (phoneMatches) {
    areaCode = phoneMatches[1];
    areaCodes = getAreaCodes();
    locationName = areaCodes[areaCode];
  }
  return locationName ? locationName : 'somewhere';
}
```

Listing 10.7   `getLocation` **After Refactoring and Without Updated Comments**

```
/**
 * getLocation asks a user for a phone number, then returns a location based on
 * that phone number. NO ARGUMENTS NECESSARY!
 */
function getLocation(phoneNumber) {
  var phoneNumberPattern = /(?:1-)?\(?(\d{3})[\-\)]\d{3}-\d{4}/;
  var phoneMatches = phoneNumberPattern.exec(phoneNumber);
```

```
var areaCodes, areaCode, locationName;
if (phoneMatches) {
  areaCode = phoneMatches[1];
  areaCodes = getAreaCodes();
  locationName = areaCodes[areaCode];
}
return locationName ? locationName : 'somewhere';
}
```

Find Bugs Using Documentation

One advantage of documenting intentions is that your documentation can help you find bugs in your code. If you have properly documented your intentions and your code does not match your documentation, something is wrong with your code. For instance, the documentation in Listing 10.8 says that we want to get the total price, suggesting that we will need to multiply itemPrice by itemsQuantity. However, the code is not multiplying, but adding itemPrice with itemsQuantity. The answer is not 13—the answer is 42. The documentation helps uncover the bug.

Listing 10.8   Correctly Documented Intentions Can Reveal Bugs in Your Code

```
var itemPrice = 7;
var itemsQuantity = 6;

// Get the total price
var total = itemPrice + itemsQuantity;
console.log('The total price is ' + total);
```

Document for Yourself

You might think that documentation is worthwhile only if you are working on your program with other people. If you are working alone, you already know all the things you might write down in your documentation, so what's the point, right? Actually, there are a lot of benefits to writing good documentation, even if you are the only person working on the project.

How Good Is Your Memory?

I'm going to assume that you don't have perfect recall (mostly because I think that pretty much only people in TV shows have perfect recall). If I'm wrong and you never forget anything, you can go ahead and skip to the next section. The rest of us forget things. Sometimes it really doesn't matter that we forget things. Why did you choose to wear a green shirt on a Tuesday six months ago? Maybe it was St. Patrick's Day. Maybe it was the only clean shirt that matched your shoes. Maybe it was the only clean shirt, period. It probably doesn't matter why you wore green six months ago. When programming, however, forgetting why you made a decision can be a big problem. Why did you choose to structure your data as an array of arrays instead of some other data structure, such as an array of objects? Was it because you didn't realize an array of objects was an option? Was it because you believed an array of arrays would make your code run faster? Was it because you were using an open source project that expected data to be structured as an array of arrays?

The decisions you make and the reasons you are making those decisions will seem obvious at the time you make them. However, things change over time. Six months down the road, you might learn about new ways to structure your data. You might realize that your code will run just as fast if you choose a simpler option. You might start using a different open source project that has different expectations. After six months have gone by and you're faced with a new decision, will you remember the reasoning behind your first decision? I'm going to guess that the answer is "no" (if you had perfect recall, you would have skipped this section). Now that things have changed, does your original decision still make sense? If you didn't document, you will again have to do all the work and research that went into that decision, to be sure.

Document to Learn

Writing good documentation requires you to really understand what your code is doing. If you don't understand your code, how can you possibly document what it is doing? Therefore, writing documentation forces you to gain a solid understanding of how your code works. On multiple occasions, I have learned something while documenting my code that has made me realize that I was doing something wrong. I learned something and fixed my code at the same time. That's a win-win situation if I've ever seen one.

Documentation Beyond Comments

Comments are usually the best place for documenting how a single piece of code works. Comments aren't as useful when you want to document how all the pieces of code work together (that is, how the program works). Flowcharts, diagrams, drawings, and narratives are much better suited for this type of documentation. Figure 5.12 from Chapter 5, "Data (Types), Data (Structures), Data(bases)," documents the structure of the library database, and Figure 7.2 from Chapter 7, "If, For, While, and When," documents how prompt.js works. Diagrams such as these can be useful for describing big-picture ideas in your program. Comments are more useful for the nitty-gritty details.

Now it's time to take our kittenbook documentation to the next level. First, we should add a description of the project to a README file. Generally a README file describes the software from the perspective of a developer, not the perspective of an end user. The README file contains information about the purpose and goals of a program, and it might also contain information about how the program is designed. You might have noticed from Chapter 4, "Build Tools," that every time you run npm install, npm complains that you don't have a README.md file (see Figure 10.2). Add one now, and fill in the description however you want. Listing 10.9 shows an example of what README.md could look like.

Listing 10.9   **An Example README.md for kittenbook**

#kittenbook

A Chrome extension that makes your Facebook timeline cuter, by replacing images in the feed with images of:

- kittens
- puppies

> ## Note
>
> ### Markdown
>
> README.md is intended to be a Markdown file. Markdown is a simplified way of writing basic HTML, using symbols instead of tags. You don't have to use any of the symbols, though: You can just write your README.md file in plain text. If you want to try out some of the Markdown features, check out http://daringfireball.net/projects/markdown/, and use http://daringfireball.net/projects/markdown/dingus to see your Markdown converted to HTML. Figure 10.3 shows the Markdown in Listing 10.9 rendered as HTML.

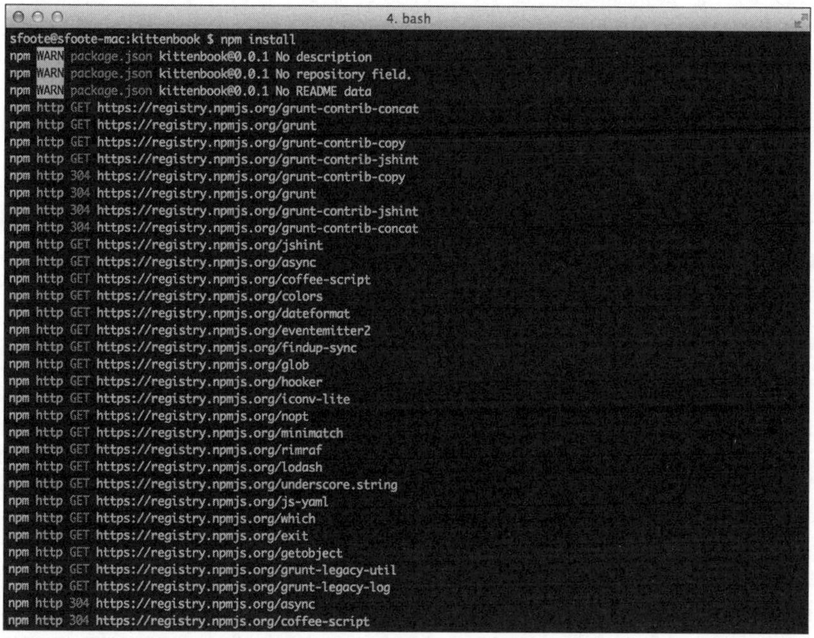

Figure 10.2   NPM tries to help you document your code by complaining when you don't have a README.md file.

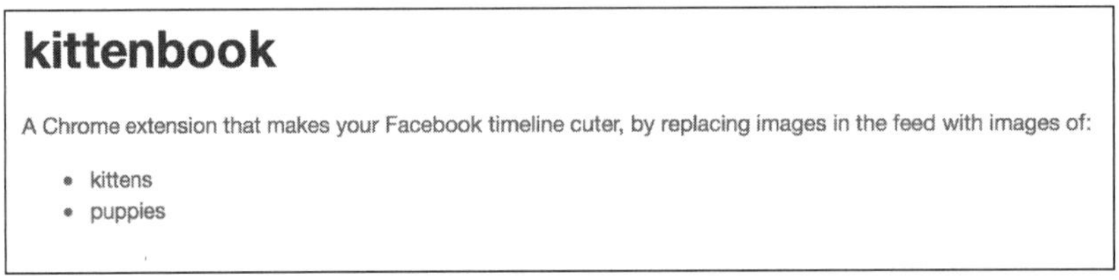

kittenbook

A Chrome extension that makes your Facebook timeline cuter, by replacing images in the feed with images of:

- kittens
- puppies

Figure 10.3   The Markdown in Listing 10.9 rendered as HTML

The next step in improving the kittenbook documentation is writing descriptions for each of the functions. If you write your descriptions in the right format, you can use Grunt to make the documentation look really good (using a program called JSDoc). Listing 10.10 shows the format, using validatePhoneNumber from prompt.js.

Listing 10.10   **Documenting validatePhoneNumber Using JSDoc**

```
/**
 * Check the validity of a phone number
 * @method
 * @param {string} phoneNumber The phone number to be validated
 * @return {boolean}
 */
function validatePhoneNumber(phoneNumber) {
  return phoneNumber.match(/(?:1-)?\(?(\d{3})[\-\)]\d{3}-\d{4}/);
}
```

The comments are placed directly above the function they are describing. The first line is a general description of the function. The other lines have special meaning for JSDoc. @method means that you are describing a method or function. The next line (starting with @param) describes the function's parameter. {string} indicates that the parameter is supposed to be a string, phoneNumber is the name of the parameter, and the last part is a description of the parameter. The final line (starting with @return) describes what the function will return, which, in this case, is a Boolean.

After you have added some JSDoc-style documentation to a few of your functions, you need to install grunt-jsdoc (see Listing 10.11) and add a jsdoc task to Gruntfile.js (see Listing 10.12). When all that is done, you can run grunt jsdoc from the kittenbook directory on the command line and then run open doc/index.html (or double-click the index.html file icon in your file browser) to open the web page grunt-jsdoc generates (see Figure 10.4). When you have documented all your functions, you will be able to see all your documentation in one (pretty slick-looking) place (see Figure 10.4). Suddenly your documentation looks organized and professional. Your task is to follow the pattern in Listing 10.10 to fill out the documentation for all the other functions in the project.

Listing 10.11   **Install grunt-jsdoc**

```
kittenbook $ npm install grunt-jsdoc --save-dev
```

Listing 10.12   **Add a `jsdoc` Task to `Gruntfile.js`**

```
module.exports = function(grunt) {
  grunt.initConfig({

    ...

    jsdoc: {
      dist: {
        src: ['js/*.js'],
        dest: 'doc'
      }
    }
  });

  // Load Grunt plugins

  ...

  grunt.loadNpmTasks('grunt-jsdoc');

  // Register tasks
  grunt.registerTask('default', ['concat', 'jshint', 'copy']);
};
```

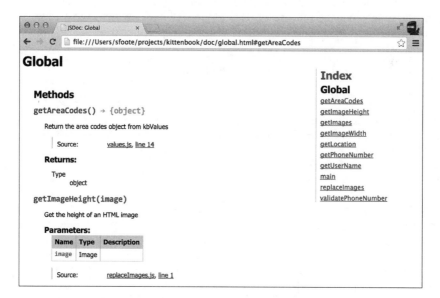

Figure 10.4   JSDoc turns your documentation into a nice-looking web page.

Document for Others

If you work with other people, you need to write documentation for their benefit as well. Writing documentation with an audience in mind will make your documentation more direct and useful. Ask yourself, "When a new developer reads this comment, will he understand why I made this decision?" If you don't work with other people yet, you should still write documentation for other people—eventually, someone else might take over your project. I built my first big project (that website I keep talking about) alone over the course of about two years. I spent very little time writing documentation, partially because I was so busy writing code and partially because I didn't really see the value in writing documentation; I was the only person working on the project. The website was my main assignment in my college job. About four months before I graduated, I realized that when I left, the website was going to die if I didn't take action. I spent those last four months writing documentation for two years' worth of code. I could not, for the life of me, remember why I had written some of the code as I had. I had to spend a lot of time relearning what my code was doing so I could write documentation for it. Four months of writing documentation is not fun, but by the end of it, I was ready to pass the baton to my successor. I wish I had just written documentation as I was writing my code, for my sake and my successor's.

Document Your Decisions

Documenting your decisions is more important for the benefit of others than for yourself. The documentation proves that you made a conscious decision and considered alternatives. That way, when someone else needs to make changes to your code, that person will know why you made the decision you made and also whether it's possible to safely switch to an alternative solution. Listing 10.13 shows an example of a well-documented decision.

Listing 10.13   **Using `while` instead of `for`, with Good Documentation**

```
var letters = ['t', 'p', 'i', 'c', 's', 'a', 'v', 'a', 'j'];
var currentLetter;
// Using a while loop instead of a for loop because the array is modified
// inside the loop, and modifying an array inside a for loop breaks everything
while (letters.length) {
  currentLetter = letters.pop();
  console.log(currentLetter);

  // Add a new letter to the array.
  if (currentLetter === 'c') {
    letters.push('r');
  }
}
```

One night, after I had gotten home from work, I got a text message informing me that I needed to immediately fix a blocker bug (a blocker is a bug so bad that you must drop everything else you are doing to fix it). The bug was being caused by a single line of code that I had not written; I wasn't even familiar with it. Deleting that line of code seemed to fix the bug and did not appear to have any effect on the rest of the application. That left me wondering why that line of code had been added in the first place. There must have been a reason. I was afraid to remove that line, just in case removing it caused another bug. Had that line of code been well documented, I would not have had this problem.

Document Your Resources

Documentation can be used not only to explain what your code is doing and why you made a decision, but also where you came up with the idea. If you are struggling to solve a problem and you find a solution online in a blog post or online forum, you should mention your inspiration in your comments. By doing so, you are giving credit where credit is due; you are, after all, using someone else's solution. If your inspiration comes from a trusted source, such acknowledgment can also give your code more credibility (it's like saying that you made your investment decisions based on advice from Warren Buffett). You are also making that resource known and available to other developers who read your comments. Those developers can go and read the original blog post, and they, too, can learn and be inspired.

Document to Teach

I have learned a lot about programming by reading other people's code, especially other people's comments. When you are using an interesting technique, you have an opportunity to teach your fellow developers about that technique and show why it's great. By taking the time to document to teach, you also learn more about the technique yourself. Listing 10.14 shows one of my favorite techniques for looping through an array. I learned about this technique from the JSHint documentation.

Listing 10.14   **Assignments in the Conditional of a `for` Loop**

```
var letters = ['a', 'b', 'c'];
var letter, i;

// Instead of using the length of the array, use the for loop's conditional to
// make assignments. When there are no more items to be assigned, the
// conditional will be falsy, so the loop will stop. As an added bonus, you
// don't have to do the assignment inside the for loop.
for (i=0; (letter = letters[i]); i++) {
  console.log(letter);
}
```

Summing Up

This chapter taught you more than you ever wanted to know about documenting software (and there's still more!). Documentation might not be the most exciting part of programming, but it really is valuable and worth doing right. In this chapter, you learned about:

- Documenting your intentions
- Documenting for yourself
- Documentation beyond comments
- Documenting for others

In the next chapter, you will learn about:

- Specifications
- Iterative planning
- Software architecture

Planning

I have said before that coding is only a part of programming, and not even the most difficult part. You might be wondering: If coding isn't the hardest part of programming, what is? Planning just might be the answer. When coding, you make small decisions about how a single piece of your program works (for example, which instructions should you include inside an if *block?). When planning, you make big decisions about how your entire program works (What programming language should you use? What data structure should you use? How should you store your data?).*

Planning involves answering an important question: What problem will this program solve? If you can't answer that question, you're not done planning. Your planning should also answer another question: What problems will this program not solve? As with the functions of Chapter 8, "Functions and Methods," programs should have a well-defined purpose and should not try to solve any problems outside that purpose. A software program consists of a system of pieces working together to achieve a purpose. When you have identified the purpose, you can get a much clearer picture of the system that is necessary to achieve that purpose. Thinking about the system as a whole helps you identify areas of your program that may give you trouble. This process allows you to come up with a realistic estimate of how long your project will take to build.

Think Before You Build

I hope you have seen how much fun programming can be. Writing code that works can be so exciting. When I am working on a hard problem and I finally get my code to work, I often throw my hands into the air as if I just sank the winning basket at a championship basketball game (that situation is probably just as nerdy as you imagine it). Writing code can be really fun and rewarding—so much so that as soon as you start a project, you want to jump right in and start writing code. The step of planning your project and designing your software is easy to overlook.

The design step is especially easy to skip because designing software can be difficult, confusing, and frustrating. You have to use your imagination. You have to imagine what your software will be like when it is complete. However, designing software does not mean that you build the entire application in your mind before building it in your text editor. When you're designing a car, you probably don't need to decide what kind of screws you will use to secure the engine in place; you can work out such implementation details when the design is actually implemented. However, during design, you do need to decide where the engine will be secured in place and how the steering wheel will be hooked up to the other systems in the car. Designing the system as a whole before building helps to ensure that you don't put a spare tire where the engine should be. Good design leads to cleaner code. So, although writing code that works is fun and exciting, code works much more often when written in a well-designed system.

Create a Specification

A great approach for designing your software is to start with a detailed specification. The specification is a written explanation of what you are planning to build. When writing a specification, try to be as specific as possible without getting into implementation details. A specification should include such details as how to handle errors. For example, a specification for kittenbook would include something such as "If a user gives an invalid phone number, give them a second chance. If the phone number is still invalid, accept it and set the user's location to somewhere."

The specification (usually called the "spec") can be either very detailed or merely a high-level description of your program. In either case, writing something down helps you control the scope of your project. You should build everything that is in the spec and nothing outside the spec. Realize that any decision that you don't make when writing the spec will have to be made when you are actually writing the code. In some cases, that's good because you will be in a better position to make some decisions when you have already built a portion of the program. Your spec should not dictate every single decision, but it should be detailed enough to give you strong guidance while you are writing code. Getting the balance right comes with time and experience.

Design an Architecture

Your specification tells you *what* you are going to build, but it does not tell you *how*. The specification doesn't help you fit all the pieces together. In fact, specifications rarely include details about the different pieces that make up a program. It's time to design an architecture for your program after you have created the spec but before you start writing code.

When designing your software's architecture, you should identify all the different parts of your program and then decide how those different parts will fit together. Architectural decisions are, in my opinion, the hardest part of planning. You have to use your imagination to see what your software will be like when it is complete. You have to identify all the different parts of your imaginary software and then figure out the best way to fit them together. Although it is possible to make these architectural decisions after you have already started writing code, each time I have tried to do so, I have run into these two problems:

1. Some crucial components do not fit logically in the program (see Figure 11.1). Either I have written so much code that I have to start over to include the out-of-place component, or I have to put my component wherever I can make it fit and then do a bunch of extra work to get it to work correctly.

2. The way we think when solving design problems is very different from the way we think when solving coding problems. Solving design problems is more of a creative, even artistic process, whereas solving coding problems is analytical and concrete. If you don't solve your architectural design problems before you start coding, you will end up trying to solve both coding and design problems at the same time, and you will not be doing either optimally.

Figure 11.1   If you build before you design, you might end up putting things where they don't belong.

Draw Diagrams

If you are having trouble designing your software, try drawing the design. Drawing helps you visualize the problem so you can see all the different pieces and how they fit together. I like drawing (as evidenced by all my drawings in this book)—although I'm not that great at it (also evidenced by all my drawings in this book)—so drawing really works for me. The great thing about drawing is that it can be really quick. You don't have to build or even write anything.

You might not get the design quite right in your first drawing, but at least you didn't waste much time; just grab another piece of paper and start over. When you get it right, your drawing can also serve as documentation. Figure 11.2 is one of many diagrams I drew while planning a recent project.

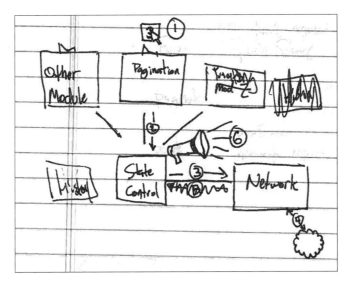

Figure 11.2   One of the many diagrams I drew while trying to come up with a good architecture for a recent project

Try to Break Your System

When you have come up with an initial design, think about the design's weaknesses. Under what circumstances would your system break down? What things might users want to do with your program that your design cannot handle? What features might your users request in the future? How hard will it be to add those features to the program you have designed? Thinking through your design like this will help you identify its weaknesses and will also help you decide what features and use cases your program should support. You don't have to support every feature or use case, but through this process, you should have a better idea of which ones you do want to support.

When building web applications, a lot of time gets spent supporting older browsers, especially Internet Explorer. If your design doesn't include the idiosyncrasies of Internet Explorer, your web application will likely be broken for Internet Explorer users. You will run into trouble if you try to bolt on Internet Explorer support after your design is complete. Support for an Internet Explorer solution should instead be included in the design phase. On the other hand, you might decide that your web application will not support Internet Explorer users at all, so you explicitly exclude the Internet Explorer fixes from your design. In either case, you have considered a way your program could be broken, and you have incorporated that consideration into your design. The design for kittenbook does not need to consider Internet Explorer because kittenbook is a Chrome extension—it can never be used in Internet Explorer.

> ### Spaghetti Code
>
> I like spaghetti. I even had spaghetti for lunch today (no joke). Spaghetti is good. But spaghetti in your code is bad. Spaghetti code describes code that, as in a bowl of spaghetti, is messy, twisted, and tangled. You can't do anything to a single noodle without affecting the entire bowl. Up until Chapter 8, the kittenbook code was very much spaghetti code. The problem with spaghetti code becomes obvious when you try to fix a bug or add a new feature. When you add or modify any part of your code, you end up modifying every part of your code to get things working. My first web application was the worst kind of spaghetti code, and I thought that was just how programming worked. Every change I made to the application was a huge pain because I didn't realize there was a better way. With good software design (and object-oriented programming, which you learn about in Chapter 15, "Advanced Topics"), you can avoid spaghetti code entirely.

Iterative Planning

For me, probably the biggest challenge of software design is trying to come up with a complete, future-proof solution entirely in my head before I have even built anything. What if I am wrong about some part of my design? What if the future is not quite how I planned it? The truth is, I am nearly guaranteed to get it a little wrong, and that's actually a good thing. As you realize your mistakes, you should continue planning. Planning should start before you start writing code, but planning should not end until you have completed the project.

One great technique for planning is creating prototypes. In this context, a prototype is code that is quickly written to prove that your design does or does not work. If your prototype works, you can move forward with your design. If not, you can go back to the drawing board without having invested too much time in building a faulty design. Prototypes can make the work of designing software fun, too.

Design for Extensibility

Another problem with not being able to see the future is that you will not be able to anticipate every feature that you or your users will want to add to your program. You should build your program in such a way that new features are easy to add (and remove). Software designed with extensibility in mind is fun to work with because adding features is so easy. An extensible program is like a TV with several HDMI ports. Your TV might not have a DVD player built in, but the TV is extensible, so you can plug in a DVD player. And when Blu-ray players replace DVD players, you don't have to buy a new TV because you can just remove the DVD player feature (unplug it) and add the Blu-ray feature. Similarly, if you want to add a Roku, you don't have to rebuild the whole TV; you can just plug in the Roku.

What Are Your Priorities?

You can't have everything. This is as true for software as it is for most everything else in life. The fact that you must make tradeoffs among user experience, performance, security, scalability, and deadlines might not be obvious until you are done designing your software and you have started building it. However, considering these tradeoffs really should be part of the design of your software. The architecture you choose for your software depends a great deal on which of these priorities is most important, and the timeline depends on the compromises you are willing and able to make.

User Experience

If you are building software, someone is going to be using it (and that someone is probably going to be someone other than just you). That means you have users, and if you have users, you should build a good user experience for them. Building a good user experience takes time, and the user experience must be part of your planning and prioritizing. As you design your software, you should consider the following items as they relate to the user experience:

- **Who are your users?** Are they programmers? Are they moderately experienced computer users? Are they novice computer users? You need to design different software for each of these different groups.

- **Is the software intuitive?** Would an average user understand how your program is supposed to work, preferably without having to read a long instruction manual?

- **Does your application respect your user's privacy?** Privacy is closely related to security. If you ask users for data, you need to keep that data safe. If your users expect their data to be completely private, you need to design your software so that the data is transmitted and stored securely and privately.

- **Does it work?** Your software doesn't have to do everything. You don't need to build every feature you or your users have ever dreamed of. But the features that you have built should work every time.

Performance

When you talk about the performance of your software, you are talking about how fast the software does its job. You can improve performance in several ways, and they depend on the environment in which you are working. In general, though, you can improve performance by minimizing the number of instructions that your program has to execute to do its job. For example, if your program uses a loop, remove any instructions from the loop that don't absolutely have to be there. A big part of studying algorithms is understanding why programs run slow and how to make them run faster. If you are interested in learning more about performance, you can find a lot of online algorithms classes (see Chapter 13, "Learning to Fish: How to Acquire a Lifetime of Programming Knowledge," for more info on finding these classes).

One of the best examples of software designed for performance is Google Search. From front to back, the Google Search experience is designed for speed. First, the web page at https://www.google.com/ loads really fast because there is almost nothing on it—basically, just the Google logo, a search box, and two buttons. One of the reasons for this minimalist design is that it is really fast. When you perform a search, the search results come back almost instantaneously because the software that Google writes to find and prioritize search results is designed for speed. Performance is clearly a priority for Google software.

Security

If you have users, security needs to be a priority, especially if you are asking your users for data. Unfortunately some people out there want to use your software to take advantage of your users (these people are hackers in the malicious sense of the word). You have a responsibility to your users to keep their data secure and to prevent hackers from using your software to do bad things. This is why Microsoft, Apple, and Adobe (among other software companies) regularly release "security updates" for their software. For security to be a priority, it needs to be a part of the design of your software. For example, you should design your software so that user passwords are never stored as plain text; passwords should be encrypted.

Scalability

A major consideration in software design is scalability. If you will only ever have 15 users (or even 150 users), or if your software will only be used to perform small tasks, you don't really need to worry about scalability in the designs of your programs. If your user base unexpectedly grows beyond the capacity of the software you have written, you will probably need to redesign and rewrite your software, but that's a good problem to have. The study and design of highly scalable systems is far beyond the scope of this book. Just keep in mind that scalability is an important design consideration.

Deadlines

How soon does your software need to be done? Sometimes a program's deadline is a top priority, so the design of the software needs to change based on that deadline. You might have to sacrifice user experience, performance, or scalability to meet the deadline. As such, setting a deadline as the top priority usually results in lower-quality software. All the software's real priorities should be examined, and then you can set a realistic deadline based on those priorities. This can be an iterative process: When the realistic deadline you set seems too far into the future, you can remove some performance or user experience features and recalculate your time estimates. Deadlines can be helpful in design and planning, but they generally shouldn't be your top priority.

The Balancing Act

These and other priorities compete with each other, and, again, you can't have it all. Sometimes, though, competing priorities can be aligned. For example, improving performance can improve user experience. But if you start improving performance too much (for example, by removing important features), the user experience will suffer. At some point, you need to determine the relative importance of each of your priorities. This decision ultimately determines the design and functionality of your software.

Identify and Create Constraints

As you design your software, you need to recognize the limitations and constraints of the system within which you are working, and you should set your own constraints. You learned the importance of setting standards in Chapter 9, "Programming Standards." By setting standards, you are setting constraints, saying that not everything is okay—even if something is possible, that doesn't mean it's a good idea. For example, the first version of kittenbook completely wiped out everything on every page on Facebook, and what a terrible experience that was. It was helpful for teaching and was kind of cool, but it was still a really bad experience. A good self-imposed constraint to help prevent this sort of bad experience is "Never annoy your user." That way, if you later have an idea to show a flashing red message when an error occurs, you can remember your self-imposed "Don't be annoying" constraint.

Know What You Can and Can't Do

Understanding the capabilities of the environment in which you are working is powerful. You might be able to do cool things in your software that you didn't realize were possible. Did you know that you can create desktop notifications in Google Chrome (see Figure 11.3)? With desktop notifications, you can easily inform your users about things happening in your app, even if users don't have your window open at the moment. Let's say you are building a to-do list app, and the items in your to-do list have deadlines. You could create a desktop notification reminding your user that a deadline is approaching, but only if you know that desktop notifications exist. If you understand what your system can do, you can include those capabilities in the design of your program.

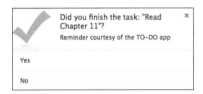

Figure 11.3   Learn about your environment's capabilities.

Computers can do a lot of cool things, but they can't do everything. Understanding the limitations of your system is just as important as understanding its capabilities. Mobile devices can do some great stuff with cameras, geolocation, and device orientation, but mobile devices have relatively little memory and battery life. When you design an application for a mobile device, the use of memory and battery are important constraints. It is a sad day when you realize that the software you have designed is not technically feasible because of an unyielding system constraint. You should design your software to work within these constraints instead of fight against them.

Permissions

Chrome Extensions, Android apps, and iOS apps all have the concept of permissions. With permissions, the environment sets up constraints and you have to explicitly ask for permission to remove those constraints. For example, in the Chrome extension environment, a constraint prevents you from loading your extension's JavaScript on just any web page. However, you can ask for permission to load JavaScript on specific web pages. In kittenbook's `manifest.json`, we asked the user for permission to load JavaScript on `*://www.facebook.com/*`. When users install the extension, they have to approve the permissions we are asking for. Permissions help you set reasonable constraints for your application and break out of those constraints only when you really need to do so for the functionality of the application. Permissions also help your users better understand the capabilities and constraints of your application.

Summing Up

You have learned a lot about what goes into planning and designing software. The best way to really internalize these concepts is to practice them. If you want, you can retroactively design kittenbook, but I think you'll have a lot more fun coming up with your own project. After you have thought of a good project, identify all its different parts and make a plan for how those parts will work together. What are your priorities? In what environment will you build your application? (Web application? Chrome extension? iPhone app?) What are your constraints? Write down all these things and draw some diagrams, and you will be well on your way to building a great application.

In this chapter, you learned about:

- Software architecture
- Priorities and tradeoffs in software design
- Constraints

In the next chapter, you will learn about:

- Strategies for manually testing your software
- How to write code to test your code
- How to use debugging tools when things go wrong

12

Testing and Debugging

| Note

Project: Write unit tests for the JavaScript code in kittenbook. Run the unit tests using Grunt.

In this chapter, you learn how to be a really effective programmer. Software testing is the practice of setting expectations for your software and then running your software to see if it meets those expectations. That might sound like the description of an overbearing parent, but software testing is actually good for the software. When your expectations are not met, you can modify the software until it works correctly. When all your expectations are met, you are ready to send your software out into the world (sniff, sniff—they grow up so fast).

To fix software that isn't meeting expectations, you have to figure out why the software is misbehaving. The process of solving this mystery is called debugging. With the right tools, debugging can actually be a lot of fun. The bug you are looking for is like a master thief, and you are the detective. If you use your tools wisely, you can follow the clues and find the culprit. Good testing and good debugging make your programs better for you and your users.

Manual Testing

The idea of manual testing is pretty straightforward. Write some code, and then run your program. Did it work? Did it do what you expected it to do? As simple as that seems, manually testing is quite powerful. In manual testing, you are actually using the software you are writing. If you were building a chair, wouldn't you try sitting on it to make sure it were comfortable and could support your weight (see Figure 12.1)? Other types of testing exist, but there is no substitute for actually using your software.

Figure 12.1   This chair is not as great as it seems.

Test As You Work

Execute your program often. I like to execute my program basically every time I make a change to the code. Each time you execute, you are checking that your program does what it is supposed to be doing. If you make a whole bunch of changes between executions, you will have a hard time remembering to check that each one of those changes is working. And if one of your changes breaks your program, you will have a very difficult time figuring out which change is guilty. I have made the mistake of writing a lot of code at once and testing at the end. I sometimes write a bunch of code without testing, all the while thinking, "I know what I'm doing. All of this will work." On rare occasions (three in the last seven years), it all does work. Usually, though, I am stuck undoing almost all my work while trying to track down the bugs I created. The many small wins you get from testing often are much better than the big (and extremely rare) win you might get if you test only after you've written all your code.

Try Something Crazy

As you find bugs in your program through manual testing, you can find and fix the problems in your code and then run the program again to verify that your changes fixed the bug. Sometimes you will make a change, run your program, and find nothing different, even though your change should have fixed the bug. You then go back to your code and make some other changes, and you run the program again. Your changes still don't seem to have any effect. This situation has happened to me several times, and it can be frustrating. I recommend doing something crazy. Delete the entire file (after creating a backup), or write some code that you know will cause an error. Then run your program again. If your latest, crazy changes seem to have no effect, you know that your program is not actually reading the file that you're changing. Figure 4.7 showed how forgetting to compile code before executing could cause this problem, and there are other possible explanations as well. For example, I once copied my project's entire directory to a different place on my computer. The next time I wanted to work on that project, I had forgotten that I'd moved the directory to a new place, and I started editing files in the old project directory. Before you start banging your head against the wall, try something crazy to see if your program is even picking up the changes you are making.

Eat Your Own Dog Food

Employees at software companies often use whatever software the company builds to do their work. This is practice is given the not-so-appetizing name of *dogfooding*, or "eating your own dog food." The story goes that the CEO of Kal Kan Pet Food would eat a can of the company's dog food at the annual shareholder's meeting, and suddenly the idea of consuming your own product had a name. I don't recommend eating dog food, but I do recommend using the software you are building for its intended purpose. If you know that you have to rely on your software, your motivation to build a high-quality product increases.

When I worked as an accountant, I hated keeping track of my billable hours, but I had to do so accurately to be able to bill clients correctly for the work I had done. I decided to build a Chrome extension that would help me track my hours by giving me reminders. As I was building the extension, I had to continue tracking my hours, so I kept using pen and paper because I knew it would work, even though it was a pain. Eventually, I felt that my extension was ready for me to use. That first week, I tracked my hours using my extension *and* pen and paper, just to make sure my new software didn't miss anything. I found and fixed a lot of bugs that week, and by the beginning of the next week, I felt confident enough to lose my pen-and-paper crutch and rely exclusively on my extension for tracking my time. After two more weeks and many more bugs, I was ready to start sharing my extension with my coworkers. The time I spent "dogfooding" was crucial to the quality of my extension.

Automated Testing

Although manual testing is and always will be an essential part of ensuring that your program works, automated testing is where things get interesting. You are a programmer now, and you automate everything from copying files to making your bed, so why not automate testing. We're going to write code that tests our code. Confusing, right? I definitely thought so, but with a few examples, you'll see that it's really not so bad. The test code actually runs all or part of the application code and compares what happens to what was expected to happen. Testing how the entire application works together is called integration testing, and testing how a single part of the application works in isolation is called unit testing.

Unit Tests

I think the name *unit testing* is confusing. What is a *unit*, and how do I test it? I was so confused, in fact, that I decided not to write unit tests for my code for a long time. I've learned a lot more about unit testing by now, though, and I think the name is accurate—but it's still confusing. For our purposes, we will simplify matters by saying that a unit is a function. So to test a function, we need to run that function with some input and check that the function does what it is expected to do.

Suppose that we have a function called sum, and we want to write unit tests for it. Before we start writing unit tests, we need to make sure that we know very well what sum is supposed to do (perhaps a specification would help). For this example, we'll say that sum takes two numbers as input and returns the sum of those two numbers. We don't want to write a test for every possible combination of two numbers; such an endeavor would prove impossible. Because testing every possible input is impossible, you should instead test a sample from each category of input. I would say that the sum function has the following input categories:

- Two positive numbers
- Two negative numbers
- One positive number and one negative number
- 0 and 0
- 0 and a positive number
- 0 and a negative number

Although there could be other categories (for example, a very small positive number with a very large positive number), this list is sufficiently comprehensive. Now let's write some tests, starting with the example in Listing 12.1.

Listing 12.1   **An Example of How to Test Code Using Code**

```
// Definition of the actual sum function
function sum(x, y) {
  return x * y;
}

// We'll put all of our tests in this testSum function
function testSum() {

  // A utility function to run the tests.
  function test(x, y, expected) {

    // Actually run the sum function and save the result
    var result = sum(x, y);

    // Is the result what we expected?
```

```
  if (result === expected) {

    // Yes! The test passed.
    console.log('Pass!\n');
  } else {

    // No. The test failed, so output some information about what actually
    // happened and what we expected to happen. console.error works a lot
    // like console.log, but is meant for logging errors.

    console.error('FAIL: expected the sum of ' + x + ' and ' + y +
                  ' to be ' + expected + ', not ' + result + '\n');
  }
}

console.log('Testing sum of two positive numbers');
// Expect 2 + 2 to equal 4
test(2, 2, 4);

console.log('Testing sum of two negaive numbers');
// Expect -3 + -2 to equal 5
test(-3, -2, -5);

console.log('Testing sum of one positive and one negative number');
// Expect 3 + -5 to equal -2
test(3, -5, -2);

console.log('Testing sum of 0 and 0');
// Expect 0 + 0 to equal 0
test(0, 0, 0);

console.log('Testing sum of 0 and a positive number');
// Expect 0 + 3 to equal 3
test(0, 3, 3);

console.log('Testing sum of 0 and a negative number');
// Expect 0 + -3 to equal -3
test(0, -3, -3);
}

// Finally, call testSum to run all our tests
testSum();
```

Listing 12.1 gives you a lot to take in. First, try running the code. In this case, I recommend saving it in a file called testSum.js and then executing the file from the command line using Node. Navigate to the directory that contains testSum.js, then run node testSum.js—the code will execute. The output should look something like Figure 12.2. You should notice that most of the tests failed, which suggests that there's a bug in the sum function. Find the bug and fix it, and all the tests should pass. Unit tests save the day!

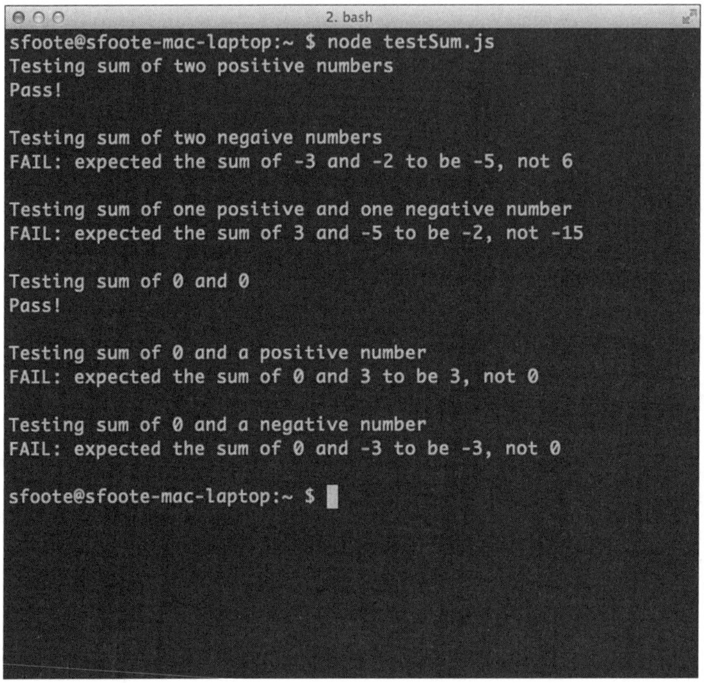

Figure 12.2   Running testSum from the command line shows that a few tests are not passing.

Try reading through the code and comments, which explain what is happening pretty well. This code is meant only to demonstrate what I mean by writing code to test code. In reality, you would almost never have your real code (often called application code) written in the same file as your test code.

Notice how descriptive all the messages are in the code. First, I declare what I am testing, as with console.log('Testing sum of two positive numbers');. Then I run the test using the utility function test. If the test passes, I print that, with console.log('Pass!\n'). The \n is a new line, which puts some space between each test for better readability. If the test doesn't pass, I print out a descriptive failure message, which includes the input, the expected output, and the actual output. Descriptive messages such as these make it much easier to see what is going wrong when your tests fail.

Another point to note is how I used the utility function, test. I did this so I didn't have to rewrite the failure message for every test I ran. The actual testing happens inside the test function, so I'd better get it right. This brings up one of the questions I have always had about writing automated tests. If I am writing test code to test my application code, how do I test my test code? Do I write test code to test my test code? Where does it end? I have come up with a few possible options:

1. When you start writing test code, you must continue writing tests for tests for the rest of your life.

2. Don't write any tests at all.

3. Limit your tests to three levels deep.

4. Write tests, but make them so simple that they don't need automated testing.

Option 1 doesn't look fun or possible, so we'll say it's not really an option. Option 2 does solve the problem of not writing tests forever, but tests are necessary, so this option won't work. Option 3 sounds like a scene from *Inception*, and I try to avoid taking programming advice from movies. That leaves us with Option 4. I think writing simple tests is the correct solution to this problem. While you are writing your test code, you can perform manual testing to make sure the test code is working as expected. At that point, the test code should be simple enough that no automated tests are necessary.

Set Up Tests for Kittenbook

There's something about the testSum example that I really don't like. I think the unit tests are good, and I think the example does a good job of demonstrating what types of components to include in a unit test. The problem is that testSum does a great job of teaching the basics of unit testing, but it doesn't show you how to test real code. Unit tests for a sum function might not be hard to write, but how would you write tests for a real program such as kittenbook?

The first step is to think about the kittenbook code in units. The entire kittenbook project is a lot more complex than sum, but each unit (function) can be just as simple. In fact, this is one of the big advantages of writing unit tests: For code to be unit testable, the code must be written in small, manageable units. Code that is written in small, manageable units is cleaner, more organized, and generally less prone to error. Before we organized the kittenbook code into functions, it would have been almost impossible to test. We will not try to test all of kittenbook at once, but we will test each function in isolation.

The good news is that Grunt can help us with our unit tests. We will be using a testing library called Jasmine to write and run our unit tests. Jasmine basically provides testing utility functions such as test, plus a lot more. To get Jasmine set up, you first need to install grunt-contrib-jasmine (which installs Jasmine and all its dependencies). Then you need to add a Jasmine task to Gruntfile.js (see Listings 12.2 and 12.3).

Listing 12.2   **Install `grunt-contrib-jasmine` from the Command Line**

```
## First navigate to the kittenbook directory, then run the following command

~/project/kittenbook $ npm install grunt-contrib-jasmine --save-dev
```

Listing 12.3   **Add a Jasmine Task to** `Gruntfile.js`

```
module.exports = function(grunt) {
  grunt.initConfig({

    ...

    jasmine: {
      test: {
        src: ['js/values.js', 'js/prompt.js', 'js/getImages.js',
              'js/replaceImages.js', 'js/main.js'],
        options: {
          specs: 'test/*.js'
        }
      }
    },

    ...

  });

  // Load Grunt plugins

  ...

  grunt.loadNpmTasks('grunt-contrib-jasmine');

  ...

};
```

Listing 12.3 shows only the new parts of `Gruntfile.js`. The new Jasmine task has familiar options. We tell Jasmine where to find the source code with the `src` attribute. I have listed the files in the same order as in the `concat` task because I found that this avoided some problems when trying to run the tests. Next, we tell Jasmine where to find the test files with the `spec` attribute (inside the `options` object). You need to create a new directory called `test`, which is where we will be putting all our test files. After you have done that, try running `grunt jasmine` from the `kittenbook` directory on the command line. You should get a warning message that says something like this: "Warning: No specs executed, is there a configuration error? Use --force to continue." That means the Jasmine task is correctly set up, but Jasmine can't find any tests to run. When you actually have a test to run, that warning will go away. So let's write our first test for kittenbook.

Specs

Unit tests are often called specs (short for *specifications*) because they describe in detail what the software can and cannot do. In the last chapter, you learned about writing a specification as a part of planning. Writing unit tests is one good way to write a specification. If all the unit tests are passing, the software meets the specification.

I think functions with simple input and simple output are the easiest functions to test, so we will start with one of those: `validatePhoneNumber` takes a string as input and then outputs a Boolean. You can write several tests for a single function; each test should be testing one small feature of the function. Our first test checks whether `validatePhoneNumber` returns a Boolean, as shown in Listing 12.4. You can see a few of Jasmine's utility functions as well. These functions are here to help, so try not to feel intimidated or confused.

- The `describe` function describes what is being tested. `describe` accepts two arguments: a string that describes what is being tested and a function that contains the tests being described. In Listing 12.4, you can see a `describe` inside a `describe`, which is perfectly okay. The outer `describe` says that we are testing functions found in `prompt.js`, and the inner `describe` says that we are testing the `validatePhoneNumber` function.

- The `it` function runs a single test. I would have picked a more descriptive name (such as `test`), but no one asked me. `it` accepts two arguments: a string describing the single test and a function containing the test code. The string usually starts with the word *should*, so the code reads "it should return a boolean."

- The `expect` function tests an expectation. If your `expect` passes, your test passes. If your `expect` fails, your test fails. If you don't have an `expect`, your test always passes, so you should always have at least one `expect` within each `it` function. The `expect` is always accompanied by another utility function (such as `toBe`), so the `expect` line of code reads something like this: "Expect [actual result] to be [expected result]." If the actual result doesn't meet your expectations, the test fails.

Listing 12.4 **Test That `validatePhoneNumber` Returns a Boolean**

```
describe('prompt.js', function() {

  describe('validatePhoneNumber', function() {

    it('should return a boolean', function() {
      var result = validatePhoneNumber('23456');
      expect(typeof result).toBe('boolean');
    });

  });
});
```

The test code in Listing 12.4 is describing the `validatePhoneNumber` function in the `prompt.js` file. Only one test has been written so far, and it states that `validatePhoneNumber` should return a Boolean. Within the test, `validatePhoneNumber` is called, and the value it returns is saved in the `result` variable. The next line says that we expect the (data) type of `result` to be a Boolean (`typeof` is an operator in JavaScript, which gives the data type of its operand). Note that we don't care whether the `result` is `true` or `false`, as long as it is a Boolean. If the data type of `result` is a Boolean, the test passes; if it is not a Boolean, the test fails and we know that something is wrong with our application code. Run the tests from the command line using `grunt jasmine`, and you will see that our test fails. This is because `validatePhoneNumber` uses the String method `match` (which returns an array or `null`) instead of the Regular Expression method `test` (which returns a Boolean). Our unit test helped us find a bug in our code. After the bug is fixed, you should see something like Figure 12.3.

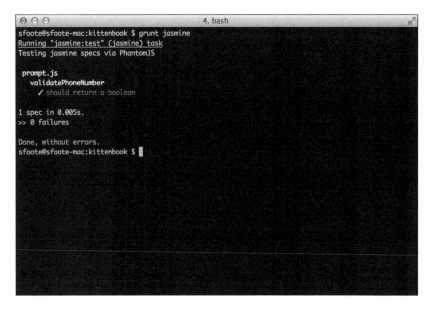

Figure 12.3   The Jasmine output shows a satisfying green checkmark for each passing test.

Epic Fail!

At this point, you are probably thinking that a good test is a passing test. Test failures are bad, right? They mean something is broken, and broken is bad. I would argue that you always want your tests to fail before they pass. When I first started writing unit tests, I was really enjoying myself. I loved all those green checkmarks indicating that all my tests were passing. I was pretty proud of myself. I started sharing my code and test code with the other programmers I worked with. Soon, though, I discovered through manual testing that my application code had a really serious bug. My unit tests were supposed to be testing for that bug, but for some reason, the tests were still passing. It turns out that I had written my tests so poorly that the `expect` function was never being called, so the expectation could never be tested, and therefore the tests could never fail. Now I always make my tests fail first before I make them pass. If I can't make the test fail, I know something is wrong.

Let's write another test for `validatePhoneNumber` and make it fail before we make it pass. We want to test that `validatePhoneNumber` returns `true` when it is given a valid phone number as an argument. We will add another `it` function inside the `describe` that contains `validatePhoneNumber`, as shown in Listing 12.5. After you have successfully made this new test fail, you can update the code to make the test pass.

Listing 12.5   Jenny, I've Got Your Number—and I Can Confirm That It Is Valid

```
describe('prompt.js', function() {

  describe('validatePhoneNumber', function() {

    it('should return a boolean', function() {
      var result = validatePhoneNumber('23456');
      expect(typeof result).toBe('boolean');
    });

    it('should return true when given a 1-800 number', function() {
      var result = validatePhoneNumber('1-800-867-5309');

      // Change to the following when we know this test can fail:
      //
      // expect(result).toBe(true);
      //
      expect(result).toBe(false);
    });
  });
});
```

Spies Like Us (and We Like Spies)

When testing a function that does not have input or output, you can't test that the output is what you expect, so you usually want to test that the code *did* what you expected it to do. For example, the `main` function takes no input and returns no output, so we want to test that `main` has called all the functions that it is supposed to call. In Jasmine, you can test that a function has been called by "spying" on the function. Spying on a function lets you know whether that function has been called, how many times it has been called, what arguments it was called with, and so on. Spying is not really useful in application code, but is great for unit testing. Let's test `main` by spying on the functions that it is supposed to call (see Listing 12.6).

Listing 12.6   **Being a Spy Is So Cool**

```
describe('main.js', function() {
  describe('main', function() {

    it('should call getUserName', function() {
      spyOn(window, 'getUserName');
      main();
      expect(getUserName).toHaveBeenCalled();
    });

    it('should call getPhoneNumber with the value from getUserName', function() {
      spyOn(window, 'getUserName').and.returnValue('Jimmy');
      spyOn(window, 'getPhoneNumber');
      main();
      expect(getPhoneNumber).toHaveBeenCalled();
      expect(getPhoneNumber.calls.mostRecent().args[0]).toBe('Jimmy');
    });
  });
});
```

The first test in Listing 12.6 shows a simple case of spying. The spyOn function creates the spy. The first argument of spyOn is the object that contains the function. The getUserName function is in the global scope, and in JavaScript, all global functions are a part of the window object. The second argument is the name of the function to be spied on (as a string). When the spying is set up, we can call the main function. Finally, we test our expectation: expect(getUserName).toHaveBeenCalled();. The toHaveBeenCalled expectation passes if the spy has been called at least once, and it fails if the spy has not been called.

The second test demonstrates an important concept in unit testing: Each test should test only one thing. In the second test, we want to test that getPhoneNumber is called with an argument that is the return value from getUserName, but we do not want to actually test getUserName in any way. We want to test only one thing in each test because we want to know exactly what went wrong if the test fails. If I test any part of getUserName inside my main tests, I won't know whether the problem is in getUserName or main. I can use a Jasmine spy to force getUserName to return a specific value (in this case, 'Jimmy'), which ensures that I am testing functionality only in main. After the test code calls main, I expect that, in the most recent call of getPhoneNumber, the first argument (index 0) is 'Jimmy': expect(getPhoneNumber. calls.mostRecent().args[0]).toBe('Jimmy');.

Now that you know how unit tests work (and a little bit about how Jasmine works), you can go write some more unit tests for kittenbook. Thinking about what to test and how to test it can be difficult at first, so if you get stuck, you can refer to the unit tests I have posted on the book's website under Chapter 12. Writing unit tests can be quite difficult, but it really does pay off: remember, we found a bug in validatePhoneNumber while writing the kittenbook unit tests for this chapter. When all your tests are written, running grunt jasmine should give you output that looks something like Figure 12.4.

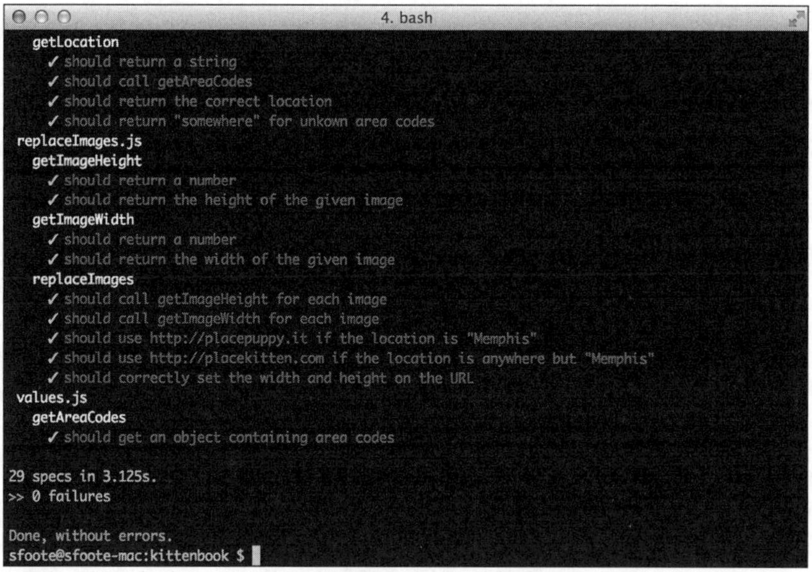

Figure 12.4   I wrote a total of 29 tests (or "specs") for kittenbook—and they all pass!

Test-Driven Development

If writing unit tests is so valuable and can find bugs, why should we wait until we're done writing our code to start writing unit tests? One method of writing code proclaims that tests should be written before application code. This method, most commonly called test-driven development, might seem crazy at first but is actually quite effective. Writing unit tests first ensures that your code is written in well-organized units. As mentioned earlier, writing tests is a lot like writing specifications. If you write your tests first, you ensure that you do proper planning before you start writing application code. Admittedly, it is hard to think about what your code should do before you have written any code, but if you can learn to think that way, test-driven development provides great benefits.

Integration Tests

I have three brothers and two sisters. Growing up in a family of eight (six kids, two parents) taught me that even if all of us kids were perfect angels on our own, we wouldn't necessarily behave nicely when all six of us were crammed in the back of a van. Even if all of your unit tests are passing, you might still have problems when the units are working together. Integration tests test your entire program, with all the units working together. I like to think of integration tests as automated manual tests. As with Jasmine for unit tests, software can help you create automated integration tests for your software. This type of software allows the computer to act like a human user, taking actions such as clicking and typing. Some robots even literally touch and swipe smartphones to automate integration tests for mobile devices. Integration tests are generally the final step before the software is ready to be presented to users—the last line of defense. Writing automated integration tests is beyond the scope of this book, but if you are interested in learning more, you can find plenty of resources online to get you started.

Catch Problems Early

One of the biggest reasons for all this testing is that you want to catch problems early. If you find a bug while you are writing code, you can easily fix it before anyone else even knows about it. If you don't find the bug until you perform integration testing, you might have already written other code that relies on your buggy code. To fix the bug, you might have to change your code *and* the code that relies on your code. If you find a bug that is in software that has already been packaged and shipped to users, you risk losing your users. Perhaps the worst situation is when users start depending on the bugs in your software and then get upset with you when you fix those bugs (see Figure 12.5).

Figure 12.5   Your users probably won't come to depend on your bugs, but if they do, they will get mad if you fix them. (Cartoon courtesy xkcd.com)

Debugging

Debugging is what happens when your program is not working and you are trying to figure out how to fix it. In my experience, debugging can be one of the best or worst parts of programming. If you know how to use debugging tools and you know what to look for, debugging can actually be a lot of fun. However, if all you know is that your program is broken and you don't know how to fix it, debugging can be frustrating and demoralizing.

My first attempts at debugging were frustrating and demoralizing. When I was starting to program Perl, the only way I knew to execute my code was by double-clicking the file I wanted to execute using Windows Explorer. Doing so opened a command prompt that stayed open only as long as the code was executing (usually less than half a second). When my code didn't work correctly, I could see a whole bunch of output in that command prompt window for the split-second before the window closed. I had no idea what the output was trying to tell me. When I realized that something was wrong with my code, I had to search through each line of code (in Notepad, remember?), trying to find a missing semicolon or mismatched parentheses. Debugging like this feels like a ridiculous guessing game. It was mind-numbing work, and I did it only because I didn't know there was a better way. Fortunately, there *is* a better way.

When working on the Web, browser developer tools are the place to go for debugging. In Chapter 5, "Data (Types), Data (Structures), Data(bases)," you learned that the console in the Chrome Developer Tools is a good place to try out JavaScript. Now we're going to dive deep into how to use the other features of the Developer Tools, starting again with the console.

Errors

For demonstration purposes, let's create an error in the kittenbook code. Open the `main.js` file in the `release` directory and remove the closing parentheses on from the first line of the `getUserName` function. That first line should now look like this:

```
var userName = prompt('Hello, what\'s your name?';
```

Now open the Chrome Extensions page (chrome://extensions/) and reload the kittenbook extension; then load https://www.facebook.com/. Open the Chrome Developer Tools (the keyboard shortcut is Ctrl+Shift+I for Windows and Linux, and Cmd+Alt+I for Mac). In the Developer Tools, click the Console tab and look for red text. You should see something like Figure 12.6. If your JavaScript code has any errors, those errors will show up in the console. Admittedly, this error message is a bit confusing. The error won't always tell you exactly what is wrong, but if you know where to look, it will tell you that an error *was* found and on what line.

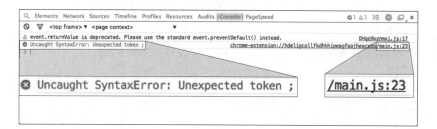

Figure 12.6   It's a bit cryptic, but this error tells us a lot.

The error in Figure 12.6 is telling us that something is wrong on line 23 in `main.js`. The error message is useful in this case, even though it doesn't tell us exactly what is wrong. The message does tell us that a semicolon (`;`) was found before the JavaScript runtime was expecting to find a semicolon. In the case of line 23, the runtime was expecting to find a closing parenthesis before it found a semicolon. The error doesn't tell us the whole story, but it gives us a pretty good hint to what is wrong; at the very least, it tells us what line has the problem. The first thing to do when something goes wrong is to check the console for errors.

Logs

When things are going wrong and you find no errors in the console, you can try using logs. We have used logs several times with `console.log`, but we have not yet used them for debugging purposes. Generally, logs have the program output information at certain places in the program. If things don't seem to be working, a `console.log` can help you check when your code is even being executed. When you run your program, if the log message doesn't show up in the console, you know that the rest of the code wasn't executed. You can also use logs to output the value of a variable at a given point in the program's execution. These log messages won't actually fix your bugs, but they can help you find what is causing the bug.

Before I found out about Developer Tools, the console, and `console.log`, I used a rather primitive form of logging: the `alert` function. Every time I wanted to check a value at a certain point in my JavaScript, I put an `alert` in my code. Sometimes I put an `alert` inside a `for` loop, which means the alert showed up each time the body of the `for` loop executed. I remember one particular `for` loop that executed about 100 times, so I had to press the Enter key about 100 times (see Figure 12.7). Using `alert` is not a fun way to do logging. It does work, but fortunately, you have much better options.

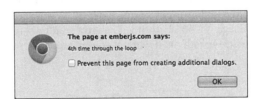

Figure 12.7   The "Prevent this page from creating additional dialogs" option wasn't around when I was using `alert` for debugging. It could've saved me quite a bit of time.

Breakpoints

Errors and logs are useful, but the most powerful method of debugging is through breakpoints. Setting breakpoints lets you pause the execution of your code on a particular line in your program. When the code is paused, you can inspect the current value of all the variables. You can execute the instructions after the breakpoint one at a time to see which instructions get executed and how the values of your variables change. Breakpoints let you slow things down to see exactly what is going on when your code is executed.

You set a breakpoint in two ways using the Chrome Developer Tools. The first and easiest way is to put a `debugger` statement in your code. The `debugger` has no effect on the rest of your code, but it pauses the code at that line if the Developer Tools are open. The `debugger` is useful, but you need to make sure you remove all `debugger` statements before packaging your code to send to your users. Breakpoints in your code might be useful to you, but they are extremely annoying to your users. Listing 12.7 shows `main.js` with a breakpoint, and Figure 12.8 shows the code paused at that point in the Developer Tools.

Listing 12.7 **Press Pause with `debugger`**

```
function main() {
  debugger;
  var userName = getUserName();
  var phoneNumber = getPhoneNumber(userName);
  var location = getLocation(phoneNumber);
  var images = getImages();
  replaceImages(images, location);
  setInterval(function() {
    images = getImages();
    replaceImages(images, location);
  }, 3000);
}

main();
```

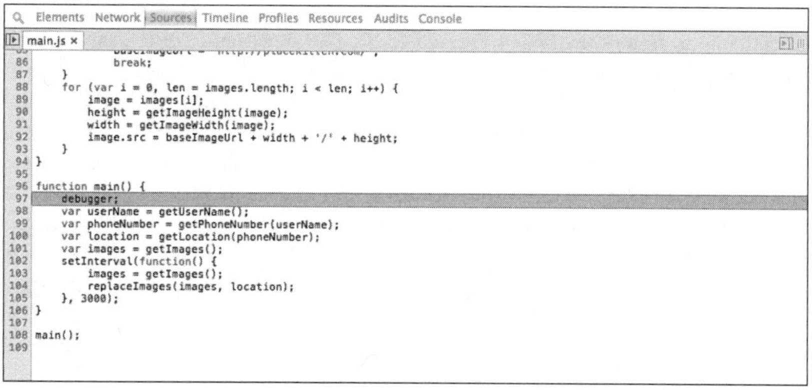

Figure 12.8 Pause your code using `debugger`.

The second way to set a breakpoint is done inside the Developer Tools. Click the Sources tab, find the line where you want to put the breakpoint, and click the line number next to that line (see Figure 12.13). Finding the line where you want the breakpoint can be the hardest part, especially when you're working on a page that has a lot of JavaScript files (such as Facebook). You can navigate to the file by clicking the Expand icon (see Figure 12.9) and then finding your file in the list. When the page has a lot of JavaScript files, finding your file can be quite tricky (especially when you are writing an extension—extension JavaScript files are found under the Content scripts subtab instead of the Sources subtab).

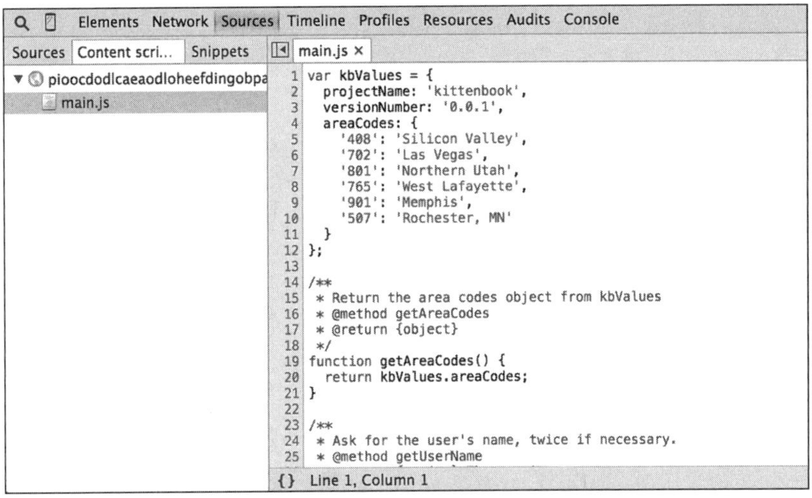

Figure 12.9   Expand the navigator and then find your file in the list.

A much easier way to find your file is to search for it. The Developer Tools' search feature lets you search through every file on the page, so all you have to do is click the correct result to open the file (see Figure 12.11). You can access the search feature with the keyboard shortcut Ctrl+Shift+F (Cmd+Alt+F on Mac). When searching for a file, you want to search for something that will likely exist only in the file you are looking for. Don't search for var or function—instead, search for a unique variable name or function name, such as replaceImages. Even if you aren't looking for a line that has replaceImages on it, you will more easily find the right file, and then your line shouldn't be hard to find. You might need to enable the Developer Tools setting for searching in content scripts (also known as extension JavaScript) for this to work with kittenbook (see Figure 12.10). You can open the settings menu by clicking the cog in the top right of the Developer Tools.

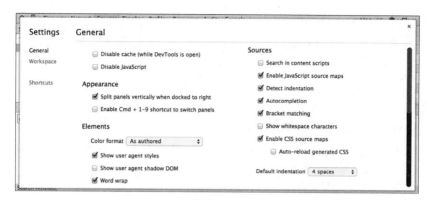

Figure 12.10   Enable searching content scripts.

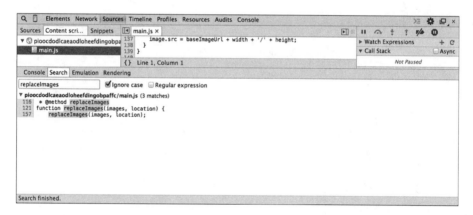

Figure 12.11   Find your file easier by searching sources.

Another method is to search for the file by name. To search for the file by name, click the main Sources tab, use the keyboard shortcut Ctrl+O (Cmd+O on Mac), and then type in the filename (see Figures 12.12 and 12.13).

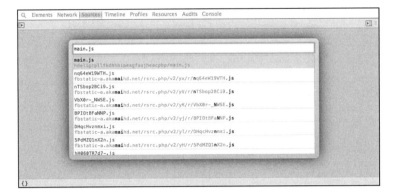

Figure 12.12   Let Chrome do the work for you: Open your file by name.

```
function main() {
    var userName = getUserName();
    var phoneNumber = getPhoneNumber(userName);
    var location = getLocation(phoneNumber);
    var images = getImages();
    setInterval(function() {
        images = getImages();
        replaceImages(images, location);
    }, 3000);
}

main();
```

Figure 12.13   Clicking line 97 sets a breakpoint at line 97.

Inspecting, Watching, and the Console

With your code execution paused at a breakpoint, you can do some really cool things. First, you can view the value of a variable by hovering your mouse over it (you have to admit, that's a lot better than using `alert` or even `console.log`). If you don't want to keep hovering over a variable, you can add it to your list of watch expressions, and the values of the variables will update as your code executes. You can add a variable to watch expressions by clicking the + and then typing the variable's name. See Figure 12.14.

You can also use your variables in the console. Any variable that is currently in scope is available in the console (and the Developer Tools even autocomplete for you as you type). If your code doesn't seem to be working, you can try out other code in the console to see if it works better. For example, as I was experimenting with the `getImages` function, I set a breakpoint in `getImages` function and tried a few different arguments for the `document.querySelectorAll` function before I found one that got all the images I was trying to find. See Figure 12.15.

Figure 12.14   Watch expressions let you quickly see updates to variables you want to keep an eye on.

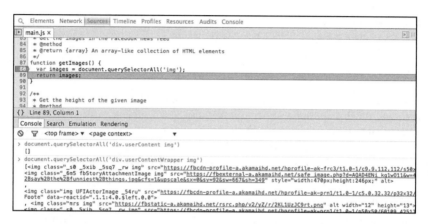

Figure 12.15   Run code in the console using the variables currently in scope.

Stepping Through the Code

One of my favorite ways to use breakpoints is to step through the code. Stepping through the code means setting a breakpoint and then executing the following code one line at a time. This is possibly the best way to diagnose what is wrong when your code is misbehaving. As an example, let's make a change to the replaceImages function in replaceImages.js. Right now, the only location we care about is Memphis, but let's say we suddenly care about Utah as well. We'll update replaceImages to look like Listing 12.8.

Listing 12.8   Add Utah to `replaceImages`, but Break the Extension in the Process

```
function replaceImages(images, location) {
  var baseImageUrl, height, width, image;
  switch (location) {
  case 'Memphis':
    // Use puppies for Memphis
    baseImageUrl = 'http://placepuppy.it/';
    break;
  case 'Utah':
```

```
    // use kittens everywhere else
    baseImageUrl = 'http://placekitten.com/';
    break;
  }
  for (var i=0,len=images.length; i&lt;len; i++) {
    image = images[i];
    height = getImageHeight(image);
    width = getImageWidth(image);
    image.src = baseImageUrl + width + '/' + height;
  }
}
```

Reload the updated code with grunt, click the Reload button on the extensions page, and then open Facebook. When asked for a phone number, use a 702 number, such as 702-555-9345. You'll notice that the images are not being replaced with puppies or kittens. What gives? We can solve this problem by stepping through the code. First, set a breakpoint on the first line of the replaceImages function. Now we'll need to use the step controls shown in Figure 12.16. The controls, from left to right, are a follows:

- **Play:** Return to normal execution speed.

- **Step Over:** Execute the next line of code and don't step into function calls. This is like pressing Play on the code inside the function call and then pressing Pause again when the function is done executing.

- **Step Into:** Execute the next line of code. If the next line of code is a function call, step into the function being called.

- **Step Out:** Step out of the current function. This is like pressing Play until the current function is done executing and then pressing Pause on the line where the function was called.

- **Disable breakpoints:** When this option is selected, Chrome ignores your breakpoints.

- **Pause on errors:** When this option is selected, Chrome pauses execution when an error occurs.

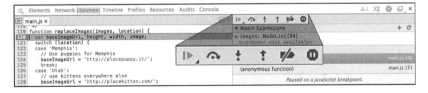

Figure 12.16   Step in, step out, and step over.

Stepping through the `replaceImages` function by clicking Step Into (over and over again) shows that the execution skips over all the cases in the `switch` statement. Therefore, the `baseImageUrl` is never set—and because `baseImageUrl` is never set, the browser doesn't know where to find the images. When we changed our code, we forgot to add a `default` to our `switch` statement, so if the location is anywhere other than `'Memphis'` or `'Utah'`, the program will be broken. Stepping through code can solve a lot of mysteries.

Call Stack

In Chapter 8, "Functions and Methods," you learned about the call stack, the list of functions that have been called. The Chrome Developer Tools give you a visual representation of the call stack on the right side, under Watch Expressions (see Figure 12.17). If we are stepping through the code, and execution is paused inside `getImageHeight`, we can see in the call stack that `getImageHeight` was called by `replaceImages`, which was called by `main`, which was called by `(anonymous function)`. You can click any of the function names to see what line was being executed when the next function was called. This tool is useful for seeing how your code got to the point where it is currently paused.

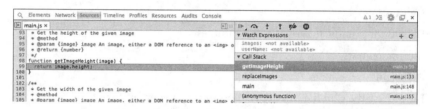

Figure 12.17   Chrome Developer Tools give you a visual representation of the call stack.

Find the Root Cause

Debugging is tricky business. You really have to act like a detective and sift through all the clues to discover why your program isn't doing what it is supposed to do. As you search for the problem, you will often find many symptoms, and you will be tempted to fix those symptoms. I have done this many times, and not once has it been a good idea. Keep digging until you find the root cause of the problem—when you fix that root cause, you will fix all the symptoms at once. A good indication that you are fixing a symptom instead of the root cause is that the fix makes your code messier and harder to work with. For instance, if you have to add a new parameter to one of your functions, you are probably fixing a symptom and not the real problem.

Code, Test, Debug, Repeat

When you are writing code, you should include testing and debugging in your workflow. First write some code, then run your tests, then debug the test failures, and then write some more code. When you have written enough code, you can do some integration testing (manual or automated) by actually using your program. You can debug any problems you find while doing integration testing and then repeat the entire cycle. When you find a bug, create a new automated test to ensure that the bug never shows up again. Including testing and debugging in your workflow helps you write high-quality code much more quickly.

Summing Up

I didn't learn about testing until years after I started programming, and my first attempts at debugging were embarrassingly primitive (`alert`, remember?). Your newfound knowledge of testing and debugging will help you become a much better programmer much faster. In this chapter, you learned about:

- Manual testing
- Unit testing
- How to use Jasmine to write and run unit tests
- Integration tests
- Debugging
- How to use the Chrome Developer Tools to debug your JavaScript

In the next chapter, instead of being given a fish, you will learn how to fish. In other words, you will learn how to keep learning about programming when you're done reading this book. Specifically, you will learn about:

- How to use the Web to search for the answers to your programming questions
- Where to ask questions, and how to ask them
- How to learn by teaching others

## 13

Learning to Fish: How to Acquire a Lifetime of Programming Knowledge

> **Note**
>
> **Project:** Start a blog to write about what you have learned so far, and register on Stackoverflow.

Your head is so full of programming knowledge, it's about to explode. Still, you have much more to learn than could possibly fit in this book (or any single book). I would say you've barely scratched the surface, but in some ways, you have only been made aware that the surface exists. I don't say that to discourage you or put you down; what you have done so far in this book is amazing, and you should be proud. You have gained a foundation upon which you can build, and you should know that you can do a lot of building.

With this foundation in place, you will be able to process new programming information and learn new concepts much faster. For example, when you hear friends talking about the build tools they are using for their project, you will know what they are talking about. You already know what build tools are, what they are meant to do, and what they are capable of. If your friend is not using Grunt, you will have the opportunity to learn about a new set of build tools, and what you learn will fit nicely into the foundation you have already started building. The real challenge is not so much in understanding these new concepts as it is in finding them. The following pages help teach you the skills to find the information you need.

How to Search

Let me paint a picture for you. Let's say you are working on a JavaScript program in which you get a date as a string (for example, `'2014-10-08'`), and you want to know what the next day is. You already know that you can convert from string to number using `parseInt`, so you use that (see Listing 13.1). Everything is going great. Then one day you notice that your program is producing some really strange results, but only in older versions of Internet Explorer: Your program thinks the day after `'2014-10-08'` is `'2014-10-01'`, not `'2014-10-09'`. You set some breakpoints and step through your code, and you find that `parseInt` seems to be broken: When the argument is `'08'`, you get 8 on most browsers, but you get 0 in Internet Explorer (see the upcoming note for more info on why this happens). You've found the problem, but you have no idea how to fix it. Now what do you do? As you continue programming, you will run into similar situations all the time. The only thing more frustrating than being stuck is having no idea how to get unstuck.

Listing 13.1   **Using `parseInt` to Convert a String to a Number**

```
function nextDay(str) {
  var num = parseInt(str);
  return num + 1;
}

var date = '2014-10-08';
var dateParts = date.split('-');
alert(nextDay(dateParts[1]));
```

The age of Google has turned us all into expert searchers. In seconds, you can find all kinds of information, such as obscure facts about an actor in a movie you're watching. Because the Internet was and is built by programmers, the Internet has a disproportionate amount of information about programming. When you run into a problem such as the previous `parseInt` example, you can almost always find an answer, as long as you know how and where to look.

> `parseInt` **Explained**
>
> Why do older versions of Internet Explorer do such strange things with `parseInt`? The reason is that `parseInt` works for numbering systems other than decimal (such as binary, octal, and hexadecimal). If you don't tell `parseInt` what type of numbering system you are using, `parseInt` uses whatever numbering system seems to make sense, and `'08'` looks like an octal number. Newer browsers tend to default to using decimal, even when the string has a 0 at the front, but older versions of Internet Explorer still think `'08'` is an octal. Regardless, you should always specify the numbering system when you are using `parseInt`: `parseInt('08', 10);` (base 10, or decimal) always returns 8 in all browsers.

Finding the Right Terms

If you don't know what you're searching for, you won't find it. I had this problem the first time I needed to use an escape character. I didn't know there was such a thing as an escape character, much less what it was called. All I knew was that apostrophes were breaking my strings. In the parseInt example, you probably don't really know what is wrong, so how do you search for a solution? The key is in picking the right search terms. If you're looking for something specific to a programming language, include the name of that programming language in your search. Then describe your problem how you think other people with the same problem would describe it. For example, when searching for an answer to the parseInt problem, a good query might be "javascript parseInt returns 0." When I ran this search, the first result gave me the answer I was looking for.

If you're not sure what to search for, Google's search suggestions can help you there. As you type in the start of your query, the suggestions can help guide you to the searches that will produce the best results. The suggestions mean that other people searched for these terms and had success, so you might have success, too. Figure 13.1 shows some of the useful (and not so useful) suggestions when looking for parseInt solutions.

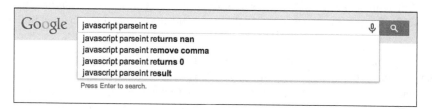

Figure 13.1   Google's suggestions can help you know what to search for.

Leveling Up

The resource you are trying to find depends on what level you are at in your learning. For example, if you are considering learning to write Python programs, you want to find introductory information on the benefits of using Python. In such cases, you will want to use search terms such as "why use Python" and "Python features." When you've decided that Python is the right language for you, you will want to learn the basics of Python. At that point, you will want to search for something such as "Python tutorial." After you've been working with Python for a while, you might run into a problem and need to use a regular expression. You already know what regular expressions are and when to use them; you just need to know how to use them in Python. You would then search for "Python regular expressions" or "Python regular expression documentation" to find documentation on how regular expressions work in Python. Now suppose that the documentation is too dense and difficult to understand; you can search for "Python regular expressions tutorial" or "Python regular expressions example" to find information on Python regular expressions that is easier to digest. In all of these cases, you will more likely find the information you need if you specify in your search terms what level you are at.

Error

Errors can be super frustrating because both your code isn't working and the error messages can seem quite vague or obtuse. Error messages have one redeeming quality, though: The words in an error message are pretty much always the same. That means other people have seen the same error message and likely found a solution. When you get an error message that you don't understand, copy and paste the entire message into Google, and you will likely find the answer to your problem.

Working Backward

You might not know from the outset what you are searching for. You might not fully understand what problem you are trying to solve or even how much you need to learn to solve it. Just because you aren't entirely sure what you are looking for doesn't mean you can't search for it. Start at the end and work backward. First, search for your end goal and, as you search through the results, look for unfamiliar words and phrases. Next, search for all those terms that seem relevant, again making note of all the unfamiliar words and phrases you find in the results.

When you get to the point that you understand almost everything in the search results, you can start learning about the things you didn't understand until you get to the point that you know enough to build whatever you have been trying to build. This process will help you learn a lot of amazing things on your way to achieving your goal or, at the very least, help you realize that your goal might require more work and learning than you are willing or able to do.

The process of searching backward led me to learn web programming. I have already mentioned the "typeahead" I built for my first website. I didn't know it was called a typeahead, so I searched for something like "google search suggestions," which led me to discover the term *autocomplete*. I read some articles about autocomplete, confirmed that it was what I was looking for, and discovered the term *AJAX*. I learned that AJAX is how the new suggestions appear, based on what the user types. I did some research on AJAX and discovered that you have to write JavaScript to use AJAX. So I started learning JavaScript until I knew enough to start using AJAX, and then I was able to build my typeahead. On the way, I learned a lot about HTTP, web servers, and data structures. I believe that working backward to solve a programming problem can be extremely rewarding.

Identifying Quality Resources

Sadly, not everything on the Internet is high quality. This is true for programing information as much as anything else. Beware of websites and books that are not high quality. I picked up a lot of false information and bad habits by trusting sites that were outdated and poorly written. Unfortunately, you might have to make this mistake a few times before you can distinguish between high- and low-quality resources. Beware if the site you are visiting has a whole bunch of ads, especially if they have little or nothing to do with programming. Look out for sites that try to cover every topic under the sun (for example, About.com covers taxes, gardening, programming, and hairstyles). Be careful when you see claims that what you will learn is easy; if it's too easy, you are probably learning to do it the wrong way. Most programming languages, libraries, and frameworks have dedicated websites with thorough, high-quality documentation. These sites generally include thorough introductory information, guides on getting started, tutorials, and reference materials. The information you find on such sites is almost always high quality and correct.

Personal Blogs: Hidden Gems

Although you should be wary of information found on random websites, you can find some valuable information on blogs. Professional programmers like to write about the problems they have solved, and this writing usually ends up on their blogs. Documentation and tutorials are great, but nothing can beat the value of a real person describing a real-world problem and its solution. Still, before you trust the information, research the authors. Check out their LinkedIn profile, StackOverflow profile (see the upcoming section, "StackOverflow"), GitHub profile (see Chapter 15, "Advanced Topics"), Twitter profile, and any other resources you can find. If they seem to know what they are talking about, you have found a great source for information. These types of blogs are like programming mentors; they give you free advice on how to program better. Remember, if you use the advice, mention the blog in your documentation.

Where, When, and How to Ask Programming Questions

Teaching yourself to program is a difficult task because you probably don't have anyone you can go to with your programming questions. Fortunately, we have the Internet, so even if you don't personally know any programmers, you can still ask programming questions to real people and can get real (good) answers. The key to getting your questions answered is knowing where, when, and how to ask.

Where

Finding the right place to ask your programming questions is probably just as important as asking the right questions. If you ask the right question to the wrong people, you might get an answer, but you won't get a good answer. Because you want a good answer, you need to learn about the right places to ask.

Phone a Friend

If you are teaching yourself to program because you have no one to teach you, coach you, or mentor you, that needs to change. In truth, you can get pretty far on your own, but you will learn so much more and much faster if you have a friend who can point you in the right direction. Chances are, you already do know a programmer or two, and they will probably be happy to answer your questions (especially now that you have a foundation and you can ask good questions). If you don't know any programmers, go meet one. Thanks to websites such as www. meetup.com/, you can find groups of programmers meeting in your area. Go find one of those groups, meet some people, and learn some great stuff.

Asking your questions to a real person is the most effective method for learning and getting good answers. A real person can look at your code, help you debug, and help you find a solution. A real person can give you personalized help because that person knows your background and your current level of knowledge—because he or she has answered your other questions and is familiar with the project you are working on. Instead of just giving you a specific answer for the problem you are having right now, a friend can teach you and help you find your own answers. If at all possible, ask a friend.

StackOverflow

Even if you have a programmer friend, he or she won't have the answers to all your questions. In such cases, StackOverflow (http://stackoverflow.com/) is an amazing resource. StackOverflow is an online Q&A community for programmers. Everything on the site is ranked by points. If you ask a question that a bunch of people find useful, those people up-vote your question (see Figure 13.2). If you give a very good answer to a question, people up-vote your answer (see Figure 13.3). Conversely, bad questions and bad answers get down-votes. The best questions get preference in the search results, and the best answers are displayed at the top of the page. Reputation points are awarded to (or taken from) users for each up- and down-vote, and the accumulated reputation score appears wherever the user's name appears on the site. The idea behind all these votes and points is to surface the good stuff and hide the bad stuff. The system works really well; you can find an answer to almost any programming question. If the question hasn't already been asked, you can ask it and usually get an answer within the hour.

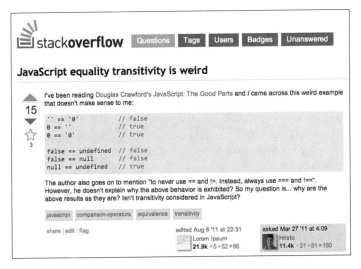

Figure 13.2   A question on StackOverflow, with the total number of votes and the asker's name and reputation score

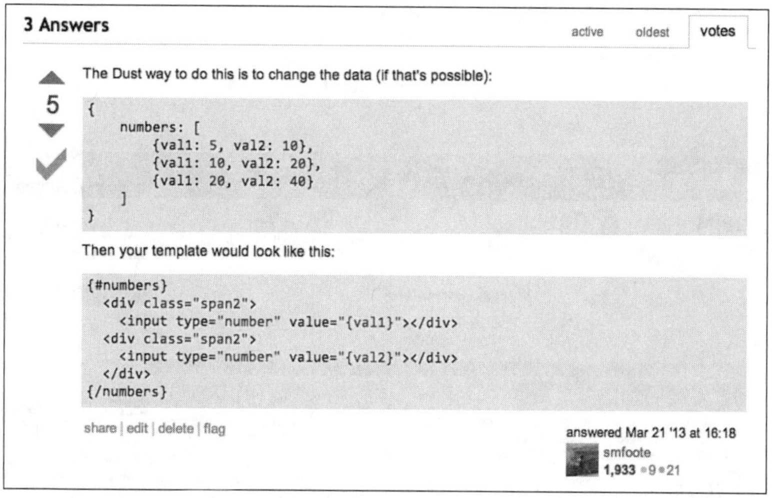

Figure 13.3   An answer on StackOverflow—the answers are sorted by votes, and the check mark indicates that this is the "accepted answer."

Forums

When I started programming, online forums were the best way to find answers to programming questions. As I was learning Perl, I spent a lot of time on Perl forums (see Figure 13.4). Although I owe a lot to these forums, I am glad that StackOverflow and other similar ranked-Q&A sites have largely replaced them. You see, forums were hard to sift through. A single question could result in pages and pages of replies, and the best answer to the question could be on any of those pages, or there could be no good answers at all. The only way to know was by reading through every reply on every page. And as you can see in Figure 13.4, the forums usually aren't too easy on the eyes. However, one advantage of forums is that they are often specific to a particular programming language and, therefore, attract the world's leading experts in that language. The concentration of experts can make forums an intimidating place for beginners. I generally recommend sticking with StackOverflow for your questions, but forums can be useful when StackOverflow fails.

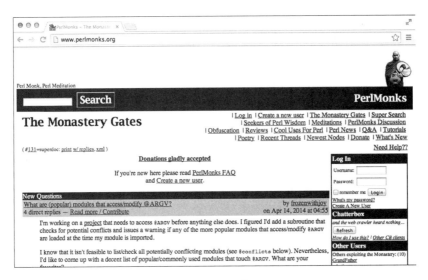

Figure 13.4   The not-so-visually-appealing PerlMonks forum

When

Programmers value efficiency, both in code and in the rest of life. They like to help, but they also value their time. Don't ask a question until you have first done your best to find an answer on your own. Before I post a question on StackOverflow, I ask myself:

1. Have I Googled it? What results did I get from Google, and why did they not answer my question?

2. Have I read through the documentation? What sections of the documentation did I read, and why did they not answer my question?

3. Has anyone else already asked this question? Why do the answers of the previously asked question not work for my situation?

As a programmer, I value efficiency, too. I want to find the answer on my own, but I don't want to search aimlessly. So if I have tried Google, tried the documentation, and tried searching StackOverflow and I still can't find an answer, then I know it's time for me to ask.

The Stuffed Duck

You can often find the answers to your questions just by asking the question. The process of articulating the problem in the form of a succinct question frequently helps you better understand the problem and might even reveal the answer. Get a stuffed animal (ducks are nice) and put it next to your computer. When you get stuck, ask the duck. The duck is a good listener and has plenty of free time. If after asking the duck you still haven't figured it out, go ask a real person. Let him or her know you already asked your duck.

How

When the time comes to ask a question, you should realize that the phrase "there are no stupid questions" does not apply on programming forums such as StackOverflow. I say this not to be mean, but to let you know that if you ask a bad question, you will probably get a lecture instead of an answer. Community members will focus on how to fix your bad question rather than how to fix your problem. On the other hand, if you ask a good question, you will get a good answer—and you may even get a compliment on how good your question is.

Make It Easy

The people answering questions on StackOverflow and other forums are volunteers. They don't get paid to answer your questions (except with reputation points), so you should do as much work as possible to make your question easy to answer. Write a clear description of your problem. Describe the resources you found while searching for an answer on your own and why those resources didn't answer your question. Your question should be thorough but not long-winded. If the question is long, you should include a summary. The less time readers need to spend understanding your problem, the more time they will have to find a solution and write a good answer.

Don't Be Shy: Post Your Code

When I asked my first question on StackOverflow, I did not include my code because I was embarrassed. I was afraid people would make fun of my code instead of answering my question. In reality, programming questions are difficult to answer without seeing the code that is causing the problem. It's like a doctor trying to diagnose over the phone. "It sounds like you have a stomach flu—or maybe appendicitis." Posting your code with your question will help you get a much better answer.

Learn by Teaching

You learn a lot by doing, but you learn even more by teaching. As you learn how to program, you are in the perfect position to teach others how to program. As you teach the things you have just learned, and the things you are still learning, you develop a point of view that is exactly what other beginners need. Seasoned (that is, hardened) programmers might know more than you, but that can mean the way they explain things is complicated and difficult to understand. In that sense, you are more qualified to teach than anyone.

Answer Questions

You don't need to go find a job as a programming teacher to start teaching. You can just start answering questions. Look through StackOverflow for questions that you might be able to answer. You already know a bit about HTML, JavaScript, and Google Chrome extensions, so you can try answering questions on those subjects. If you don't yet feel comfortable answering questions on StackOverflow, you can still answer questions. Find someone else who is learning to program (or convince a friend that he or she wants to learn to program), and then you can answer each other's questions. You will both learn more than if you tried to learn alone.

Write a Blog

Writing can be a great way of learning (I guess that's why you have to write so many essays in school). You have already learned a lot of good things you can write about, such as how JavaScript functions work, what source code is, how and why to start using Grunt, how to use Chrome Developer Tools, and how to create a Chrome extension. As you start to write about these topics, you will discover the gaps in your understanding. As you research to fill in the gaps, your understanding of the concept will solidify. Remember, you are in an excellent position to teach others because you are learning the concepts yourself. If you don't feel comfortable writing a blog post for the world to see, you could write a letter to your stuffed duck, who happens to be a great listener.

Summing Up

In this chapter, you learned some important tools that will help you continue to build on the foundation of programming knowledge you have already built. Specifically, you learned about:

- Searching for answers
- Asking good question
- Learning through teaching

In the next chapter, you will learn about:

- What to do when you finish reading this book
- How to start your own project
- Online education tools, free and paid

14

Building Your Skills

> **Note**
>
> **Project:** Sign up for and start a class on Udacity, Coursera, codecademy, or a similar site, and pick the next book you'll read.

You made it! You have built for yourself a solid programming foundation, and you created a cool Chrome extension along the way. You know how to solve your own problems, and you know where to look when you get stuck. So now what should you do? With the skills and knowledge you have now, you can already build some powerful stuff. So go build something great. Then keep learning so you can build something even greater. Your journey has only just begun.

Make kittenbook Your Own

You have done great work with kittenbook, but the project is clearly not complete. Those two pop-up windows asking for a name and phone number are annoying, and they shouldn't pop up every time the user loads any page on Facebook (names and phone numbers don't change that often, so why keep asking?). A lot of features can be added, too. What if the user wants a mix of puppies *and* kittens? What if the user wants pictures of him- or herself (how vain, right?)? What if the user doesn't want to see any pictures at all? Kittenbook was intentionally left in an unfinished state so that you can make the project your own by adding the features you want to it. You are already familiar with the kittenbook code and how it all works together, so you are in a great position to expand on it. Have some fun with kittenbook, and make it your own.

Restyle Facebook

Have you always imagined Facebook would look better in green instead of blue (see Figure 14.1)? Have you wished that the chat sidebar on the right were a little wider? Do you have your own ideas about what the icons should be? You can change it all by adding some custom CSS using your extension. You now have the power to modify Facebook—or any website you want. Remember, though, to always follow the terms of service of the site you are modifying, and don't do anything malicious. Use your power for good.

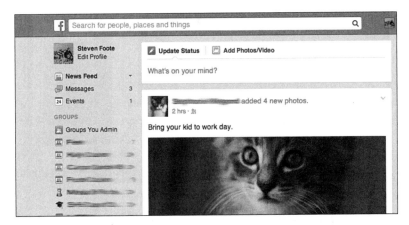

Figure 14.1   Well, maybe Facebook really does look better with blue. At least we tried.

Add New Functionality

You can do more than just change the way Facebook looks. You can add new functionality to Facebook as well. Do you wish you could see your friends' latest Tweets or Pins right from Facebook? With a little bit of work, you can learn about the Facebook, Twitter, and Pinterest APIs and add completely new features to Facebook.

The decision to use Facebook for kittenbook was arbitrary; we could have used any website we liked. In fact, we still can use any website we like. By modifying the `content_scripts` array in `manifest.json`, you can add cute puppies and kittens to other sites. Scratch that—you can add whatever functionality you dream up to other sites. The possibilities are endless. Listing 14.1 shows how to get your JavaScript to run on www.pinterest.com, but you have to make some changes to `getImages.js` to get the images to be replaced on Pinterest (Figure 14.2 shows kittenbook running on Pinterest).

Listing 14.1   **Pinterest Gets Puppies and Kittens!**

```
{
  "manifest_version": 2,
  "name": "kittenbook",
  "description": "Replace all the pictures on facebook with pictures of kittens or puppies",
  "version": "0.0.1",
```

```
"content_scripts": [
  {
    "matches": ["*://www.facebook.com/*", "*://www.pinterest.com/*"],
    "js": ["main.js"]
  }
]
}
```

Figure 14.2   Pinterest with kittens. Can you tell the difference?

Share Your Version of Kittenbook

When it's ready, show off your version of kittenbook to your friends. Teach them how to install it on their own computers (and probably teach them how to disable it, too). If you have made something really worthwhile, you can even share your extension with the world by publishing it on the Chrome Web Store (https://chrome.google.com/webstore/category/apps).

Find Your Own Project

If I could give you only one recommendation as you finish this book, it would be to start your own project. I hope you found the kittenbook project to be fun, even if it was a bit silly. Kittenbook was just a fun project contrived to help you learn various programming concepts. The end product isn't useful for you—or for anyone, really. But now that you have learned all those concepts, you have the tools to start a project that is truly useful. Is there an iPhone app you've always wanted? Have you imagined a tool that would make life so much easier for you and your coworkers? Be creative, and make the world a better place while you're at it.

Solve Your Own Problem

Your project will be a lot easier to build if you are solving your own problem. Maybe your problem is that you have to repeat the same mundane tasks over and over again (remember the example of renaming hundreds of files from Chapter 3, "Getting to Know Your Computer"?). Maybe your problem is that you have a great idea for a video game, but no one has built it yet. When I was working as an accountant, my problem was that I was really bad at keeping track of my hours (an essential skill for accountants), so I built the Chrome extension shown in Figure 14.3. No one understands your problem better than you do, and you don't understand anyone's problems better than you understand your own, so the best problems to solve are your own. Even if no one else ever wants to use your software, the work is still worthwhile because it is useful for you. Having said that, if you have a problem, other people like you probably have the same problem, so others will probably benefit from your work. Regardless, when building software, the best problems to solve are your own.

Figure 14.3   Because I was so bad at tracking my hours, I built a Chrome extension to give me reminders every 15 minutes. Eventually, a few hundred coworkers and strangers started using the tool I built for myself.

Be Ambitious

When you are picking a project, aim high. The best way to keep learning is to imagine an ambitious project, even though you know you don't yet have the skills necessary to build that project. When you have started a project you are passionate about, no amount of bad documentation or poorly designed forums will stand in your way of figuring out how to make that project a reality. My first big project was a website; and through that project, I learned how to use Linux, HTTP, relational databases, PHP, HTML, CSS, and JavaScript. Those skills eventually got me a job as a programmer at LinkedIn, one of the major technology companies in Silicon Valley. If you already know how to do everything you are going to need to build, you won't grow or learn very much—and you certainly won't have as much fun.

Get Help, Give Help

If you have the opportunity, find a friend to work with you on your project. You will actually learn more by working with a friend than you would by trying to do all the work yourself. If you don't already have an idea for a project to work on, you can help your friend with his or her project. You and your friend will have different ideas about how things should be done, and you can learn from each other. Perhaps the most important reason to collaborate with someone else is to learn how to work with another person on a software project. Programming might seem like a solitary activity, but really, programming is best done in groups. The next chapter introduces you to Git, which is an important software collaboration tool. Collaborating on a software project is a skill unto itself—and a very important one, at that.

Make a Website

I love the Web. If you are thinking about creating an application, I highly recommend using the Web as your platform. The easiest way to share your software is by giving someone a link to your website. The Web is capable of amazing things, and you have what it takes to build them. And the Web is fun, too.

Open Source Projects

You have learned a lot about using the work of others to do your work faster. By contributing to an open source project, you make your work available to others. Contributing to an open source project can be a great experience, and you can learn a lot by working with talented developers. You are already familiar with some open source projects, including Google Chrome, Mozilla Firefox, and Linux. If you've done some research on JavaScript, you have probably heard of open source JavaScript libraries such as jQuery and underscore. Even programming languages such as Perl, Python, and Ruby are open source. The world runs on open source software, and you have a chance to be a part of it.

GitHub

GitHub is a company that provides excellent tools for collaborating on software projects. GitHub is free to use for open source projects. This incentive, plus the quality of the tools, means that GitHub has become the de facto home for new open source software projects. Many popular open source projects are hosted on GitHub, so if you are looking to contribute to an open source project, GitHub is a good place to start your search. Other websites are similar to GitHub, including Google Code and BitBucket, although GitHub does have the strongest collection of open source projects.

Finding a Project

For me, finding an open source project to which I can contribute is the hardest part. You want to find a project on which you can make meaningful contributions, or even any contribution at all. That means projects such as Mozilla Firefox, Google Chrome, and Linux might seem a little out of reach. Instead, you might get started by contributing to one of the open source libraries that you actually use while building your software. A Grunt plug-in might be a good project to start with because these are relatively small in scope. Small projects are easier to get started on because there is less code and documentation to read through. Most of these projects have a link to the GitHub page where you can find the code and instructions on how to contribute. Look for the Fork Me on GitHub ribbon, shown in Figure 14.4.

Figure 14.4   This ribbon indicates open source projects that are seeking contributors.

Different Ways to Contribute

Contributing by adding or modifying code might be intimidating or difficult at first, but that's not the only way to contribute. You have other ways to contribute so you can get familiar with the project and the code before you actually start changing it. For example, you can consider these options:

- Find and file bugs
- Add and update documentation and user guides
- Find and fix typos and other errors in documentation or code comments
- Answer questions about the project on StackOverflow

When you have become more familiar with the project by contributing in these ways, you will feel more comfortable making actual code changes, and the owners of the project will feel more comfortable accepting your code changes. Start small and work your way up.

Create Your Own

One of the best things about open source projects is that anyone can create one—including you. In fact, I strongly recommend that you create an open source project of your own—even if you don't think anyone else will ever use it. Maybe no one ever will use it, but creating an open source project will teach you a lot of important lessons. Things that seem pretty important, such as code quality, structure, documentation, and testing, will become even more important as you publish your code for the world to see. And who knows? Maybe someone will find your project and start using it or, even better, contribute to it.

Free Online Education

Many websites are dedicated to teaching you how to write code, many of them free. With the foundation you have in programming, you are ready to take full advantage of these resources. You will find descriptions here of a few of the resources I have found to be most useful, but many more exist. I recommend exploring the following resources and finding more on your own.

Project Euler

If you enjoy math, even a little bit, then Project Euler (https://projecteuler.net/) is an amazing resource. Project Euler uses math to teach computer programming and, at the same time, uses computer programming to teach math. Project Euler is a series of challenges that require knowledge of both math and computer programming to solve. The challenges build on each other; so you use the skills that you learned in the last challenge to solve the next challenge. The programming portion of the first few challenges is relatively easy if you have a solid understanding of math, but the challenges quickly begin to get quite difficult. You can use whatever programming language you like to solve the problems, but you definitely need to use programming to solve them. If you have an interest in mathematics, you should definitely spend some time solving challenges on Project Euler.

Solve a Math Challenge, Get a Job

In 2004, Google had an interesting idea for recruiting programmers. Google wanted programmers who enjoy solving problems just for the fun of solving problems, so they put up a billboard with an interesting math problem, similar to the Project Euler problems. The problem was to go to "{first 10-digit prime found in consecutive digits of e}.com" (see Figure 14.5). A curiosity for math and computer programming can really pay off, as it did for the programmers who got jobs at Google by solving the billboard challenge.

Figure 14.5   Google's clever recruiting message

Udacity

Udacity has an ever-increasing number of programming courses, taught by experts, covering many different aspects of programming and computer science. Most of the courses use Python as the programming language, but some classes use Java, JavaScript, and others. The Udacity courses are ranked by difficulty, so you can start with the beginner-level courses and work your way up from there. The courses are organized into short videos (about 4 minutes, at most), with quizzes as you go. Most of the courses are built around a project of some sort, but the lessons learned are easily applicable outside of the class and the project. I recommend starting with these courses:

- The "Web Development" course, which teaches you how to build a blog

- The CS101 courses, which teaches the fundamentals of computer science along with how a search engine works

Coursera

Coursera is similar to Udacity, with a few key differences. The classes are taught by professors from various contributing universities, and they feel more like real university classes. The classes have a timeline, with deadlines for homework and projects as you go. As such, Coursera classes can be a bit intense, but the intensity does help you to learn a lot—and quickly. Coursera offers courses on a number of subjects (whereas Udacity focuses on computer science), and most of the programming classes are geared toward more experienced programmers. A few beginner-level courses are offered, and you can still get a lot out of the advanced courses even if you don't understand everything. I have really enjoyed the Coursera courses I have taken, but the intensity and deadlines do make it easier to drop classes and give up. I recommend starting with these courses:

- Programming for Everyone
- An Introduction to Interactive Programming in Python

codecademy

Codecademy helps you learn the basics of coding in a specific language, offering tutorials for HTML/CSS, JavaScript, PHP, Python, and Ruby. These tutorials are great for getting familiar with a language to see if you want to invest the time to learn it more fully. A codecademy course provides a text editor inside your browser where you can type your code and see the results, which means you don't have to install the programming language's runtime on your computer to get started. However, it also means that debugging your code is quite a bit harder. Also, because you don't have the runtime installed, you can use the skills you learn only while you are on the codecademy website. In other words, codecademy teaches you how to code but does not teach you how to program. I recommend starting with these courses:

- The JavaScript course—see how much you already know
- The Python course—learn the similarities and differences compared to JavaScript

Khan Academy

Khan Academy is a great place to learn about all sorts of things. Recently, Khan Academy released an Introduction to JavaScript course that teaches you how to create drawings and animations with JavaScript. Like Udacity and codecademy, the Khan Academy course provides you with a built in text editor to run your JavaScript code.

Tutorials

The websites I have mentioned so far are great for expanding your general knowledge, but tutorials are great for learning how to do a specific task. For instance, I learned how to create Grunt tasks by reading the "Getting Started" tutorial on http://gruntjs.com/. Online tutorials range in quality from excellent, to useless, to harmful. I have followed online tutorials that taught me how to do things in a terrible way. I structured a lot of data in strings instead of objects or arrays because I read a tutorial that told me to do it that way. The moral of the story is to be careful about tutorials that come from a source you don't know. However, a good tutorial can be an amazing resource to help you take your programming skills to the next level.

Paid Education

When you are serious about what you want to learn, you might consider making a financial investment in your learning. Almost everything you need to know about programming is already online for free, so whatever paid education you choose should add some sort of extra value beyond what you would get from what is already available for free.

Read a Book

I didn't read a lot of books as I was first learning to program. I figured all the information that I might find in a book was available for free online, so why should I pay for the book? I struggled for more than a year trying to understand how to use Git correctly, until I finally bought a book about Git. When I finished the book a week or two later, I had learned everything I wanted to know about Git and discovered things I didn't even know I'd wanted to know. That's when I realized how valuable programming books could be. Although it is true that all the information in a book is freely available online, that information is not organized, and there's also a lot of bad information online. An author presents all the good information that you might eventually find online in an organized manner with a consistent voice. The author also presents concepts in the right order and teaches you things you would not discover on your own. Now whenever I want to learn about a new technology, I first try to find a book. I recommend that you do the same.

Udacity and Coursera

Udacity and Coursera both offer paid versions of their courses. The paid versions contain the same content as the free versions, but they also offer verified certificates that you receive when the course is complete. These certificates don't replace a college diploma, but technology companies are starting to recognize them. If you are looking to get a job as a programmer, you should consider the paid versions.

Udacity courses try to give you real-world experience, and the paid courses take that one step further. In a Udacity paid course, you get everything you get in the free course, plus the following:

- In-class projects with feedback and code reviews
- Personalized guidance and pacing from your coach
- On-demand chat with your coach
- A verified certificate upon course completion

Coursera offers a Signature Track for each course and Specializations for groups of courses. If you pay to take a course as a Signature Track, you receive a Verified Certificate when you complete the course. A Specialization is a series of courses with a unifying theme that culminates in a capstone project. If you successfully complete each of the courses and the capstone project, you are awarded a Specialization Certificate issued by Coursera and the university that created the course material. Again, these certificates are not college diplomas, but they do look good on your LinkedIn profile and your resume.

Treehouse

Treehouse focuses on web design and development, with the goal of teaching you the skills necessary to get you a job. All the material from a Treehouse course is freely available elsewhere on the Web, but Treehouse courses curate and organize all that information into courses that make sense. You don't have to do the work of searching all over the Internet for the right infor-mation, and you don't have to wonder what you should be learning next; Treehouse does that work for you. One of the big advantages of Treehouse is the frequent updates to course content. Technology changes quickly, so the weekly updates from Treehouse ensure that you are not learning outdated material.

Summing Up

You have done great work, and you are ready to move on and do great things. You should be proud. In this chapter, you learned about:

- Starting your own project
- Contributing to open source projects
- Online resources to further your programming knowledge

The next chapter is a preview of things you might want to learn next. You will be introduced to:

- Design patterns
- Object-oriented programming
- Version control
- Git

15

Advanced Topics

> **Note**
> **Project:** Install Git and turn your Chrome extension project into a Git repository.

You made it! I want to thank you for letting me be a part of your journey to learn programming. You have learned so much already, and you are ready to keep learning. You can now have a conversation with software developers and understand what they're talking about (at least some of it). You are ready to pick up any programming book or start any programming tutorial online and actually understand what is going on, instead of being completely lost and frustrated. Most important, you are ready to start working on your own projects. You should be proud of what you have accomplished.

Your head is so full of new programming terminology and concepts right now that you might feel that nothing else will fit up there. If that is the case, you can close this book right now and walk away with a well-deserved feeling of accomplishment. This chapter is an introduction to a few advanced programming topics you should consider learning about next—a bonus, if you will. If now is not the time for advanced topics, I understand; take a break and come back in a few days. However, if you are itching to learn more, keep reading.

Version Control

You have learned about tools to write programs (text editors and IDEs), to compile and build programs (build tools such as Grunt), and to debug programs (such as Chrome Dev Tools). Like the others, a version control system is an important programming tool. A version control system is a tool for managing changes made to your program. Version control allows you to take a snapshot of your project every time a change is made to the source code. Each snapshot is accompanied by a description of what changes were made and why. This type of meticulous record keeping is useful even if you don't plan to publish a detailed biography of your project.

If your software stops working for some reason, version control enables you to easily roll back to a previous (working) version while you figure out the problem.

When a project is using version control, all the code for the project is stored in a central location, called a repository. To start working on the project, you must "check out" a local copy of the code from the repository (*local* means the files are on your computer). You make changes to your local copy of the code, and when your changes are ready, you "check in" to the repository. Checking in means sending to the repository the changes you made, along with a message where you describe those changes. By checking in, you create a new snapshot of your project at that point. See Figure 15.1 for an example of how this process works.

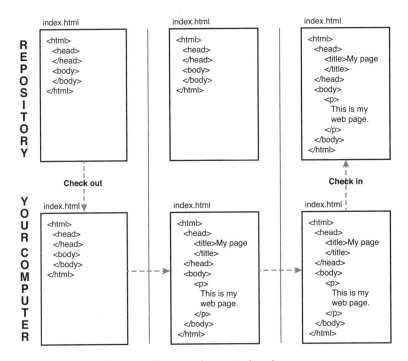

Figure 15.1   A simple visualization of how version control works

Why Use Version Control?

Beyond its capability to track changes in your project, one of the most compelling reasons to use version control is for collaboration. As you will see in the next section, the way version control is set up makes it ideal for working in small and large teams. Version control also helps you write code in a more focused manner. As with functions, each check-in should have a specific purpose. When working within a version control system, you should make only changes that relate to the current check-in, which helps you stay focused. Finally, version control enables you to experiment without fear of ruining everything. The capability to roll back means that even if you do ruin everything, you can quickly get back to a good place. Beyond rollbacks, the concept of branches (see section on Branches below) means you can experiment without ever checking in. Version control is worth the time to learn, whether you are working alone or on a team.

Working with a Team

You have already seen how you can work with a repository by checking out and checking in. This process of checking out and checking in allows many people to effectively work on the same project at the same time without getting in each other's way. If you and I were to work on a project together, we would create a central repository and then each check out a local copy. Let's say we're building a website together, and you want to start writing the JavaScript while I start writing HTML. When you check in your JavaScript changes, the repository is updated, but my copy of the code is left unchanged. When I check in my HTML changes, the repository is updated, but I still don't have your JavaScript changes and you still don't have my HTML changes. To get the latest changes from the repository, we each have to request an "update" from the repository. The repository updates us with the code that has changed since our last update. Figure 15.2 shows a visualization of how this process works.

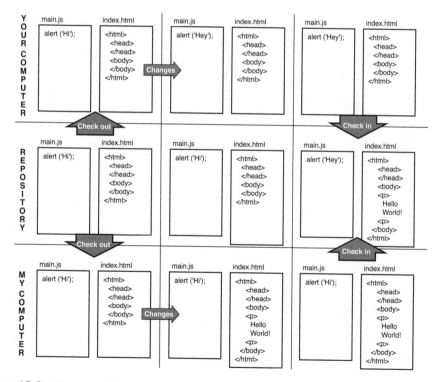

Figure 15.2   A series of check-ins and updates, to keep everyone in sync

Now let's say that you need to make some changes to the HTML file that I am still working on. How will that work? You make your change to the HTML file and check in, and then I finish my change to the HTML file and try to check in. When I try to check in, the version control system will notice that my version of the HTML file is outdated because you checked in your changes since the last time I updated. I will have to get your update from the repository before I am allowed to check in, to make sure that the changes I am checking in don't overwrite the changes you just checked in. This is where version control works its magic. When I request an update from the repository, the version control system tries to merge your changes into my copy of the HTML file. If conflicts arise, the version control system highlights the conflicts and informs me that I must resolve them before I can check in (see Figure 15.3). One example of a conflict is if you and I both try to edit the same line of a file. I can resolve that conflict by manually merging your changes into mine.

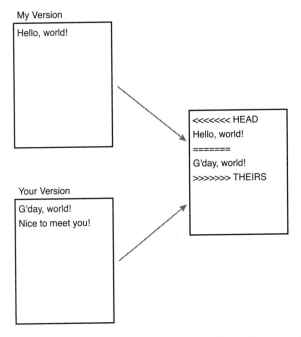

Figure 15.3 The version control system merges as much as it can for you and highlights any conflicts that it is unable to merge.

The process of merging and conflict resolution allows us both to work on the same code at the same time without fear of overwriting each other's changes. In the context of working on a team, this process can have a huge impact on productivity. I can work on any file in our project at any time, and I don't have to worry about whether you or anyone else is already working on it. The impact is even greater when you work on a team of 20 or 200 or larger. Working with a team on a programming project would be nearly impossible without version control. You would basically need to ask permission before editing any file. The following email conversation is how I imagine collaborative software development without version control might work. It's not pretty.

> Monday, April 14, 2014, 8:32 AM
> Hey team,
> Happy Monday :P I wanted to start working on some changes to index.html this morning. Is anyone else already editing that file?
> Thanks,
> Steven

> Monday, April 14, 2014, 8:50 AM
> Hey Steven,
> I think Jerry was working on index.html this morning. You better check with him.
> Paul

> Monday, April 14, 2014, 8:52 AM
> DO NOT TOUCH index.html! Jerry is working on it, and I'm next in line.
> Harry

> Monday, April 14, 2014, 9:03 AM
> Hey everyone,
> I am in line for index.html, too. Maybe we should set up a sign-up sheet in the breakroom?
> Thanks,
> Sally

> Monday, April 14, 2014, 9:08 AM
> Thanks everyone.
> Sally, that sounds like a great idea. Can you put my name on the list as well?
> Thanks,
> Steven

> Tuesday, April 15, 2014, 12:17 AM
> Just a minute, mates. A sign-up sheet in your breakroom won't help those of us down here in Sydney. I need to makes some changes to index.html, too.
> Cheers,
> Ryan

With version control, I can edit any file whenever I want and let the software handle the merging. If there are any conflicts, I can deal with them as they arise. Version control makes working on teams hugely more efficient. No sign-up sheets, no lines, no email—just do your work and let version control handle the hard part.

Code Reviews

One of the greatest advantages of working on a team of developers is that you can learn from the code the other members of your team write, and they can learn from your code. A common practice on software development teams is code reviews, in which other members of the team must review and approve your code changes before they can be checked in. These code reviews might seem intimidating at first, but they can be incredibly valuable for everyone involved. The overall quality of the project's code tends to increase, and so does the knowledge and expertise of the team as a whole. If you are not working on a team, you can still get code reviews online. The people who built StackOverflow created a public place for code reviews at http://codereview.stackexchange.com/. Don't be shy—ask for a code review!

Subversion

Subversion is one of the more popular version control systems available today. The basic features of version control are available in all version control systems, but the features and implementation of each system are slightly different. Subversion is a centralized version control system, which means that Subversion has a central server where the repository is stored. Each developer checks out a copy of the repository at a given point in time, but only the server contains the actual revision history. Whenever you want information about the history of the project, you must have a working network connection and a running server. Therefore, if the server breaks down, the entire system breaks down. If one piece of a system can cause the entire system to break down, that piece is referred to as a single point of failure, and a single point of failure is not a good thing. The server that holds the central repository is Subversion's single point of failure. Nevertheless, Subversion is still a popular version control system in use on some very large projects (including Google Chrome). As long as you take precautions to keep your server safe and running, Subversion works well. Other centralized version control systems exist, but Subversion is the most prevalent.

Git

Git is my version control system of choice. The original author of Git (Linus Torvalds) is also the original author of Linux, and Git was written to be the version control system for the Linux development team. Git was designed to be fast and to work well for both small and large teams working on small and large projects. Git also solves the single point of failure problem of centralized version control systems. With Git, the entire revision history is on every computer, not just the server. If the server breaks down, any of the other computers can immediately step in and act as the server. You have already learned a bit about Git in the context of GitHub, but now you'll learn how it actually works.

Clone

Because Git has a different philosophy about how version control works, it uses a different set of terms. First, you don't just "check out" a copy of the code on a repository; with Git, you are getting the code and the entire revision history. So instead of using the "check out" phrasing, Git uses the word *clone*—your local repository is a full clone of the server's repository. You clone a repository from the command line using the command git clone, with the URL of the server repository as an argument (see Listing 15.1).

Listing 15.1   **Cloning a Git Repository Using git clone**

```
# Create a clone of one of the first repositories I created on GitHub, a clock.
sfoote@sfoote-mac:projects $ git clone https://github.com/smfoote/html5-clock.git
sfoote@sfoote-mac:projects $ cd html5-clock
sfoote@sfoote-mac:html5-clock $ # Now I'm ready to start making changes
```

Add

After you have cloned the repository, you are ready to start making changes. Git gives you fine-grained control about how your changes are tracked. After you have made some changes, you need to tell Git which of those changes you want to track, using the git add [filename] command. Only changes that have been included in a git add will be included in the next snapshot (snapshots in Git are called commits). If you want to include all your changes in the next commit, you can use git add -A (the -A is for *all*). Note that git add does not add anything to Git's revision history; it only tells Git which changes to include in the next commit. You can see which changes will be included in the next commit by running the command git status. See Listing 15.2 for an example of using git add.

Listing 15.2   **Adding Files in Preparation for a Commit**

```
# make some changes to index.html
sfoote@sfoote-mac:html5-clock $ vim index.html

# Check which files will be included in the next commit
sfoote@sfoote-mac:html5-clock $ git status
```

```
On branch master
Changes not staged for commit:
  (use "git add <file>..." to update what will be committed)
  (use "git checkout -- <file>..." to discard changes in working directory)


      modified:   index.html


no changes added to commit (use "git add" and/or "git commit -a")



# add those changes to the next commit
sfoote@sfoote-mac:html5-clock $ git add index.html
sfoote@sfoote-mac:html5-clock $ git status
On branch master
Changes to be committed:
  (use "git reset HEAD <file>..." to unstage)


  modified:   index.html
```

Commit

When you're ready to take a snapshot of your project, you use `git commit`, which adds a new entry to the revision history with all the changes you have included using `git add`. Any changes that you have made but not included with `git add` will still be there, but they will not be committed. The new entry you make in the revision history by running `git commit` exists only in your local repository. See Listing 15.3 for example commands for this process, and Figure 15.4 for a visualization of how it works. If you are working on a project by yourself, committing is the last step. However, if you're working with a team, you must take one more step to share your changes with everyone else on your team.

Listing 15.3   Committing Changes with a Commit Message

```
sfoote@sfoote-mac:html5-clock $ git status
On branch master
Changes to be committed:
  (use "git reset HEAD <file>..." to unstage)


      modified:   index.html


sfoote@sfoote-mac:html5-clock $ git commit -m "Fix typo in index.html"
[master 1234567] Fix typo in index.html
 1 file changed, 3 insertions(+), 2 deletions(-)
```

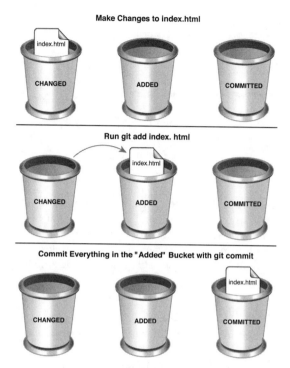

Make Changes to index.html

CHANGED   ADDED   COMMITTED

Run git add index. html

index.html

CHANGED   ADDED   COMMITTED

Commit Everything in the "Added" Bucket with git commit

index.html

CHANGED   ADDED   COMMITTED

Figure 15.4   Only files in the Changed bucket can be moved to the Added bucket, and only files in the Added bucket are moved to the Committed bucket.

Push and Pull

Up to this point, none of the Git commands we have run (with the exception of `git clone`) required an Internet connection. That is one of the powerful features of Git; you can work on a Git repository if you're on a train, a bus, an airplane, or anywhere else with no Internet connection, whereas, almost everything you do with Subversion requires an Internet connection. However, when the time comes to sync your changes with the server's repository, you do need a connection. In Subversion, you check in changes, but in Git, you have already taken the snapshot with `git commit`, so you "push" your commits. To update your local repositories with commits made by other developers, you "pull." For basic Git usage, the server's repository is called the origin, and when you push and pull, you have to tell Git the name of the server's repository (see Listing 15.4 for an example).

Listing 15.4   **Syncing with the Server's Repository Using `git pull` and `git push`**

```
# Pull updates from the server's repository
sfoote@sfoote-mac:html5-clock $ git pull origin master
```

```
From github.com:smfoote/html5-clock
 * branch              master      -> FETCH_HEAD
Updating 68125d1..4525da7
Fast-forward
 README.md | 2 +-
 1 file changed, 1 insertion(+), 1 deletion(-)


 # Push the commit I made locally to server's repository
sfoote@sfoote-mac:html5-clock $ git push origin master
```

Git Workflow

Git takes a little while to learn and get used to. You might even be wondering why you'd want to go through all the hassle of using `git add` and `git commit` and `git push` and `pull`. Seems like an awful lot of extra work just to keep track of code, right? Let me just say that version control systems exist for a reason, and it is a very good reason. I didn't know there was such a thing as version control until about two years after I started programming, and at that point, I still didn't think it was necessary. After all, I had been programming for two years and I hadn't needed version control yet, so why would I take the time to learn some crazy system of check-ins, commits, updates, and pulls?

Then one day, the entire website I was building was broken. I had no idea why, and I had only a vague idea of what code I had been updating in the past few days. I had no way to roll back to a previous version of the code because I *had* no versions. I finally found and fixed the problem, but I still didn't want to learn version control. Instead, I set up a Google doc, and every time I made a change to the website, I wrote down the date, the purpose of the change, and what files I had modified. In other words, I was trying to create a version control system, but I was missing out on all the real advantages of a version control system. When I finally learned how to use Git, I never looked back; the benefits are worth all the hassle of adding, committing, and pushing. I now use Git on every project I work on (including this book).

One of the reasons I was hesitant to learn Git was that I didn't really understand how I was supposed to use it. I don't want you to have the same problem, so consider this very basic Git workflow:

1. Make some changes to the code in your repository.

2. Add your changes to the set of changes you want to commit.

3. Commit the changes you have included with `git add` using `git commit`.

4. Update your local repository with changes made by other developers using `git pull origin master`.

5. Push the commit snapshots you have created to the server's repository using `git push origin master`.

Kittenbook Gets Git

It's time to put your skills to the test. You have learned a lot about finding answers to your own problems, and now you have a problem. Kittenbook needs version control, and you need to figure out how to set it up. The first step is to install Git (*hint:* GitHub has some great resources on how to get started with Git). Second, when you have Git installed, you need to turn your kittenbook directory into a Git repository (*hint:* this requires only a single Git command from the command line, and it's not `git clone`). Finally, you need to create an initial snapshot of your project, which you can do by following the Git workflow just described.

I recognize that the task of setting Git for kittenbook might seem unnecessarily difficult. I have done my best throughout this book to give you as much direction as possible because I know how frustrating it can be when a book assumes that I know how to do something that I don't know how to do. But you are ready to walk on your own. I know you don't already know how to install Git, but I also know that you have the tools to figure it out on your own. You'll do great—but if you do get stuck, remember to use resources such as StackOverflow or experienced friends/acquaintances.

Branches

You should be aware of one more feature of Git, and that is branches. The concept of Git branches is at first a little difficult to understand (at least, it was for me). A Git branch is a way to keep different tasks neatly organized and separated. For example, let's say you are working on adding a new feature to kittenbook (for example, kittens on LinkedIn), but you have an ongoing task of updating all your documentation. Without branches, you would need to manually track which changes are documentation changes and which changes are LinkedIn kitten changes; you wouldn't want a partially complete feature to be committed with your documentation changes, and vice versa. With branches, you can create a branch called `documentation` where you work on your documentation changes, and you can create another branch called `linkedin-kittens` where you work on your new feature. You can easily switch between your branches to work on the different tasks; the changes you make on one branch are saved to that branch, but they don't come with you when you switch to another branch. When all your changes are ready, you can merge your branches into the "master" branch using `git merge`.

This introduction to Git is clearly incomplete. Git involves so much more than I can possibly cover in a few pages. If you are interested in learning more, I highly recommend that you check out the book *Pro Git,* by Scott Chacon. I did not think Git was that great, or really even understand Git, until I read this book. After reading it, I wanted to use Git for everything. The book is very well written, good for Git beginners, and available for free online at http://git-scm. com/book.

OOP (Object-Oriented Programming)

Now for something completely different, let's talk about object-oriented programming (OOP). You might already be familiar with this term, either from previous experience or from research you've done while reading this book, but you might not really understand what it means.

First let me say that OOP is not as confusing as it might seem, but it is very powerful. OOP is an effective way to organize and share code—and as a result, the code becomes easier to work with. The name *object-oriented programming* comes from the idea that your programs should literally be based on objects (the type of objects you learned about in Chapter 5, "Data (Types), Data (Structures), Data(bases)"). I don't find the name to be that helpful in understanding what OOP is, nor in explaining why I would want to learn and use it. Instead of objects, I like to think about my OOP programs in terms of actors. Video games are probably the easiest way of thinking of computer programs in terms of actors. For example, the game *Pac-Man* has a PacMan actor, several Ghost actors, a GameBoard actor, and Fruit actors, among others. In OOP terms, each type of actor is called a class, and an actual member of a class is called an instance.

When you think in terms of actors, you can write your program so that all the behaviors of a given actor are connected to that actor. For example, the PacMan actor has the ability to move around on the screen, so we could give the PacMan class a move method. Then whenever PacMan needs to move up, our code can just call pacMan.move('up'). As PacMan moves across the screen, his mouth opens and closes, so we could create another method called chomp and call pacMan.chomp() each time PacMan's mouth should open and close. After the methods of move and chomp are written, you don't have to worry about how they work. You know that they do work, so it doesn't really matter how. In this way, OOP lets you write a lot more functionality a lot faster with a lot less code.

Classes

An object-oriented program consists of a bunch of objects that have attributes and behaviors. A class is a description of the attributes and behaviors of a type of object. For instance, the code for the PacMan class would include the move and chomp methods, which are descriptions of how a PacMan object moves and chomps, respectively. The class is just a description of what a PacMan would be like, but it does not create a PacMan (that is the job of the instance). One of the big advantages of using classes is how it organizes your code. When you have a PacMan class, you know that all the code that describes a PacMan must go into the PacMan class definition. If sometime in the future you decide that you want PacMan to be able to jump, you will know just where to put the jump method.

Inheritance

We now have a pretty good idea of what the PacMan class would look like, with methods such as move, chomp, and (maybe) jump, but what about the other actors in the game? Most notably, what about the Ghosts? If you have played *Pac-Man*, you consider the Ghosts to be the enemy. But if you're thinking about how to program *Pac-Man*, you will notice that the Ghosts and PacMan are a lot alike. For instance, they can all move around the game board, but they can't go through walls. In Chapter 8, "Functions and Methods," you learned the importance of keeping your code DRY (don't repeat yourself), but if we write a move method for the PacMan class *and* a move method for the Ghost class, we will be repeating ourselves. The answer to this problem is inheritance.

Inheritance means that a class can be a type of another class. As an example, I am from Nevada and am therefore a member of the Nevadan class. All members of the Nevadan class have certain attributes and behaviors that are specific to Nevadans (such as surviveRidiculousHeatWithLittleWater), but all members of the Nevadan class are also members of the American class. The Nevadan class (the subclass) inherits all the attributes and methods of the American class (the parent class). All Nevadans are Americans, but not all Americans are Nevadans. The Texan class, for instance, also inherits from the American class, but from not the Nevadan class. The concept of inheritance allows for code to be shared among different classes. Both the PacMan class and the Ghost class can inherit from a parent class that we'll call MovableCharacter. The move method would be defined in the MovableCharacter class and shared by both the PacMan class and the Ghost class (see Figure 15.5).

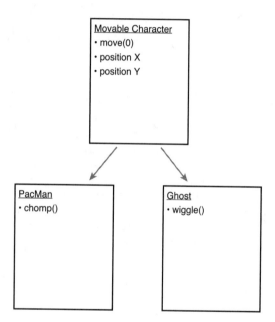

Figure 15.5   Although they have their differences, Pac-Man and the Ghosts share a common parent (class), MovableCharacter.

Instances

Like Coke, an instance is the real thing. Whereas the PacMan class is just the idea of what a real PacMan would be, an instance of the PacMan class is a real PacMan. It can move, it can chomp, it can jump (maybe?)—it's the real deal. The reason to keep classes and instances separate is so you can create multiple instances of a single class (for example, a game of *Pac-Man* has multiple Ghosts). Classes and instances keep your code organized and easy to understand.

Design Patterns

As you design and build software, remember that your software problems are not entirely unique, even if your product is. In fact, your problems are probably very similar to problems that have well-defined solutions. These well-defined solutions are referred to as design patterns. Your challenge is to choose the right design pattern and then implement it correctly to solve your problem. As you approach a difficult programming problem, don't reinvent the wheel; use a design pattern. Design patterns are meant to make your life a little easier.

The following list of design patterns is but a small sample. The purpose of this list is to give you an idea of what design patterns are good for and what types of problems they solve. Some design patterns describe how to architect an entire application; others describe how to design a relatively small part of an application. You can mix, match, and meld design patterns as you see fit. If you don't find an answer to your problem in this list, don't fret. Plenty of other established design patterns exist, and at least one of them will likely help you solve your problem.

Pub Sub

An entire software application usually consists of several parts, called modules. Consider, for example, a web browser, which has a Tabs module, an Address Bar module, a Bookmarks module, and a Webpage View module (see Figure 15.6). To keep the code clean and organized, the modules should not have direct references to each other (in programmer-speak, the modules should not know about each other), because if two modules directly reference each other, they might as well be one module. If all the modules directly reference all the other modules, you end up with one giant module that is hard to maintain and nearly impossible to understand. Yet the different modules need to be able to communicate in some way. For instance, when a tab is selected, the web page associated with that tab needs to be displayed. The Pub Sub pattern provides a solution to this communication problem.

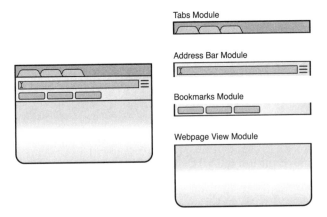

Figure 15.6   A web browser and its modules

Pub Sub (short for Publish/Subscribe) describes an events system (not unlike the events we discussed in Chapter 7, "If, For, While, and When"). When something important happens in one module, an event is published so that other modules can know that the event occurred and respond appropriately. A module must "subscribe" to an event to be notified that it has occurred. Returning to our web browser example, when a tab is selected, the Tab module would publish a tabSelected event, and the Address Bar module and Webpage View module (both subscribers of the tabSelected event) would know to update their content appropriately. One advantage of using events is that the program will behave correctly no matter where the event originates. If you want to add a feature that allows users to switch tabs by clicking a button in the Bookmarks module, all you have to do is publish a tabSelected event from the Bookmarks module, and everything else will just work.

Mediator

The Mediator pattern is like a more civilized version of the Pub Sub pattern. The Pub Sub pattern is just a bunch of modules yelling at each other: "I'M A TAB AND I HAVE BEEN SELECTED, IF ANYBODY CARES!" The trouble with all this yelling becomes apparent when there are conflicts. If two tabs publish the tabSelected event at the same time, which tab actually gets selected? If one tab publishes the tabSelected while another tab is in a frozen state (tabs can be frozen when an alert or prompt window is open), do the tabs switch anyway? Should they? When modules can communicate only through events, these types of conflicts can result in some strange behavior. If you try to fix this behavior while still using only events, your modules might start to directly reference each other, until eventually the whole Pub Sub system falls apart. Instead, your code needs a way to mediate these conflicts. The Mediator pattern provides a solution.

The Mediator is a module that is allowed to know about all the other modules. The mediator module contains the code that is used to resolve conflicts. For instance, if a tab wants to be selected (because the user clicked on it), the tab asks the mediator for permission to be selected. The mediator checks to see if any of the other modules have a reason why the tab should not be selected. If the tab is allowed to be selected, the appropriate code runs and the tab is selected. If there is a reason why the tab should not be selected, the mediator decides how to handle the conflict (see Figure 15.7). This Mediator pattern works great for programs in which modules might conflict with each other.

Figure 15.7   A good mediator resolves conflicts in a way that works for everyone.

Singleton

The Singleton pattern is a type of class that can have only one instance. Every time you try create to create an instance of a Singleton, you don't actually get a new instance—you are really getting only a reference to a single instance. For example, the `PacMan` class could be implemented as a Singleton. You might try to create an instance of PacMan in several different places in your code, but you really want only one PacMan. If the `PacMan` object has already been created, you don't actually want to create a second PacMan; you really just want a reference to the existing PacMan.

Summing Up

Congratulations! You are done, and you even made it through the advanced topics. You should celebrate. The skills you have learned in this book will change the way you see computers—and might even change the way you see the world. These skills are too valuable to keep to yourself. Now that you're done reading it, you should lend this book to a friend. Then you can joke together about using your grandma's toothbrush.

In this chapter, you learned about:

- Version control
- Subversion
- Git
- Object-oriented programming
- Classes
- Instances
- Design patterns

It's up to you to write the next chapter of your programming journey. Enjoy!

Glossary

$PATH When you try to enter a command on the (Linux or Mac) command line, your computer needs to know where it can look for the instructions related to that command. The $PATH variable is a list of all the directories where the command line should look for instructions related to a given command.

(Google) Chrome An open source web browser whose largest contributor is Google.

absolute path In a file system, an absolute path gives the full path to a file or directory, starting with the root directory.

abstraction The details of how a system work are hidden so that you don't have to understand how the system works to be able to use the system. A car engine is an abstraction, and a programming language is an abstraction. Abstractions allow programmers to work more quickly without having to know everything (although some programmers still believe they know everything).

Ada Lovelace The world's first programmer, Ada Lovelace wrote code for a mechanical computer (the Analytical Engine) that existed only in theory.

`add` (`git`) Git command used to add files to the list of changes that will be included in the next commit.

allocation (hard drive)   When a new file is created, a certain amount of space is set aside (or allocated) to store the data related to that file.

Analytical Engine   What would have been the world's first computing machine. The Analytical Engine was the work of Charles Babbage. It was never completed because it was too expensive (the English government no longer wanted to foot the bill), and Babbage lost interest (because he was more interested in Analytical Engine v2.0).

ancestor (tree)   In a tree data structure, an ancestor is a node that is connected to nodes farther down the tree.

Android   An open source operating system originally intended for mobile devices, primarily developed and maintained by Google.

anonymous function   A function that has no name because it needs no name. These types of functions are often passed as arguments to other functions.

Ant (build tool)   A build tool whose main usage is building Java applications (see "Grunt" for another example of a build tool).

API   Application programming interface. An API is the interface that allows different pieces of software to interact with each other.

application   A piece of software with a given purpose. Literally, an application (or possible use case) of the hardware.

architecture   The high-level design of a software application, which decides how the different pieces of the application will be separated and how the separate pieces will interact with each other.

argument   A value passed into a function (or program) that modifies or determines the behavior of the behavior of the function (or program).

array   An ordered list of zero or more items. Generally, the first item in the list is assigned the number 0, the second is assigned the number 1, and so forth.

ASCII   American Standard Code for Information Interchange. A way to encode characters as numbers so that computers can understand and use them.

assembly language   A low-level programming language that gives instructions directly to hardware. For most programming tasks, a high-level programming language can be used instead of assembly.

assignment   An instruction in a programming language in which a variable is given (or assigned) a value.

automated testing   Using software to test software. Two important parts of automated testing are unit testing and integration testing.

automation   Using software to perform a task that would otherwise have to be manually performed by a human.

Bash   The default program used to execute commands from the Linux and Mac OS X command lines. A series of Bash commands can be written in a file and executed in sequence; this is called a Bash script.

binary   A method of expressing values using a series of 1's and 0's. Computer hardware can understand 1's and 0's, so binary is particularly useful for working with computers. However, a programmer has little need to understand binary because such details are abstracted away by programming languages.

binary operator   In mathematics and computer science, a binary operator is a type of operator with two operands. A simple example is 2 + 4, where 2 and 4 are the two operands and + is the binary operator.

Boolean   A logical term to describe something that can be either true or false. Booleans are used widely in programming to determine such things as which code should be executed (`if` statements) and how many times (`while` loops).

branch (`git`)   A lightweight way of switching between different versions of a software project, useful for experimenting and multitasking.

`break` **statement**   An instruction used to prematurely break out of a `for` loop or `while` loop (before the loop's condition becomes false).

breakpoint   A marker set on a line of code that pauses the code's execution at that point, allowing the developer to examine the values of variables and step through the following instructions one line at a time.

bug   A problem, flaw, or error in an application that causes the application to behave in unintended ways.

build tools   Software to automate repetitive tasks (such as compiling, testing, packaging, and deploying) that a programmer would otherwise have to do manually—and programmers do not like doing things manually.

C   A general-purpose programming language originally developed at AT&T Bell Labs between 1969 and 1973.

C#   A general-purpose programming language originally developed by Microsoft as a part of its .NET Framework.

C++   A general-purpose programming language that is much like C, but with extra capabilities (hence the "++"). Most notably, C++ is an object-oriented programming language.

call stack   When a function calls another function, which calls another function, and so on, the list of functions that have been called (in order) is referred to as the call stack.

callback   A function (usually an anonymous function) that is passed as a parameter to another function. The callback function will be executed when some event occurs.

capturing group (regex)   A subpattern within a regular expression. When a string matches the regular expression, the part of the string that matches the capturing group's subpattern is captured and stored for later use.

`cat` **(command)**   A Bash command used for outputting the contents of a file (or files). The command is often used for concatenating multiple files into a single file (hence the name: con-cat-enate).

catch   When a programmer is concerned that a certain piece of code might cause an error, the programmer can "catch" the error instead of allowing the program to crash.

`cd` **(command)**   A Bash command used to change directories. If you want to use the command line, you need to learn to use `cd` to get around the file system.

central repository   In the context of version control software, a central repository is the software project's source of truth. The central repository is generally stored on a server that all the programmers working on the project can access.

character   A data type that stores a single value. For example, `a`, `7`, and `%` are all characters. Space, tab, and newline are also characters. A character can be thought of as a single unit of a string.

Charles Babbage   The inventor of the Analytical Engine, what can be considered the world's first computer (although it was never finished).

check in (version control)   When a programmer sends changes to update the central repository of a version control system.

check out (version control)   When a developer downloads all the source code for a project from a central repository.

child (tree)   A node in a tree data structure that is directly connected to a node one level farther up the tree.

Chrome Developer Tools   Tools with Google Chrome for programmers working on building web pages. These tools include a debugger with breakpoints and variable inspection, a console for quickly trying out code, and many other features.

Chrome extension   A lightweight application used to extend the functionality of the Chrome web browser, or a website accessed with the Chrome web browser.

class   A description of the attributes and behaviors of a type of object.

class (HTML)   An HTML attribute that describes and differentiates an HTML element. See also source code.

CLI   Command-line interface. A program used to interact with a computer (especially with the file system of a computer) through text commands.

`clone` (`git`)   Similar to a checkout, running the command `git clone` downloads the source code from a Git repository.

code   Instructions for a computer written in a programming language.

code encapsulation   A concept similar to abstraction, code encapsulation is gathering all the instructions for a related task in the same place (for example, in a function).

code formatting   The use of whitespace to determine how source code appears in a text editor. Different programming languages and different projects might have different rules (or conventions) for code formatting.

code reuse   Reusing the same code in more than one place. The code to format a date or time should be made reusable. Object-oriented programming, with classes and inheritance, is well suited for code reuse.

code review   When one or more programmers comment or critique the code written by another programmer. The purposes of code review include maintaining high-quality source code and teaching programmers about different techniques and best practices.

coding conventions   Code formatting and other rules that are followed in a given software project. See also code formatting.

coercion   In dynamically typed languages, coercion is a way of converting a value from one type to another. For instance, the string `'2'` could be coerced to the integer `2`.

command line See CLI.

comments   In source code, text that is ignored when the code is executed. Comments are most commonly used to document the source code, but they can also be used in debugging to ignore valid instructions (this is called commenting out code).

`commit` (`git`)   A snapshot of the Git project directory in a given state.

comparison operator   A type of binary operator that performs a comparison of its two operands and returns a Boolean. Greater than (`>`) is an example of a comparison operator.

compilation   The process of transforming source code into something that other software or computer hardware can understand.

compiled language   A programming language, the source code of which must be compiled before it can be executed.

compiler   A software program that transforms source code into compiled code.

composite data type   A data type that is made up of other data types (for example, a string is made up of a series of characters). See also primitive data type.

concatenate   To combine strings. This can be done with strings in source code. For example, `'hey'` + `' '` + `'there'`) or with strings stored in files. See also `cat` (command).

condition   An expression that evaluates to `true` or `false`, or that evaluates to a value that is truthy or falsy. Conditions are used in `if` statements and loops to control the flow of a program.

console   A text-based window used for entering commands. The Chrome Developer Tools have a console for entering JavaScript commands. The Linux and Mac command lines and the Windows command prompt are all consoles.

constraints   The limitations of a system. In software development, constraints should be considered in the planning phase.

control character   A character with no visual representation that provides information to the computer about the text. Many control characters are now obsolete.

control flow   The order in which instructions are executed. The order can be changed using `if` statements, `switch` statements, and loops.

`copy` **(command)**   A Windows command for copying files or folders. See also `cp` (command).

`cp` **(command)**   A command-line command for copying files or directories.

CPU   Central processing unit. The piece of hardware that executes the instructions given in source code.

cron job   A special type of program that repeatedly runs at a given interval. An example use of a cron job is backing up files every day.

CRUD   Create read update delete. An application that requires persistent (or long-term) storage should implement each of these four functions.

CSS   Cascading Stylesheets. CSS is the language used to define how things appear on a web page. Colors, fonts, sizes, and positioning are all defined in CSS.

curly brace   The characters that look like a mustache if rotated 90 degrees: { and }. Often used to denote a block of code (such as a function or an `if` statement).

data sanitization   The process of turning potentially malicious data (usually data that a user has input) into data that is safe to use within a software application.

data structure   A way of organizing data so that it can be more useful and more easily understood.

data type   In programming, different values fit into different categories called data types (string, Boolean, integer, and so on).

data validation   The process of checking that data a user inputs conforms to a certain set of parameters. For instance, valid American phone numbers should have 10 digits and no letters or symbols.

database   A collection of data that is organized and persistently stored. Relational databases are one of the more common types of databases.

date   A data type that represents a time and is usually stored as the number of milliseconds since a given starting point (most commonly January 1, 1970, the UNIX epoch).

deallocation (hard drive space)   The freeing of hard drive space that occurs when a file is deleted. Note that the data in that space is not actually deleted, removed, or destroyed when the space is deallocated. The data remains, but the space is open to be overwritten by some other file.

debugging   The act of manually testing software and examining source code to determine the cause of a bug. Debugging activities include manually testing the software to identify the conditions under which the bug exists (called reproducing), setting breakpoints and stepping through code, examining errors and logs, and reading source code.

defensive coding   A method of writing code that anticipates errors and problems in order to handle them gracefully without causing the software to crash and burn.

`delete` **(command)**   A Windows command for deleting a file or folder. See also `rm` (command).

dependencies   Software programs or packages that are required for an application to run properly.

deploy   A term for sending a packaged application to an environment where the end user can access it, most commonly used for web applications.

descendant (tree)   The reciprocal of an ancestor. In a tree data structure, a descendant is a node that is connected to nodes farther up the tree.

design pattern   In programming, many of the same problems appear again and again; design patterns are reusable solutions to these common problems.

`dir` **(command)**   A Windows command used to list the contents of the current directory.

directory   More commonly known as a folder, a directory is an item in a file system that can contain files and other directories.

documentation   An explanation of how a software application works. Documentation can include comments within the source code, diagrams, presentations, drawings, and other written explanations.

dogfooding   The practice of being a user of the software you are building.

dot files   On Linux and Mac, hidden files that are often used for configuration.

DRY   Don't repeat yourself. A principle of programming that urges programmers to not store the same information in multiple places. Within the book, we saw applications of the DRY principle in database design (Chapter 5) and in writing reusable functions (Chapter 8).

dynamically typed language   A programming language that does not require (or even allow) the data types of its variables to be declared. The data types are instead inferred at runtime.

edge (graph)   The connection between two nodes in a graph data structure. In a graph representing cities and roads, the cities are the nodes and the roads between the cities are the edges.

error   A condition that prevents the parsing, compilation, or execution of a program.

escape character   A character that alters the meaning of the following character. In Chapter 1, we used an escape character to be able to use a single quote (') inside a string without prematurely closing the string. In programming languages, the backslash (\) is a common escape character.

event   In software applications, an event is an occurrence that might be of special interest to the software. Events allow for code to be executed when something happens. Examples of events on a website are mouse movements, clicks, and scrolls.

event listener   An instruction that allows a part of a program to be notified when a given event occurs. See also event.

execution   The processing of the instructions found in source code.

execution environment   The software or hardware that is used to execute code. JavaScript is usually executed with a web browser as its execution environment. Java is executed within the Java Runtime Environment (JRE).

external devices   Examples of external devices on a desktop computer are the keyboard, mouse, and webcam.

falsy   In some programming languages, the value of a condition does not have to be a Boolean to evaluate to `true` or `false`. For example, in JavaScript, `false`, `0`, `undefined`, and `''` (an empty string) are all falsy even though only `false` is a real Boolean.

file path   The location (or address) of a file or directory within a file system.

file permissions   Different users of the same computer can be granted different levels of permissions for any given file or directory on that computer. The types of permissions are read (open and view the contents), write (modify and delete), and execute (applicable only to files that can be executed).

file system   The way your computer stores and organizes its files, usually as a hierarchy of directories.

file type   A description of the type of contents expected to be stored in a file. The file type determines what program will be used to open a file and whether it can be executed.

Finder (Mac OS X)   A graphical user interface of the Mac OS X file system.

`findstr` **(command)**   A Windows command for finding files that contain certain strings.

float   A data type that represents a number with a decimal.

folder   See directory.

`for` **loop**   A type of loop most commonly used for iterating through a series of numbers (usually but not always starting with `0`).

function   A set of instructions that can be called with a single command. Useful for not repeating the same code over and over again.

function definition   The description of a function's instructions, in the form of source code. The instructions are not executed until the function is invoked (or called).

function invocation   A call to execute the instructions related to a given function.

general-purpose language   A programming language that can be used for many different computing tasks, including data retrieval and analysis, command-line programs, and graphical user interfaces.

GIGO   Garbage in, garbage out. The concept that a program that is given bad data will produce a bad result.

Git   A modern, scalable, distributed version control system (see version control system).

GitHub   A service for managing Git repositories. GitHub has become a popular place for working on open source software.

global variable   A variable that can be accessed anywhere in a program, regardless of current scope.

graph   A data structure in which nodes are connected by edges, useful for storing data with many-to-many relationships (such as social networks).

greedy (regular expression)   The tendency of a regular expression to match as much of a string as possible, even if a smaller portion of the string would still match.

`grep` **(command)**   A command-line tool for finding files that contain a given string. Regular expressions are especially useful when using `grep`.

Grunt   A build tool system built using JavaScript and `Node.js`.

Gruntfile   The file that defines and describes all the tasks that Grunt will perform in a particular project.

GUI   Graphical user interface. A user interface that is generally characterized by buttons, images, and other graphical interactions that might require the use of a mouse. A non-text-based user interface.

hack   Either a quick (and perhaps sloppy) prototype built to demonstrate the potential of an idea (this is the idea behind hackathons) or the software equivalent of duct tape and bailing wire (code that works but is written in an ugly or nonscalable way).

hacker   Any programmer can be referred to as a hacker, but hackers are generally thought of as programmers who disregard rules and conventions (and even break things) in order to build something great. Note this definition is inconsistent with the more common definition of hackers being criminals who use computers to commit their crimes.

hard drive   The piece of computer hardware where data is saved for long-term storage.

hash   A data structure of key value pairs (see map and object).

hexadecimal   A method of representing numbers using base 16, which is somewhat common in programming.

HTML   Hypertext Markup Language. The language that describes the structure and content of a web page.

HTML tags   The building blocks of an HTML document. Tags should be chosen based on the type of content they contain.

IDE   Integrated development environment. A tool for creating software in which code can be written, compiled, tested, and executed.

`if` **statement**   A control flow structure with a condition and a body. The instructions within the body are executed only if the condition evaluates to `true` (or some truthy value).

IIFE   Immediately invoked function expression. In JavaScript, an anonymous function that is invoked immediately after it is defined, generally used for scoping.

infinite loop   A loop with a condition that will never be false, no matter how many times the body of the loop is executed.

inheritance   In object-oriented programming, when a class is based on (or inherits from) another class. The class doing the inheritance has access to all the methods and attributes of the original class, and it can add or modify methods and attributes as necessary.

instance   In object-oriented programming, a concrete usage of a class. If a class is a blueprint, then an instance is an actual building.

instructions   In the context of programming, instructions are commands given to a computer that describe actions the computer should execute.

integration testing   The part of software testing that verifies that the several individual parts of an application work properly when combined (or integrated).

interpreted language   A programming language whose programs are executed by an interpreter. Unlike compiled languages, the instructions in interpreted languages never have to be compiled.

interpreter   A software program that takes source code as its input and executes the instructions in the source code one at a time.

iOS   The operating system used in iPhones and iPads, developed and maintained by Apple.

iterate   To repeat a set of instructions or to loop through a list (for example, iterate through an array).

Java   A general-purpose programming language originally developed by Sun Microsystems and currently maintained by Oracle. Java is used for a wide variety of applications. Java is an object-oriented programming language.

JavaScript   The language of the Web, originally developed by Brendan Eich for Netscape in 1995. JavaScript is now officially maintained by ECMA (European Computer Manufacturers Association) as ECMAScript. Although it was originally designed to work only inside a web browser, JavaScript has more recently become a more general-purpose language with the advent of Node.js.

JSDoc   A standardized method for documenting JavaScript programs, using @ annotations.

JSHint/JSLint   JSHint and JSLint are JavaScript programs that check the quality of other JavaScript programs by identifying common errors and mistakes.

JSON   JavaScript Object Notation is a structured way to store data that is readable by computers and humans. It is understood by almost all programming languages.

Kleene star   In the context of regular expressions, the * is known as the Kleene star, after the mathematician Stephen Kleene. Among programmers, it is more commonly referred to as just "star." In regular expressions, the star is used to match zero or more of a character or group of characters.

leaf (tree)   A node in a tree data structure that has no descendants.

library   A group of related pieces of software that is not itself a full-featured software application but that can be used to more easily build full-featured software applications by abstracting away difficult, problematic, or tedious tasks. In JavaScript, jQuery is an example of a common library.

Linux   An open source operating system originally developed by Linus Torvalds beginning in 1991. The Linux project has split into several versions of Linux called distributions (or, more commonly, "distros"), such as Ubuntu, Fedora, Debian, SUSE, Redhat, and Mint.

local variable   A variable whose value is available only in a given scope (as compared to a global variable, whose value is available anywhere in a program).

logical operator   An operator whose operands are conditions. The logical operators are AND, OR, and NOT.

logs   Logs are an essential part of software development and can sometimes be important even for software consumers. When a software program is not working properly (it has a bug), the problem is much easier to find if the program is logging everything it is doing. By searching the logs, a programmer can identify when (and hopefully why) the program is doing something that is not expected.

long (data type)   A data type that stores numbers (without decimals), with enough room for the numbers to extend into the billions. See also short (data type).

long-term storage   Also known as persistent storage. Long-term storage refers to when data is written to a hard drive, CD, DVD, USB drive, or magnetic tape, as opposed to being stored only in short-term memory (in RAM).

ls **(command)**   A command-line command for listing the contents of the current directory.

Mac OS X   The operating system used on Apple computers.

make **(build tool)**   A software utility for automatically building executable programs from source code. See also Grunt.

malicious code   Code that has the intent to do harm. Malicious code can be annoying (causing a program to go into an endless loop of alerts), frustrating (distributed denial of service, or DDOS, attacks that can take down a website), or damaging (stealing someone's identity).

manual testing   Testing software by actually using the software.

many-to-many relationship   In relational database design, this is a relationship between two tables in which a single item in the first table can be related to many items in the second table, and a single item in the second table can be related to many items in the first table. An Authors table and a Books table would have a many-to-many relationship because an author might write many books, and a single book might have many authors.

match   A string that fits a regular expression is said to match.

md **(command)**   A Windows command for making a new directory. See also mkdir.

mediator pattern   A software design pattern in which different modules communicate through a mediator module.

memory leak   A problem in a software program in which the program does not release space in short-term memory, even if it will never again use the values stored in that space. The longer the program runs, the more space it takes up in short-term memory. Eventually, this can cause the program or even the entire computer to crash.

merge   In a version control system, a merge happens when the changes of two different programmers to the same file are brought together. See also merge conflict.

merge conflict   In a version control system, when a merge cannot be completed by software (for example, two programmers have made changes to the same line in the same file), merge conflicts must be manually resolved by the programmer doing the merging.

method   See function. In the case of JavaScript, there is a slight distinction between a method and a function: A method is a function that is a part of an object.

`mkdir` **(command)**   A command-line command used for making new directories.

mod   See modulus.

module   A small part of a software application with a specific and self-contained purpose. A full software application can be made up of many modules.

modulus   A mathematical operator used to find remainders (such as the remainders from long division), often represented by % in programming languages. The result of a modulus operation is the remainder of the first operand divided by the second operand (for example, 1 % 4 = 1 and 5 % 4 = 1).

monospace type font   A family of font types in which each character is exactly the same width. This type of font is valuable when writing code, where indentation and alignment matter.

`move` **(command)**   A Windows command for moving a file or directory from one place to another (see also `mv` command).

`mv` **(command)**   A command-line command for moving a file or directory from one place to another. This command is also used for renaming files and directories.

Nautilus (Linux)   A GUI application for accessing the file system in Linux.

nested loop   A loop inside the body of another loop.

node   In graph and tree data structures, a node is an entity (as opposed to a connection, which is called an edge).

`Node.js`   An implementation of JavaScript that allows JavaScript programs to be executed outside a browser, thus making JavaScript a more general-purpose programming language.

npm   Node Package Manager, a command-line program that install, updates, and uninstalls `Node.js` programs. npm may also refer to the registry of `Node.js` programs available to be installed.

object   In JavaScript, an object is a data structure of key-value pairs similar to dictionaries and maps found in other languages. More generally, in object-oriented languages, an object is an instance of a class.

object-oriented programming (OOP)   A method of programming in which related data and functions are wrapped together into objects. OOP encourages code reuse through the use of classes and inheritance.

Objective C A programming language that introduces object-oriented programming to the C programming language (C++ also introduced OOP to C, but in a different way). For many years, Objective C was the programming language Apple used for Mac and iOS applications. See also Swift.

off-by-one error A logical error in programming where the program is literally off by one. This often happens when looping through arrays and the program loops one too few or one too many times.

one-to-many relationship In relational databases, a relationship between two tables in which a single item in the first table can be related to many items in the second table, but each item in the second table can be related to, at most, one item in the first table.

one-to-one relationship In relational databases, a relationship between two tables in which a single item in the first table can be related to, at most, one item in the second table, and a single item in the second table can be related to, at most, one item in the first table. Usually the two such tables are combined into a single table.

open source software Literally, software in which the software's source code is distributed openly (as opposed to distributing only the compiled versions of software). The term open source software usually implies that the software is distributed under a license that allows the software to be reused, redistributed, and modified freely. Most such licenses require that any modifications made to open source software also be distributed under the same license. Furthermore, the development of open source software is often (but not always) opened to the public, meaning that anyone can contribute to building the open source software.

operand A value that is acted on by an operator.

operator A construct in programming languages that acts on a set of operands and produces a result.

order of operations Just as with math, the order in which the operands of an operator are evaluated.

output The result of a function or program.

parameter A special kind of variable created within a function that represents the value of one of the function's arguments.

parent A node in a tree data structure that is directly connected to a node one level farther up the tree.

performance In programming, performance refers to how fast a program executes or the amount of resources it consumes.

Perl A programming language generally used for writing relatively small programs called scripts. Very powerful when using regular expressions.

permissions In a file system, files and directories can be protected by permissions. A user needs permissions to be able to read, write, or execute a file.

persistent storage   See long-term storage.

PHP   A programming language that was popular for building websites in the early 2000s.

pointer (file system)   In a file system, an address used to look up the location where a file's data is stored.

pop (array)   A method used on arrays to remove (and return) the last item of an array.

present working directory   The current directory. See *pwd* (command).

primary key (database)   The field in a database table that is used as the unique identifier.

primitive data type   A datatype that cannot be broken down into other data types. See also composite data type.

procedure   See function.

processor   See CPU.

programmer   A person who creates software by writing source code.

programming language   A language that programmers can understand and that can be turned into instructions that a computer can understand (through interpretation or compilation).

prompt   See command line.

pub subpattern   A software design pattern in which modules communicate with each other by broadcasting (or publishing) events, and each modules listens to (or subscribes to) the events that are of interest to them.

`pull` (`git`)   A Git command to fetch changes from a remote repository and merge them into your repository.

push (array)   A method used on arrays to add an item to the end of the array (in some languages, this method is called `append`).

`push` (`git`)   A Git command to send local changes to a remote repository.

`pwd` **(command)**   A command-line command for displaying the full path to the present working directory.

Python   A general-purpose programming language that is relatively easy to learn and understand.

R   A dynamic programming language most commonly used for statistical analysis.

random access memory (RAM)   A piece of hardware in which the instructions and data related to a program wait to be executed by the CPU.

read (operation)   When the contents of a file are accessed by a program.

read/write head   The piece of hardware on a hard drive that actually reads and writes data from the hard drives disks.

record (database)   A single entry in a table of a relational database.

regular expression   In programming, a way to match strings using patterns.

relational database   A method of storing data using related tables of rows (records) and columns (fields). The data in a relational database can be retrieved using SQL.

relationship (database)   The connection between tables in a relational database. These connections are made explicit when the primary key (the identifier) from one table is used as a field in another table.

relative path   The path to a file, relative to the present working directory.

repository   In version control, the repository is the place where a project's source code is stored and tracked.

reserved word   A word that has special meaning to a programming language. It is reserved, in that you cannot use that word as the name of a variable or function.

`return` **statement**   In a function, the statement that defines the value to be returned by the function.

reusable code   Code that can be used in more than one context.

`rm` **(command)**   A command-line command for removing (or deleting) a file or directory.

robust code   Phrase you will find in a lot of job descriptions, resumés, and LinkedIn profiles. It basically refers to code that is relatively bug free and can handle most situations that it should be able to handle.

root directory   In Linux and Mac OS, the root directory is the very top directory of a file system.

Ruby   A general-purpose, dynamically typed programming language used widely in building servers for websites.

runtime environment   The environment in which code of a given language is executed.

sanitization   See data sanitization.

scalability   The capability for software to handle more users, more usage, or more data.

scope   In a software program, scope refers to the place in the code where a variable can be used.

scripting language   A type of programming language that is generally used in writing short programs for automating small tasks, as opposed to a general-purpose language that can be used in writing full-scale software applications.

security   In programming, security refers to taking measures to prevent unauthorized use and access of systems and data.

self-documenting code   The idea that code should be understandable without the use of comments. This can be achieved through descriptive variable and function names, and by not writing code that is tricky or confusing.

server   In the context of websites, a server is a computer (or group of computers) that "serves" the website's content.

set   A mathematical concept (and data structure) of a list, with no duplicates.

sibling (tree)   In a tree data structure, two nodes with the same parent are siblings.

signed integer   A data type that represents an integer than can be either positive or negative. See also unsigned integer.

singleton   A software design pattern wherein instantiating a certain class always returns a reference to the same single object (the singleton).

snippet   A small piece of example code that will generally not work on its own. The code examples in this book can be called snippets.

software   Instructions for computer hardware to execute. See also program.

software design   The way software is planned and architected, before and during the process of actually writing the code.

software engineer   A person who designs and writes software.

software testing   The process of ensuring that a software program is working as intended, through both manual and automated testing.

solid state drive   A type of hard drive that does not have moving parts.

source code   Text, written in a programming language, that can be compiled or interpreted to be used as the instructions for a software program.

spaghetti code   Code that is written in such a way that making a change in one place often means making updates in several other places. It is messy, unmaintainable code.

specification   A document that describes in detail what a piece of software should do (as well as things the software explicitly should not do).

specs   When writing unit tests, the test files are often called specs because they perform a similar function to a specification. See specification.

spy   In unit testing, a way to know whether a function has been called (and with what arguments).

SQL   Structured Query Language. A language used for retrieving data from relational databases.

square brackets   Characters often used in programming: [and].

stack   A data structure consisting of a list of items, where items can be added to and removed from only the top of the list.

StackOverflow   A programming Q&A website that will be a great resource to you as long as you program.

standard output (STDOUT)   The default location where the output of a program is sent. For a command-line program, the output is displayed in the terminal, but it can be redirected (for example, to a file).

state   The (important) conditions under which a software program is operating. State can help determine how the software should behave—for example, if the document is in edit mode (state), it should autosave every 15 seconds (behavior).

static typing   Some programming languages require the data types of variables to be declared when the variable is being declared. See also dynamic typing.

step through code   When debugging software, when a breakpoint is set, the programmer can execute lines of source code one at a time. This is called stepping through code.

string   A data type that is used to store text (a group of characters). In source code, strings are generally represented as text surrounded by single or double quotes.

subclass   In object-oriented programming, a class that inherits from another class is called a subclass.

subroutine   A small program. In some programming languages, functions are referred to as subroutines.

Subversion   A popular version control system that uses a server to store a central repository.

superclass   In object-oriented programming, a class that is inherited from is called a superclass.

Swift   A programming language created by Apple and released in 2014 to be a replacement for Objective C in iOS and Mac OS applications.

`switch` **statement**   A programming control flow tool that is given a value and compares that value to each of a set of other predefined values (called cases). When one of the cases matches the value, the code related to that case is executed. A default case is allowed if none of the other cases is a match.

symbolic link   A file in a file system that is actually just a pointer to another file.

syntactic sugar   When a programming language gives you an easy, concise way of performing a specific type of task that would otherwise take a lot more code.

syntax   The set of rules that define what is valid code in a given programming language.

table (database)   A collection of related data. A table describes a type of entity that is important to the database (such as a User table or a Product table), with fields to describe the attributes of that entity.

tags (HTML)   A component of HTML that consists of a word and some attributes surrounded by < and > that describes the content of an HTML document. For example, `<title>` is an HTML tag that contains the title of the HTML page.

TDD   See test-driven development.

terminal   A software program in which a user can access the command line.

ternary operator   An operator with three operands. The ternary operator is usually just a concise `if` statement in which the first operand is the condition, the second operand is the result if the condition is true, and the third operand is the result if the condition is false.

test-driven development   A method of writing software in which tests are written first and then application code is written to pass those tests.

testing   See software testing.

text editor   A software program used for creating plain-text files. Source code is written as plain-text files, so text editors are important for programmers. See Chapter 1 for a list of several options you have when choosing a text editor.

throw   When an error occurs while a program is being executed, the program is said to throw the error.

tree   A data structure with nodes and edges (similar to a graph), where a node can be connected only to its parent and its children.

trunk (tree)   The topmost node in a tree data structure. The trunk has children but no parents.

truthy   In some programming languages, the value of a condition does not have to be a Boolean to evaluate to `true` or `false`. For example, in JavaScript, `false`, `0`, `undefined`, and `''` (an empty string) are all falsy even though only `false` is a real Boolean. Any value that is not falsy is considered to be truthy. See also falsy.

`try catch`   In programming, a control flow tool in which you try to execute some risky code (code that might throw an error); if an error is thrown, you "catch" the error without allowing the program to crash.

`type` (**command**)   A Windows command that can be used for concatenating files. See also `cat` (command).

type coercion   See coercion.

UI   User interface; the part of the program that a human can interact with. No matter how great your program is, if the user interface is hard to use, you won't have many users.

unary operator   An operator than acts on a single operand (such as the `not` operator).

unit (**of code**)   A piece of code that has a specific purpose. A function or method is a good example of a unit of code.

unit test   An automated test that is used to test a single unit of code in isolation.

Unix   An operating system originally developed by Bell Labs in the 1960s. Unix is the basis for both Linux and Mac OS X.

Unix time   A common way for computers to measure time. UNIX time is the number of seconds since January 1, 1970.

unsigned integer   A data type that represents an integer that can only be positive. See also signed integer.

URL   Uniform resource locator. The unique address of a web page, usually seen in a web browser's address bar.

user experience   The entire experience of a consumer using a software application (also called UX). Software development is an important part of user experience, but it is not the only part. The way an application looks and feels is part of the user experience.

UTF   Unicode Transformation Format. A way to encode characters that includes more characters than ASCII.

validation   See data validation.

variable   A part of a programming language that is used to store data for later use in a program.

variable lookup   The process that the runtime environment uses to find the valuable of a variable. See also scope.

VBA   Visual Basic for Applications. A programming language that runs inside Microsoft Office products such as Excel, Access, and Word.

version-control software   Software used to track changes made to a software application. See also Git and Subversion.

web application   A software application that runs inside a web browser.

web browser   A software application used for displaying and interacting with websites and web applications.

web developer   A software programmer who builds websites and web applications. The term often refers to programmers who write the code that is executed in the browser (HTML, CSS, and JavaScript), but it can also refer to programmers who write code executed on the server.

web page   A single page in a website, identified by a unique URL.

website   A collection of web pages (such as Wikipedia).

`while` **loop**   A type of loop with a body and a condition. The instructions in the body continue to execute until the condition is false.

whitespace   Spaces, tabs, newlines, and so on.

Windows   An operating system developed by Microsoft.

Windows Explorer   A graphical user interface used to access the Windows file system.

wire up   The process of connecting different pieces of software so they can work together.

write (operation)   A file system operation in which data is added to a file, removed from a file, or modified within a file.

Index

Symbols

C

E

F

G

Q - R